MATHEMATICS IN ACTION

Mathematics in Action Group

Blackie and Son Limited
Bishopbriggs
Glasgow G64 2NZ

W & R Chambers Limited
43–45 Annandale Street
Edinburgh EH7 4AZ

7 Leicester Place
London WC2H 7BP

Illustrated by *John Martin*
Cover photograph © 1986 *Darryl Williams*/Steelcase Strafor. Computer graphics composition from 'eclipse' task lighting photograph.

British Library Cataloguing in Publication Data

Mathematics in Action
   Pupils' book 2
   1. Mathematics——1961.
   I. Mathematics in Action Group
   510   QA39.2

   ISBN 0–216–91911–8
   ISBN 0–550–75714–7 (Chambers)

ISBNs	Blackie	Chambers
Pupils' Book 2	0 216 91911 8	0 550 75714 7
Teacher's Book 2	0 216 91912 6	0 550 75715 5
Answer Book 2	0 216 91913 4	0 550 75716 3
Assessment 2	0 216 91914 2	0 550 75717 1

Printed in Great Britain by Scotprint Ltd, Musselburgh, Scotland

Robin D. Howat, Auchenharvie Academy, Stevenston, Ayrshire
Edward C. K. Mullan, Eastwood High School, Glasgow
Ken Nisbet, Madras College, St Andrews, Fife
Doug Brown, St Anne's High School, Heaton Chapel, Stockport, Cheshire

with
**W. Brodie, D. Donald, E. K. Henderson, J. L. Hodge, J. Hunter, R. McKendrick,
H. C. Murdoch, A. G. Robertson, J. A. Walker, P. Whyte, H. S. Wylie**

MATHEMATICS IN ACTION GROUP

CONTENTS

INVESTIGATIONS will always be in a right-handed box

BRAINSTORMERS will always be in a left-handed box

Mathematics is in action all around you. You need mathematics in your daily life. **Mathematics in Action** has been written to help you to understand and to use mathematics sensibly and well—to save you time and effort. Some parts of mathematics are needed in other subjects and some parts will be studied in greater detail later on.

Mathematics in Action follows the latest thinking in *what* mathematics should be studied and how hard, or easy, it should be. So you are taken forward, stage by stage, as far as you can go.

Exercises for practice, Puzzles and Games for fun, Brainstormers to make you think, Investigations to explore, Practical Activities, even Check-ups (to see how you're doing)—all are here.

Enjoy maths with **Mathematics in Action!** Let's hope that you will find a lot that is worthwhile, interesting, and above all, useful.

MiAG April 1986

MEASURING

Class discussion—seeing is believing?

Angela   Brenda   Carol   Debbie   Elaine

1 a *Guess* who is the tallest girl.
  b *Guess* who is the shortest girl.
  c Who *is* the tallest girl?
  d Who *is* the shortest girl?
  e What is the difference in height between the tallest and shortest girls?
  f At which question did you first *have* to use a ruler?
  g What unit of measurement on your ruler did you use?
  h Why did you choose this unit?

2 a *Guess* which is longer, the mast or the deck of the yacht.
  b Which *is* longer?
  c Is eyesight alone good enough for comparing lengths? Give a reason for your answer.
  d Are units of measurement necessary for comparing lengths?
  e When are units of measurement of length necessary?

3 Imagine that you are talking to the 'Thing from Outer Space' by radio.
How could you explain the idea of units of length?

MEASURING AND DRAWING

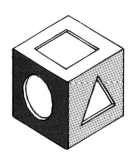

This is a 'Post-box' toy for small children. Three sets of shapes are shown below.
In each case measure the shapes to find the one which is the best fit for the hole. Can you also pick out the other shapes which would fit through the hole, and the ones which would be too big?

1 Square hole

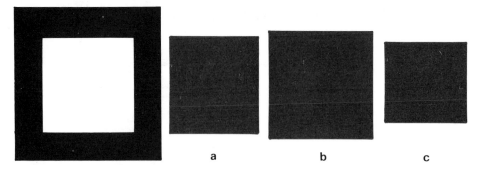

a   b   c

2 Triangular hole

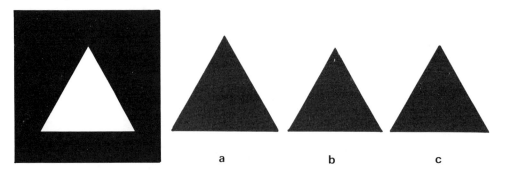

a   b   c

3 Circular hole

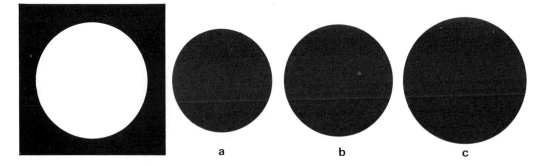

a   b   c

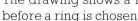

The drawing shows a ring gauge. This is used in a jeweller's shop to find the size of a finger before a ring is chosen.
Anne's finger has a ring size 7.

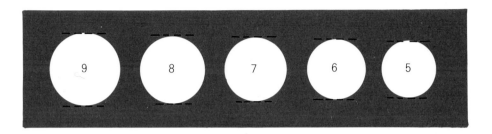

1 Which of the rings below would fit her finger?

2 If Anne cannot find a ring which fits, she can choose one bigger than the size she needs. It will be altered free of charge.
She can also pick one which is too small, but then she will have to pay for the alteration.
Which of these rings could be altered free of charge?

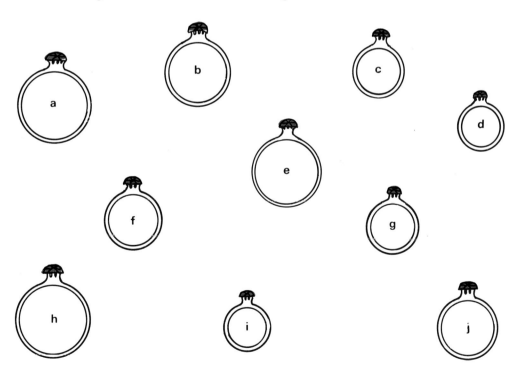

MEASURING AND DRAWING

MEASURING AND DRAWING

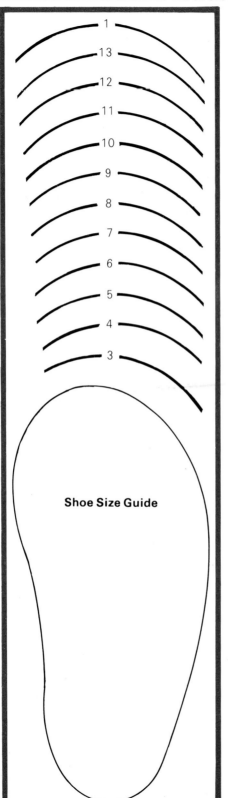

Shoe Size Guide

This diagram shows a shoe-size guide.

1 Which is larger, size 6 or size 9?

2 Which is larger, size 3 or size 1 *on the chart*?

3 How many spaces are there from size 3 to size 13?

4 Measure the difference in length, in millimetres, between size 3 and size 13.

5 Use your answers to questions **3** and **4** to calculate the difference in length, in millimetres, between one shoe size and the next.

6 How long do you think a *small* size 1 foot would be?

7 Would it be sensible to include a size zero?
  a Give a reason for your answer.
  b What length would it be?

There are small holes between postage stamps to help you to tear the stamps apart. These are called *perforations*.

Stamp-collectors can tell whether a stamp is genuine by its number of perforations. They do this by counting the number of perforations in a length of 20 millimetres. Here is an example:

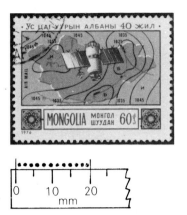

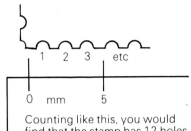

Counting like this, you would find that the stamp has 12 holes in a space of 20 mm, giving a perforation number of 12.

1 Find the perforation number for each of the stamps below.

2 Do all four sides of each stamp have the same perforation number?

3 Find the perforation number for some British stamps.

MEASURING AND DRAWING

1 Measure the width and the height of the opening in this doorway.

2 Which of the doors below would you buy to fit the doorway?

3 If you had to take one of the other doors, which one would you choose? Why?

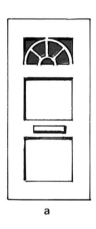

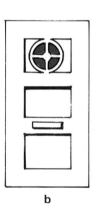

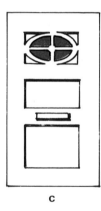

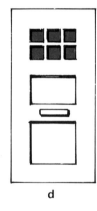

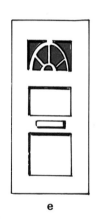

a   b   c   d   e

4 Which of the automatic washing machines below will just fit through the doorway if you keep the front facing outwards?

5 If you had to take one of the others, which one would you choose? Why?

6 In what way is the problem of fitting the door different from the problem of moving the washing machine through the doorway?

a   b   c   d

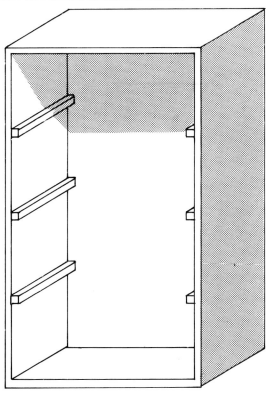

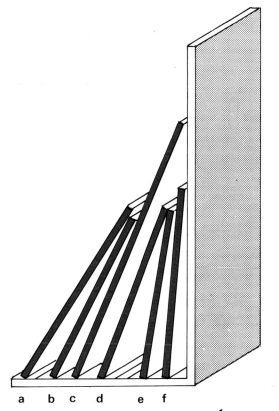

a   b   c   d   e   f

1 Which one of the six shelves fits the bookcase exactly?

2 Which ones could be cut to size to fit?

3 Which of these books would be the right size to stand on one of the shelves in the completed bookcase?

4 Estimate the number of books that the completed bookcase could hold.

5 Odd pieces of wood can sometimes be bought cheaply. Which of these pieces could be cut to make suitable shelves?

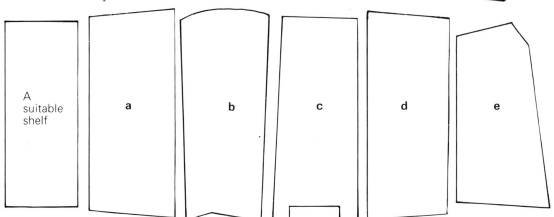

A suitable shelf   a   b   c   d   e

MEASURING AND DRAWING

Here is a 'scaled-down' ruler. You can make the ruler in card, or copy the marks from it onto a piece of paper, like this

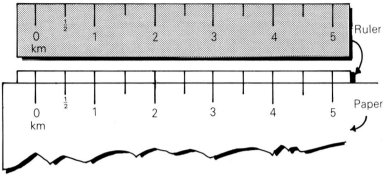

1 You can use your 'ruler' to measure the distance between points on a map. What is the distance in kilometres between the places marked X and Y?

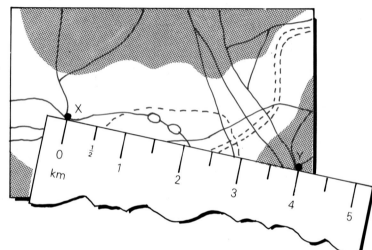

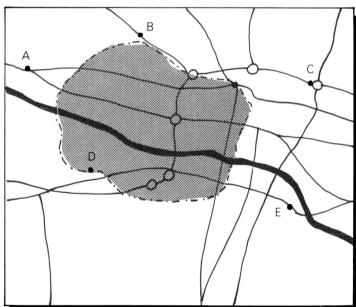

2 Here is a map of a city centre. It has the same scale as your ruler.
Measure the distances in a straight line, to the nearest $\frac{1}{2}$ km, between:
a A and B   **b** B and C
c C and D   **d** D and E
e E and A

First, decide which of these 'scaled rulers' to use for each question.
Then trace it, or transfer it onto paper or card, as in Exercise *3A*. Extend your ruler if necessary.

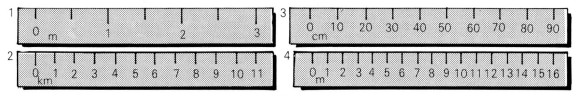

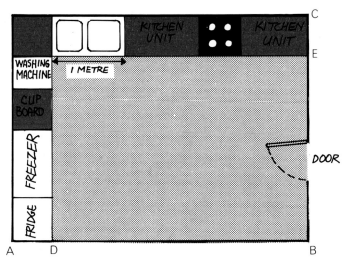

1 Which ruler would you choose to measure this kitchen?

2 a Measure the length and breadth of the kitchen (AB and BC).
  b Measure the length and breadth of the floor-area that has to be covered with linoleum (DB and BE).

3 a Which ruler would you choose to measure distances on this map?
  b Check that the distance from Alva to Tullibody as the crow flies (in a straight line) is about 3 kilometres.
  c Which town is 9 kilometres from Stirling in a straight line?
  d Which towns are between 6 and 7 kilometres from Stirling?
  e Which towns are between 3 and 4 kilometres from Alloa?
  f Which town is about 3 kilometres from Stirling and 8 kilometres from Alloa?

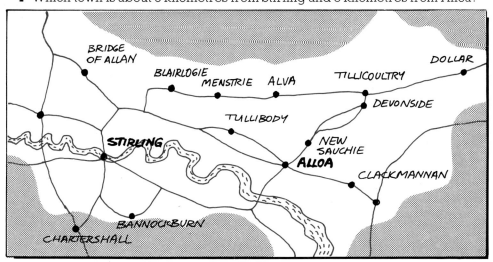

Exercise 3C   Bowls

Many people enjoy playing bowls. You might have watched them playing the game on television, or in the park. The aim is to roll your bowl closer to the jack (a smaller white ball) than your opponent's.

Here is a picture of four bowls and the jack during a game.

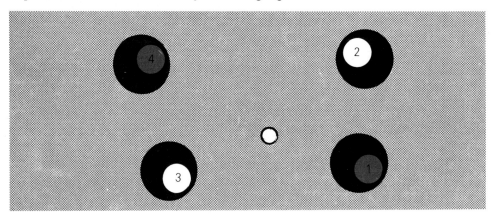

1 a Use one of the rulers in Exercise *3B* to check that bowl number 1 is 20 centimetres from the jack (measure between their nearest points).

b *Guess* the order in which the bowls lie—the nearest one to the jack first.

c Measure the distance of each bowl from the jack, in centimetres, as in question **1a**.

d Sketch one of the bowls and the jack. Mark points to show where you took your measurements from.

2 Using your ruler and protractor, and compasses if you wish, make an exact copy of the diagram. No tracing paper allowed!

Exercise 4A   In the home

Choose the correct 'scaled ruler' in each question. Again, extend your ruler if necessary.

1 Lindsay's Mum would like to have this picture framed. To calculate the cost of the frame she has to know the perimeter (the distance round the sides).

The picture is 70 cm high. Find the perimeter.

2 The length of each edge of the table in this room is 1 metre.
Find the perimeter of the room.

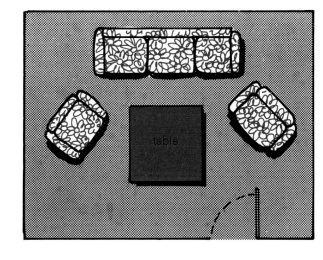

3

Some members of the Youth Club have to decorate this lorry to take part in the Summer Parade. They want to pin a frill of coloured paper round both sides and the back of the trailer, which is rectangular in shape.

Use the right-hand diagram to measure the total length of paper that they will need.

Exercise 4B   In the garden

The diagram shows a scale drawing of a lawn with clothes poles set at each of the corners. AB represents a length of 5 metres.

1 Use your ruler, or one of the scaled rulers, to find the distance between the clothes poles marked nearest to A and B.

2 What length of rope is needed to go round all four poles, ignoring any extra needed for windings and knots?

3 How much more rope is

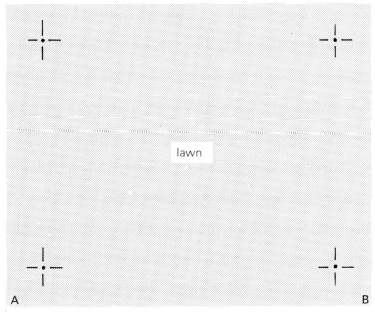

needed if the clothes lines are also taken diagonally between pairs of poles (from corner to corner)?

Exercise 4C   Fencing

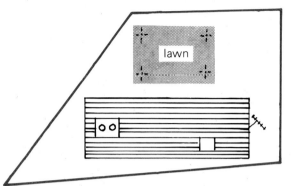

lawn

This diagram shows an *overhead view* of the garden, house and lawn.

The owner wants to put a fence round the garden, leaving a gap of 2 metres for a gate.

1 Remembering that the lawn is about 5 metres long, find the length of fencing the owner would have to buy to go right round the garden.

2 Fence posts are needed at every corner, at the sides of the gate, and at 2 metre spaces. How many posts will the owner have to buy? Make a sketch of the arrangement of fencing, posts and gate as you see it.

DRAWING

Exercise 5A   Scale drawing

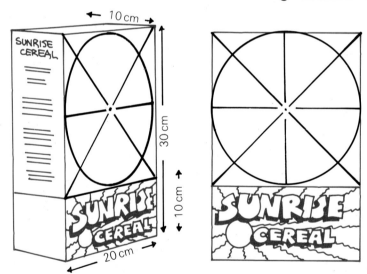

A breakfast cereal is packaged in cardboard cartons like the one above.

1 What shape is each face of the carton?

2 Using this 'scaled-down ruler' to help you, make a scale drawing of each different face, on plain or squared paper. (You will only need three drawings.)

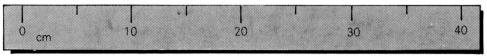

3 a On the front face draw the pattern of straight lines which you see on the front of the carton.
   b Now draw the circle shown on the front of the carton.

4 The cereal is sent to the shops in boxes of 36 cartons.
Here is one way to pack the boxes.
Check that there are 36 cartons.

5 Calculate the length, breadth and height of the box which will hold cartons packed like this.

6 Sketch another way to pack 36 cartons.

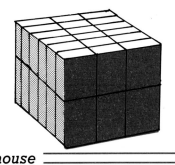

===================== *Exercise 5B   A model house* =====================

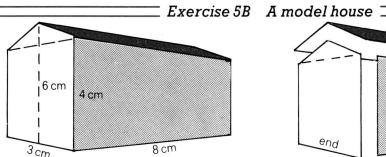

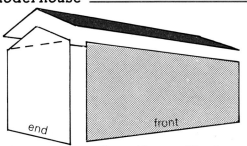

Dave has a model railway, and he has decided to make several cardboard houses like the one shown above. Before cutting the cardboard he has to make accurate drawings.

1 What shape is the front of the house?

2 Using your ruler and squared paper, make an accurate drawing of the front of the house.

3 How would you describe the shape of the end of the house? Make an accurate drawing of the end.

4 Measure the length of the sloping sides of the triangular part of your drawing.

5 The roof is made from a rectangle which is creased and folded as shown. Make an accurate drawing of this rectangle.

6 You can now make the model house if you wish.

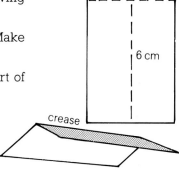

===================== *Exercise 5C   A lean-to shed* =====================

Dave decides to add a 'lean-to' shed to one of his houses.
Its roof has to have the same slope as the roof of the house.

1 Make an accurate drawing of the end of the shed. You will have to use your drawing of the side of the house.

2 Measure the height of the front of the shed.

3 Draw the front of the shed.

4 Draw the roof of the shed.

5 If the end of the shed was to be 3 cm long, what difference would this make to the front and roof of the shed?

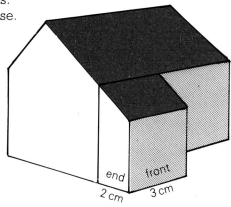

Exercise 6A   Straight line designs

1 Follow the flowchart carefully. The data are listed at the foot of the page. The diagrams at the right-hand side are to help you. They have been drawn using different data, so you will get a different picture.

To draw a straight line picture

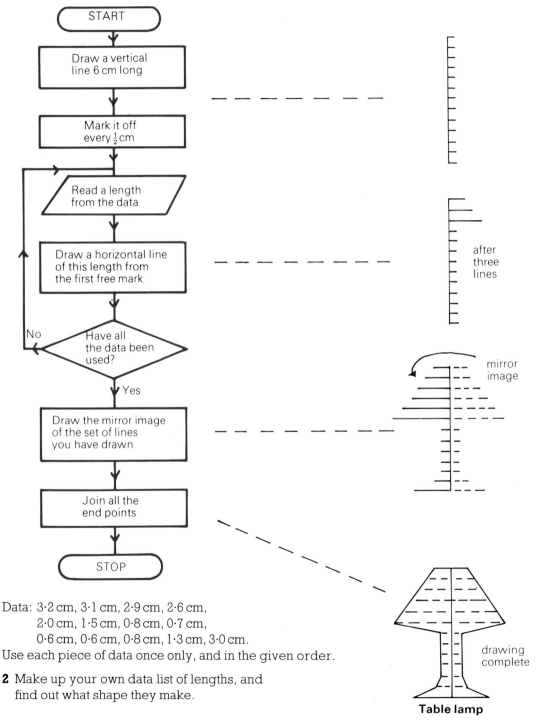

START

Draw a vertical line 6 cm long

Mark it off every $\frac{1}{2}$ cm

Read a length from the data

Draw a horizontal line of this length from the first free mark

Have all the data been used?

No

Yes

Draw the mirror image of the set of lines you have drawn

Join all the end points

STOP

after three lines

mirror image

drawing complete

Table lamp

Data: 3·2 cm, 3·1 cm, 2·9 cm, 2·6 cm,
     2·0 cm, 1·5 cm, 0·8 cm, 0·7 cm,
     0·6 cm, 0·6 cm, 0·8 cm, 1·3 cm, 3·0 cm.
Use each piece of data once only, and in the given order.

2 Make up your own data list of lengths, and find out what shape they make.

1 Follow this flowchart. The data are listed below the flowchart.
  Once again the diagrams at the right-hand side should help you to follow the instructions.

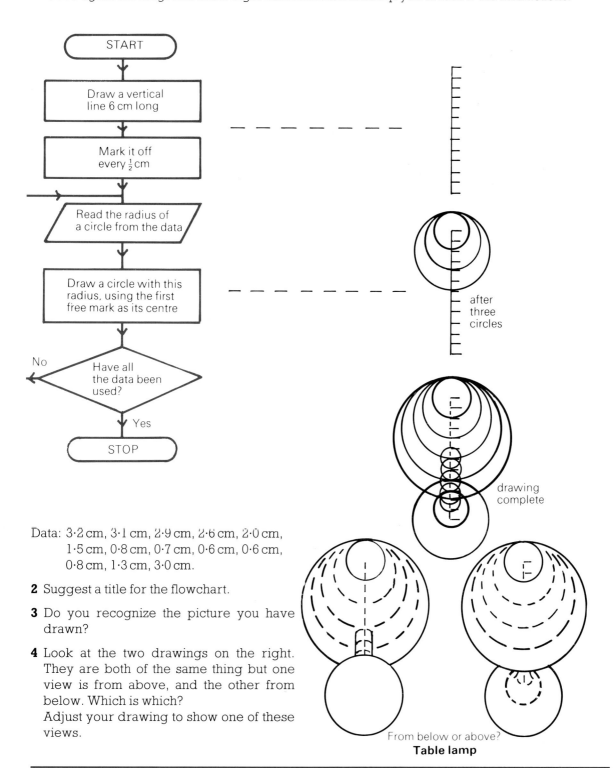

after
three
circles

drawing
complete

Data: 3·2 cm, 3·1 cm, 2·9 cm, 2·6 cm, 2·0 cm,
      1·5 cm, 0·8 cm, 0·7 cm, 0·6 cm, 0·6 cm,
      0·8 cm, 1·3 cm, 3·0 cm.

2 Suggest a title for the flowchart.

3 Do you recognize the picture you have drawn?

4 Look at the two drawings on the right. They are both of the same thing but one view is from above, and the other from below. Which is which?
  Adjust your drawing to show one of these views.

From below or above?
Table lamp

15

A games company wants new designs for a pack of cards. Can you draw the four aces?

1 ACE OF DIAMONDS

Draw the card first—a rectangle 57 mm by 85 mm.
Find the exact centre, and draw the
diamond symbol accurately.

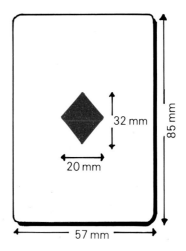

2 ACE OF HEARTS

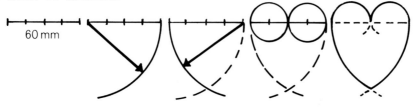

Follow the diagrams carefully, and draw the heart symbol.

3 ACE OF SPADES

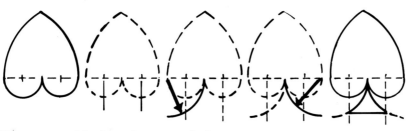

Draw an upside down heart symbol.
Then follow the diagram to make the spade symbol.

4 ACE OF CLUBS

 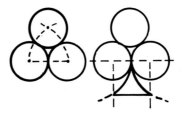

Follow the diagrams, and draw the club symbol.

MEASURING AND DRAWING

16

Lynn decides to make Easter cards for her friends. She wants to know how to draw eggs. She is given the following instructions and diagrams. Try to follow them and draw an egg.

Step 1   Draw a circle with centre A and radius 3 cm.
Step 2   Draw a diameter BC.
Step 3   Draw an arc with centre B and radius BC.
Step 4   Draw another arc, with centre C and radius CB.
          Call the point where the two arcs meet 'D'.
Step 5   Join A to D, using a ruler.
          Call the point where this line cuts the circle 'E'.
Step 6   Draw a line from B through E.
          Call the point where it cuts the arc 'F'.
Step 7   Draw a circle with centre E and radius EF.
Step 8   You should now be able to draw the egg in a heavy line.

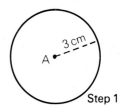

Step 1

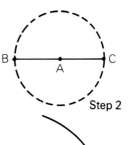

Step 2

For her cards, Lynn wants to draw an egg 13 cm high.
She has to find out the starting radius.

1   What is the height of the egg you have drawn?
2   Divide this height by 3 (number of cm in the starting radius).
3   Draw another egg, with a starting radius of 4 cm.
4   Divide its height by 4.
5   What do you notice about your answers to questions **2** and **4**?
6   What radius should Lynn use?

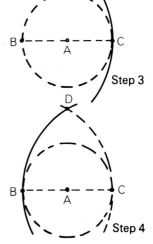

Step 3

Step 4

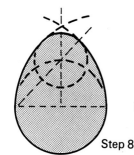

Step 8

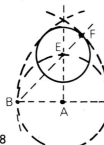

Step 7

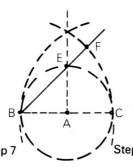

Step 6

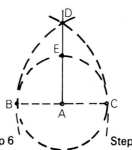

Step 5

MEASURING AND DRAWING

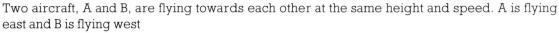

MEASURING AND DRAWING

Two aircraft, A and B, are flying towards each other at the same height and speed. A is flying east and B is flying west
A has a radio range of 50 km, and B has a radio range of 70 km.
This drawing shows the position when the aircraft are 140 km apart.

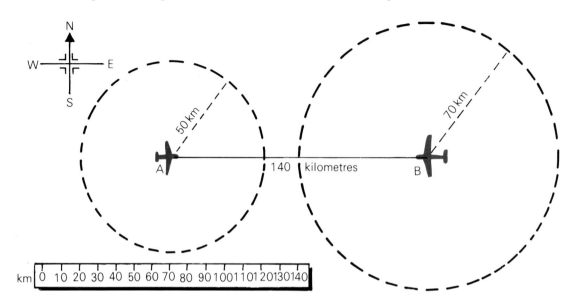

km | 0 10 20 30 40 50 60 70 80 90 100 110 120 130 140

The circles show the limit of radio range of each aircraft.

1 Can either pilot hear the other?

2 Is it possible for anyone to hear both pilots?

3 What is the distance between A and B after the aircraft have flown a further 10 km? Make a scale drawing of the position then, like the one above.

4 Mark the position of a person who can now pass messages from one pilot to the other and back again.

5 Draw the position after the aircraft have flown a further 10 km.

6 Show, by shading, all possible places where radio calls from both pilots can be heard.

7 Mark the position of the person furthest north who can receive calls from both pilots. Call this position C.

8 How far is: **a** C from A   **b** C from B   **c** A from B?

*Questions **1**–**8** should suggest answers to the following:*

9 Could you draw a triangle with sides 50 mm, 70 mm and 100 mm long? If your answer is 'Yes', then draw the triangle. If 'No', explain why.

10 Repeat question **9** for the following lengths of sides:
a 50 mm, 70 mm, 120 mm   **b** 50 mm, 70 mm, 140 mm   **c** 50 mm, 70 mm, 70 mm
d 50 mm, 70 mm, 50 mm   **e** 50 mm, 70 mm, 30 mm   **f** 50 mm, 70 mm, 20 mm

11 Can you make up a rule for deciding when three lengths will make a triangle?

MULTIPLES

Cards and envelopes

This is a blank 'multiples envelope'.

The numbers shown on these cards are the **natural numbers**.

$$3 \times 1 = 3$$
$$3 \times 2 = 6$$
$$3 \times 3 = 9$$
$$3 \times 4 = 12$$
$$3 \times 5 = 15$$

This strip was cut from the multiplication table.

If 3 is written on the envelope then [3], [6], [9], [12] and [15] can all go into it.

3, 6, 9, 12 and 15 are the first five multiples of 3.
3, 6, 9, 12 and 15 are all **divisible** by 3;
this means that 3 divides into them exactly, with
no remainder.

$3 \div 3 = 1$ (no remainder).
$6 \div 3 = 2$ (no remainder).
$9 \div 3 = 3$ (no remainder).
$12 \div 3 = 4$ (no remainder).
$15 \div 3 = 5$ (no remainder).

$20 \div 5 = 4$,
no remainder.

20 is divisible by 5
so 20 is a multiple of 5.

$7 \div 6 = 1$,
remainder 1.

7 is not divisible by 6,
so 7 is not a multiple of 6.

1A a List all the multiples of 2 from 2 to 20. (2, 4, 6, 8, . . .).
   b List all the multiples of 3 from 3 to 15.
   c List all the multiples of 4 from 4 to 20.
   d List all the multiples of 5 from 5 to 30.

Say whether or not each number can go into the envelope in questions **2A–9A**.

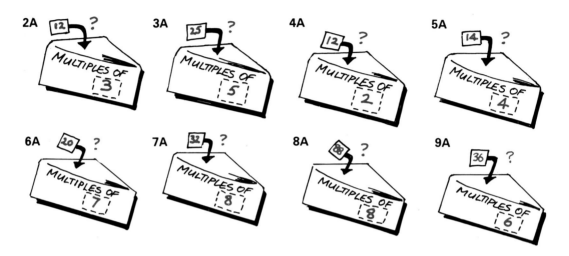

List the numbers that can go into the envelopes in questions **10A–18B**.

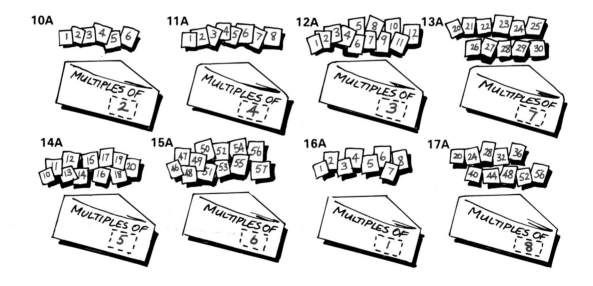

Explain why it is difficult to choose one envelope each for , and

Exercise 2   Out or in?

All the cards have been tipped out of these envelopes. In each pile the largest number is on top. List all the numbers that could be on the other cards in the pile.

Example

Multiples of 4. The largest number in the pile is 20. The numbers could be 4, 8, 12, 16, 20.

1A

2A

3A

4A

5A

6A

7A

8A

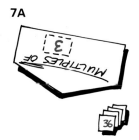

9B

10B

11B

12B

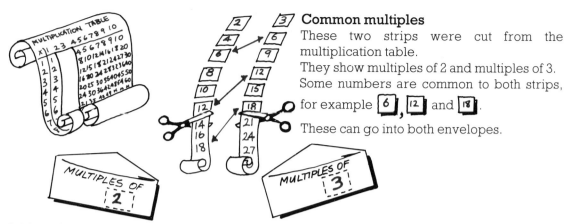

Common multiples

These two strips were cut from the multiplication table.

They show multiples of 2 and multiples of 3. Some numbers are common to both strips, for example 6 , 12 and 18 .

These can go into both envelopes.

6, 12 and 18 are divisible by both 2 and 3, so they are **common multiples** of 2 and 3.
6 is the **least common multiple (lcm)** of 2 and 3.

=================== *Exercise 3   In both* ===================

Write down the first three common multiples of the numbers shown on each pair of envelopes. Say which is the least common multiple (lcm).

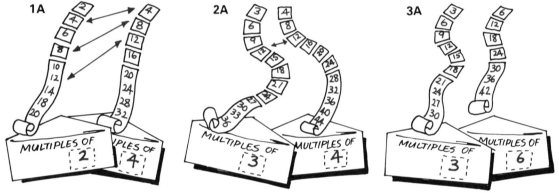

Make lists of the multiples of the numbers on the envelopes until you have at least two common multiples. Say which is the least common multiple (lcm).

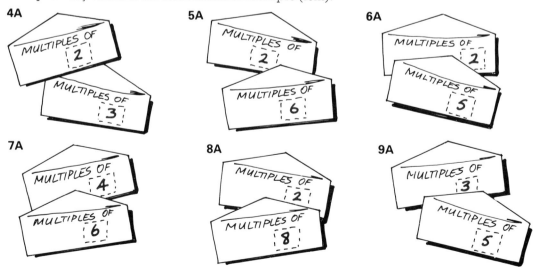

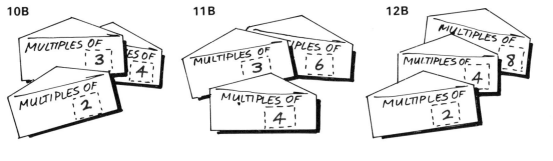

10B MULTIPLES OF 3 / ...ES OF 4 / MULTIPLES OF 2

11B MULTIPLES OF 3 / ...PLES OF 6 / MULTIPLES OF 4

12B MULTIPLES OF 8 / MULTIPLES OF 4 / MULTIPLES OF 2

================= *Exercise 4   Both out* =================

MULTIPLES OF 2 / MULTIPLES OF 3 (with 6 and 6)

The lcm of 2 and 3 is 6. 6 is the least number that is divisible by 2 and 3.

Without writing lists of multiples, find the least common multiple (lcm) of the numbers in the envelopes.

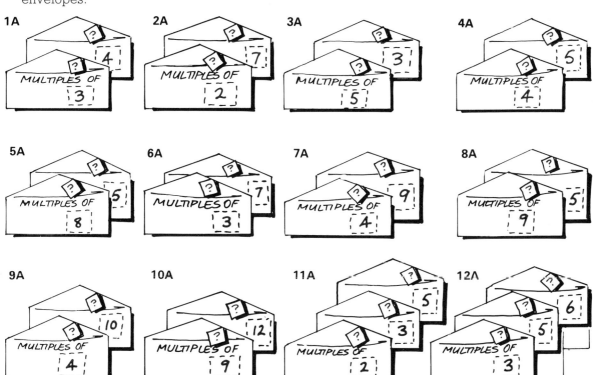

1A MULTIPLES OF 3 / 4

2A MULTIPLES OF 2 / 7

3A MULTIPLES OF 5 / 3

4A MULTIPLES OF 4 / 5

5A MULTIPLES OF 8 / 5

6A MULTIPLES OF 3 / 7

7A MULTIPLES OF 4 / 9

8A MULTIPLES OF 9 / 5

9A MULTIPLES OF 4 / 10   (not 40!)

10A MULTIPLES OF 9 / 12   (not 108!)

11A MULTIPLES OF 2 / 3 / 5

12A MULTIPLES OF 3 / 5 / 6

Find the lcm of:

13B 2, 17	**14B** 6, 18	**15B** 8, 10	**16B** 10, 14
17B 5, 13	**18B** 5, 10, 15	**19B** 4, 6, 9	**20B** 3, 4, 8
21C 24, 30	**22C** 18, 25	**23C** 42, 60	**24C** 56, 120

An application of multiples

=== *Exercise 5   Video tapes* ===

1A
This video tape lasts for 1 hour.
How many programmes can be recorded on one side if each programme lasts:
a 30 minutes   **b** 20 minutes   **c** 15 minutes   **d** 60 minutes?

2A Here is a 2 hour tape. How many programmes could be recorded on it if each programme lasts:
a 30 minutes   **b** 90 minutes   **c** 40 minutes   **d** 1 hour?

3A Which of these programme lengths could be recorded on a 90 minute tape *without* any waste? For example, four 20 minute programmes = 80 minutes so 10 minutes would be wasted.
a 30 minutes   **b** 60 minutes   **c** 45 minutes   **d** 40 minutes
e 15 minutes.

Write down the shortest playing time for the tapes in questions **4A–8B** so that there would be no waste. For example, 30 and 40 minute programmes would both fit exactly into 120 minute tapes.

4A
Meant for
20 minute and 30 minute programmes.

5A
Meant for 15 minute and 20 minute programmes.

6A

7B

8B

9C

b

a The MIA video company wants to make a new tape designed to record 20 minute, 25 minute and 30 minute programmes without waste. Their research scientists tell them that $4\frac{3}{4}$ hours is the maximum possible playing time for any tape.
Is it possible for the company to make this new tape?

Is this tape possible, with a $4\frac{3}{4}$ hour maximum playing time?

A natural allsort: prime numbers

How can these ten cards be sorted into the multiples envelopes?

Here's how:

Write 1 on the first envelope. Then the envelope can swallow the lot!

The numbers on the cards are all divisible by 1. So they are all multiples of 1.

That's too easy! Let's put 1 aside since 1 is too greedy.

Without using greedy 1, how can these cards be sorted into the multiples envelopes?

Here's how: follow this flowchart

Prime numbers

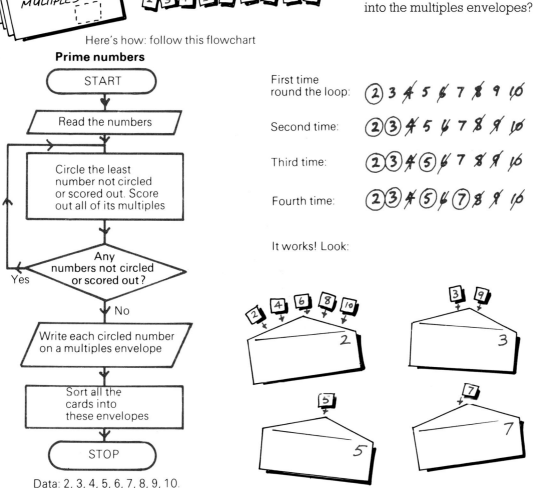

First time round the loop: ② 3 4̸ 5 6̸ 7 8̸ 9 1̸0̸

Second time: ② ③ 4̸ 5 6̸ 7 8̸ 9̸ 1̸0̸

Third time: ② ③ 4̸ ⑤ 6̸ 7 8̸ 9̸ 1̸0̸

Fourth time: ② ③ 4̸ ⑤ 6̸ ⑦ 8̸ 9̸ 1̸0̸

It works! Look:

Data: 2, 3, 4, 5, 6, 7, 8, 9, 10.

Only four envelopes were needed. The numbers on the outside of these envelopes are 2, 3, 5 and 7.

These numbers are multiples of only themselves and, of course, greedy 1.

This means each is divisible only by itself and by 1.

They are called **prime numbers**.

AMONG THE NATURAL NUMBERS

1A Sort these numbers into multiples envelopes. Then list the prime numbers.

a 2   3   8   9   11   12
b 3   5   10   12   13   15
c 5   7   10   14   19   20
d 3   5   6   7   11   14   15   18
e 2   4   5   6   7   10   11   12   15   19

2A By sorting the list   2   3   4   5   6   7   8   9   10   11   12   13   14   15   16   17   18   19   20, find all the prime numbers up to 20.

3A Here are some bigger lists. Decide which one you want to try.

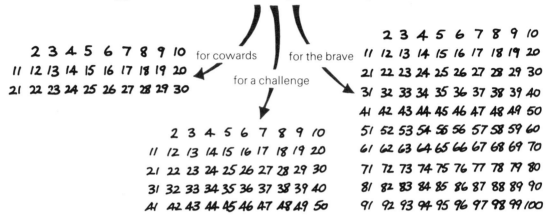

for cowards   for the brave   for a challenge

4A

Here is part of the first page of the book 'The Prime Number Sorter's Guide to the Natural Numbers'.

2	547	1229	1993	2749	3581	4421	5281
3	557	1231	1997	2763	3583	4423	5297
5	563	1237	1999	2767	3593	4441	5303
7	569	1249	2003	2777	3607	4447	5309
11	571	1259	2011	2789	3613	4451	5323
13	577	1277	2017	2791	3617	4457	5333
17	587	1279	2027	2797	3623	4463	5347
19	593	1283	2029	2801	3631	4481	5351
23	599	1289	2039	2803	3637	4483	5381
29	601	1291	2053	2819	3643	4493	5387
31	607	1297	2063	2833	3659	4507	5393
37	613	1301	2069	2837	3671	4513	5399
41	617	1303	2081	2843	3673	4517	5407
43	619	1307	2083	2851	3677	4519	5413
47	631	1319	2087	2857	3691	4523	5417
53	641	1321	2089	2861	3697	4547	
59	643	1327	2099	2879	3701	4549	
61	647	1361	2111	2887	3709		
67	653	1367	2113	2897	3719		
71	659	1373	2129	2903	3727		
73	661	1381	2131	2909			
79	673	1399	2137	2917			
83	677	1409	2141				
89	683	1423	2143				
97	691	1427					
101							

Put the numbers above into the correct barrels. (List them opposite A, B, C).

5A

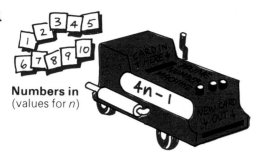

Numbers in
(values for *n*)

Numbers in	Calculation	Numbers out
1	$4 \times 1 - 1$	3
2	$4 \times 2 - 1$	7
$\vdots$	$\vdots$	$\vdots$

Copy and complete the calculations for ten 'Numbers in'.
How many prime numbers came out?

6B, C

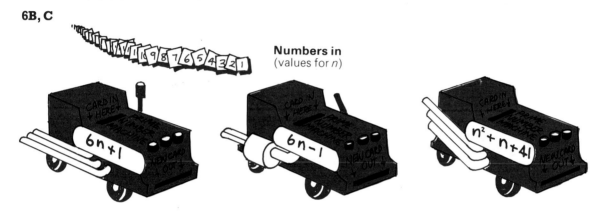

Numbers in
(values for *n*)

$6n + 1$ $6n - 1$ $n^2 + n + 41$

a Put 1 2 3 into each machine. (Remember $n^2 = n \times n$.) Is each machine making prime numbers?

b Put 4 into each machine. One of the machines has had a 'hiccup' by producing a non-prime. Which machine is it?

c Put 5 in. Are all three machines working properly again?

d Put 6 in. Describe what has happened now.

e Put 7 8 in. Have there been any more 'hiccups'?

f Put 9 10 in. For these ten numbers which machine has worked best (fewest 'hiccups'), and which machine has been worst (most 'hiccups')?

g Now put in 11 12 13 14 15 16 17 18 19 20 . How do the machines compare for the first twenty numbers?

Here are some questions to investigate:

(i) WILL THE BEST MACHINE EVER HAVE A 'HICCUP'?

(ii) HOW MANY OF THE FIRST TWENTY PRIMES DO THE '6n+1' AND THE '6n-1' MACHINES MAKE BETWEEN THEM? INVESTIGATE FURTHER

(iii) IN THE LONG RUN, WHICH OF THE '6n+1' AND '6n-1' MACHINES HAS MORE 'HICCUPS'?

(iv) TRY TO MAKE UP A 'HICCUP' RATE FOR THE MACHINES.

(v) HOW DO THE MACHINES WORK FOR BIG INPUT NUMBERS, eg 334 335 ?

(vi) CAN YOU INVENT YOUR OWN PRIME NUMBER MACHINE. SEE IF YOURS WILL BEAT YOUR NEIGHBOUR'S (FEWER 'HICCUPS')? $4n+1$ $4n^2+1$ $12n+1$ $2n^2+3$ n^2+n+1

The largest known prime number is $2^{216091} - 1$. This is a number with 65 050 digits. Think of a way to estimate the number of pages of this book that would be needed to print this number. Write out your method.

FACTORS

Another envelope

This is a blank 'factors envelope'.

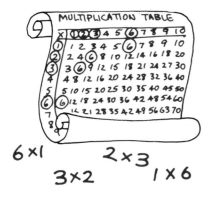

6×1 $\quad$ 2×3
3×2 $\quad$ 1×6

THE FACTORS OF

If '6' is written on the envelope then

THE FACTORS OF 6

$\boxed{1}$, $\boxed{2}$, $\boxed{3}$ and $\boxed{6}$

can all go into it.

1, 2, 3 and 6 are the factors of 6.
6 is divisible by 1, 2, 3 and 6;
this means that 1, 2, 3 and 6 divide into 6 exactly.

═══════════════ *Exercise 7   All in* ═══════════════

In each of the following questions say whether or not the number can go into the envelope.

1A

THE FACTORS OF 6

2A

THE FACTORS OF 5

3A

THE FACTORS OF 7

4A

THE FACTORS OF 10

Each of these envelopes holds *all* the factors of the number on it.
Copy and complete the list of factors in each envelope.

1, 2, . . ., 10.

. . ., 11.

1, . . ., 3, . . ., 6, 12.

1, . . ., . . ., 27.

1, . . ., . . ., 21.

1, . . ., . . ., 35.

1, 2, 4, . . ., . . ., . . ., . . .,

. . ., 2, . . ., 8.

. . ., . . ., . . ., 15.

. . ., 2, . . ., 6, . . ., 18.

. . . .

. . . .

List the numbers in each envelope.

Prime factors

After all her work on factors, Molly noticed that every number had a set of prime factors. Can you see the set of prime factors of 60?

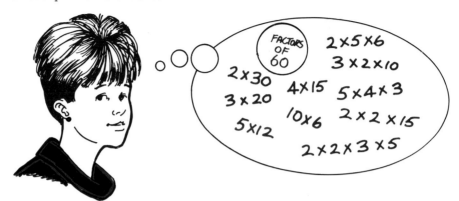

She tried to think of a good system for finding these prime factors. 'Like peeling an onion,' she thought. 'One prime factor at a time.'

For 60, peel off 2: 2×30
Peel off 2 again: $2 \times 2 \times 15$
Now peel off 3 (the next 'skin'): $2 \times 2 \times 3 \times 5 = 2^2 \times 3 \times 5$.

'Or like branches of a tree':

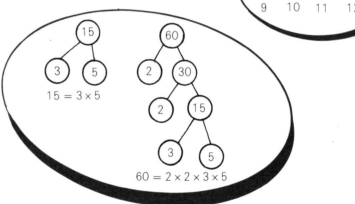

$15 = 3 \times 5$

$60 = 2 \times 2 \times 3 \times 5$

═══════════════ *Exercise 8   In their prime* ═══════════════

Write each number as a product of prime factors. For example, $60 = 2 \times 2 \times 3 \times 5$.

1A 6	**2A** 14	**3A** 21	**4A** 22	**5A** 35
6A 10	**7A** 26	**8A** 33	**9A** 65	**10A** 77
11A 4	**12A** 9	**13A** 25	**14A** 49	**15A** 121
16A 18	**17A** 20	**18A** 28	**19A** 45	**20A** 50

Another example: $48 = 2 \times 24$
$= 2 \times 2 \times 12$
$= 2 \times 2 \times 2 \times 6$
$= 2 \times 2 \times 2 \times 2 \times 3$
$= 2^4 \times 3$

Write each number as a product of prime factors in its shortest form.
For example, $48 = 2^4 \times 3$.

1B 8	**2B** 27	**3B** 125	**4B** 24	**5B** 54
6B 16	**7B** 100	**8B** 84	**9B** 180	**10B** 81
11B 64	**12B** 374	**13B** 483	**14B** 1000	**15B** 1 000 000

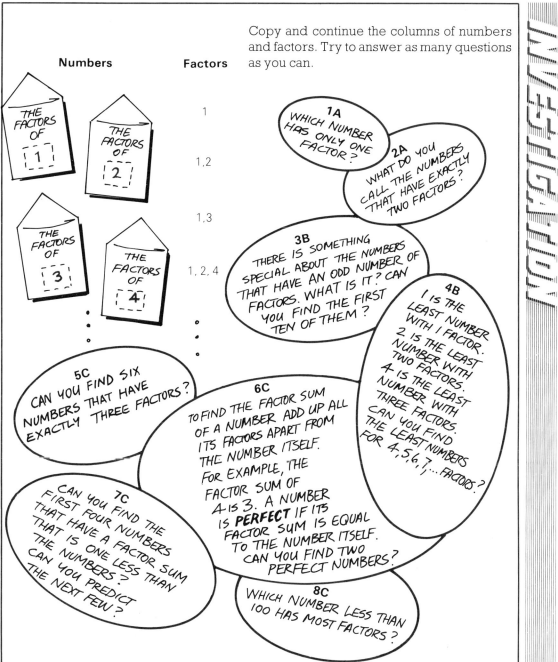

Copy and continue the columns of numbers and factors. Try to answer as many questions as you can.

Numbers   **Factors**

THE FACTORS OF 1

THE FACTORS OF 2

THE FACTORS OF 3

THE FACTORS OF 4

1
1, 2
1, 3
1, 2, 4

1A WHICH NUMBER HAS ONLY ONE FACTOR?

2A WHAT DO YOU CALL THE NUMBERS THAT HAVE EXACTLY TWO FACTORS?

3B THERE IS SOMETHING SPECIAL ABOUT THE NUMBERS THAT HAVE AN ODD NUMBER OF FACTORS. WHAT IS IT? CAN YOU FIND THE FIRST TEN OF THEM?

4B 1 IS THE LEAST NUMBER WITH 1 FACTOR. 2 IS THE LEAST NUMBER WITH TWO FACTORS. 4 IS THE LEAST NUMBER WITH THREE FACTORS. CAN YOU FIND THE LEAST NUMBERS FOR 4, 5, 6, 7 ... FACTORS?

5C CAN YOU FIND SIX NUMBERS THAT HAVE EXACTLY THREE FACTORS?

6C TO FIND THE FACTOR SUM OF A NUMBER ADD UP ALL ITS FACTORS APART FROM THE NUMBER ITSELF. FOR EXAMPLE, THE FACTOR SUM OF 4 IS 3. A NUMBER IS **PERFECT** IF ITS FACTOR SUM IS EQUAL TO THE NUMBER ITSELF. CAN YOU FIND TWO PERFECT NUMBERS?

7C CAN YOU FIND THE FIRST FOUR NUMBERS THAT HAVE A FACTOR SUM THAT IS ONE LESS THAN THE NUMBERS? CAN YOU PREDICT THE NEXT FEW?

8C WHICH NUMBER LESS THAN 100 HAS MOST FACTORS?

Copy and complete this flowchart for finding the factors of a number. Then test it by finding the factors of 20, 36 and 91.

To find the factors of . . .

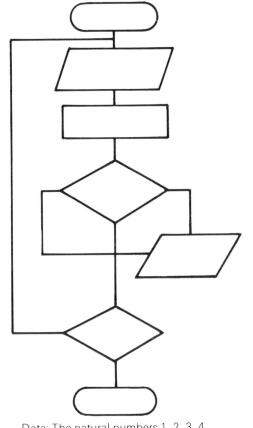

Data: The natural numbers 1, 2, 3, 4, ...

CHECK-UP ON **AMONG THE NATURAL NUMBERS**

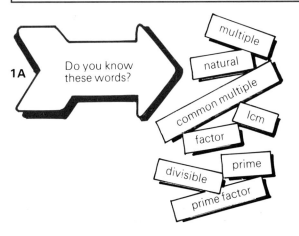

1A Do you know these words?

multiple
natural
common multiple
lcm
factor
divisible
prime
prime factor

Copy and complete the following.

2, 4, and 8 are _____ of 2.

Each is a _____ of 24.

8 is a _____ _____ of 2 and 4,

since it is _____ by both of them.

6 is the _____ of 2 and 3.

6 is not a _____ number, since

it is divisible by _____ and _____.

1, 2, 3, 4, . . . are all _____ numbers.

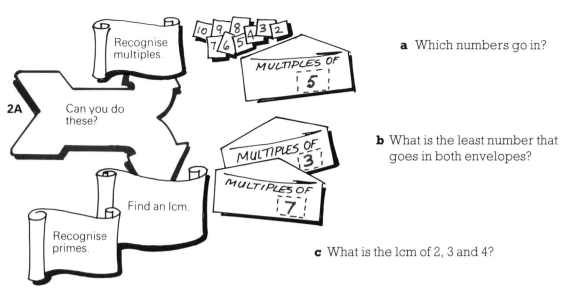

2A Can you do these?

Recognise multiples.

Find an lcm.

Recognise primes.

a Which numbers go in?

b What is the least number that goes in both envelopes?

c What is the lcm of 2, 3 and 4?

d List the first six prime numbers.

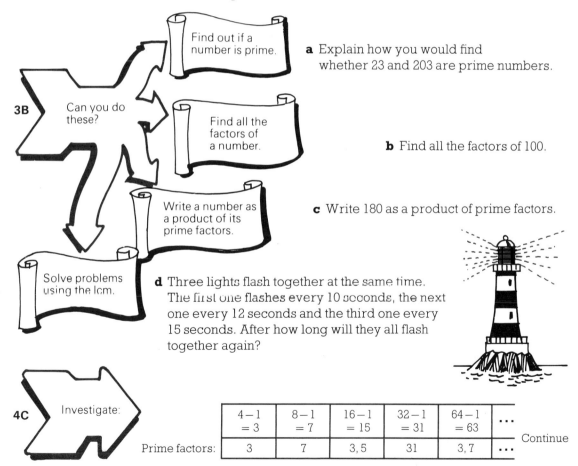

3B Can you do these?

Find out if a number is prime.

Find all the factors of a number.

Write a number as a product of its prime factors.

Solve problems using the lcm.

a Explain how you would find whether 23 and 203 are prime numbers.

b Find all the factors of 100.

c Write 180 as a product of prime factors.

d Three lights flash together at the same time. The first one flashes every 10 seconds, the next one every 12 seconds and the third one every 15 seconds. After how long will they all flash together again?

4C Investigate:

	$4-1$ $=3$	$8-1$ $=7$	$16-1$ $=15$	$32-1$ $=31$	$64-1$ $=63$	$\cdots$
Prime factors:	3	7	3, 5	31	3, 7	$\cdots$

Continue

Describe any patterns that you discover in the prime factors of these numbers. Some of the patterns may help you to continue the table. How far can you go?

FRACTIONS AROUND US

Class discussion
Each of these pictures has something to do with fractions.
Explain the connection in each one.

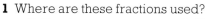

1 Where are these fractions used?

a Half-price   **b** Half-hour   **c** Half-dozen   **d** Half-back

e Half-day   **f** Half-century   **g** Half-time   **h** Half-holiday

i Quarter-deck   **j** A coin called a quarter   **k** Wing three-quarters

l Semi-quaver   **m** One and a half lengths   **n** Time and a half

o Half-life   **p** Half-moon shaped   **q** Quarterly account

r $2\frac{1}{2}$ inches to 1 mile   **s** Three-quarter length coat   **t** Half-share

u One and a half somersaults   **v** 27 inches by $1\frac{1}{4}$ inches (_HINT_ On a bicycle.)

2 Can you think of any others?

THE MEANING OF A FRACTION

Four people sat their driving test.

3 out of 4 passed; $\frac{3}{4}$ of them passed.

1 out of 4 failed; $\frac{1}{4}$ of them failed.

In the fraction $\frac{1}{4}$, 1 is the numerator and 4 is the denominator.

1 This cake has been cut in half.
Sketch or trace it.
Shade one half of it.

2 This pie has been cut into quarters.
Sketch or trace it.
Shade one quarter of it.

3 Sketch or trace these shapes. Each has been divided into equal parts. Shade the fractions shown.

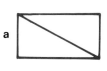   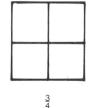   

a $\frac{1}{2}$ b $\frac{3}{4}$ c $\frac{1}{2}$ d $\frac{1}{4}$ e $\frac{5}{6}$

FRACTIONS IN ACTION

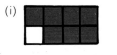

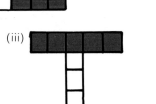

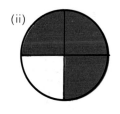

4 a Copy and complete this table for the diagrams (i)–(v):

	(i)	(ii)	(iii)	(iv)	(v)
Fraction shaded	$\frac{7}{8}$				
Fraction unshaded	$\frac{1}{8}$				

b What do you notice about each pair of answers?

c Now complete this table in the same way:

Fraction shaded	$\frac{2}{3}$	$\frac{5}{8}$	$\frac{7}{10}$	$\frac{2}{5}$	$\frac{5}{6}$
Fraction unshaded					

(i) (ii) (iii) (iv) (v)

5 Sketch a car's petrol gauge. Mark in E (Empty), $\frac{1}{4}$, $\frac{1}{2}$, $\frac{3}{4}$, F (Full). Draw the pointer at $\frac{3}{4}$. What fraction of a tankful of petrol has been used?

6 What fraction of the normal price do you have to pay during this sale?

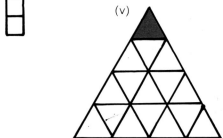

7

What fraction of the keys on this keyboard are:
a black **b** white?

8 a How many days of the week begin with the letter S?
b What fraction of the days of the week begin with the letter S?

9 Fold a rectangular sheet of paper into:
a halves **b** quarters **c** eighths **d** sixteenths

10 Fold a rectangular sheet of paper into:
a thirds **b** sixths **c** twelfths

===================================== *Exercise 3B/C* =====================================

What unit is:

1 $\frac{1}{10}$ of a centimetre **2** $\frac{1}{100}$ of a metre **3** $\frac{1}{100}$ of £1

4 $\frac{1}{1000}$ of a kilometre **5** $\frac{1}{1000}$ of a metre **6** $\frac{1}{1000}$ of a kilogram

7 $\frac{1}{1000}$ of a litre **8** $\frac{1}{100}$ of a litre **9** $\frac{1}{1000}$ of a tonne

10 $\frac{1}{3}$ of a yard **11** $\frac{1}{12}$ of a foot **12** $\frac{1}{8}$ of a gallon

13 $\frac{1}{8}$ of a mile **14** $\frac{1}{14}$ of a stone **15** $\frac{1}{16}$ of a pound (lb)?

What difference do you see between the decimal units of measure and the old imperial units of measure?

ANOTHER WAY OF LOOKING AT A FRACTION

Here are 5 parcels, all the same, and one piece of string 4 m long to tie them up.

Each parcel needs the same length of string, so the 4 metre length is cut into 5 equal parts. Each part will have a length of $4 \div 5$ metres, that is $\frac{4}{5}$ of a metre.

The fraction $\frac{4}{5} = 4 \div 5$

Exercise 4B

1 Write each of these in another way. For example, $\frac{2}{3} = 2 \div 3$.

   a $\frac{3}{4}$ **b** $\frac{4}{5}$ **c** $\frac{1}{3}$ **d** $5 \div 6$ **e** $1 \div 2$

2 Write, as fractions, the sizes of the parts when:

   a a 2 metre length of ribbon is cut into 5 equal lengths,

   b a 3 metre plank of wood is cut into 8 equal lengths,

   c 2 bars of chocolate are divided equally between 3 people,

   d the £200 cost of a holiday is shared equally by 8 friends.

3 Draw sketches to show how:

   a 3 pies could be shared equally between 4 people,

   b 4 bars of chocolate could be shared equally between 5 people.

4 How can you divide:

   a £6 equally between 4 people?

   b £2 between 3 people?

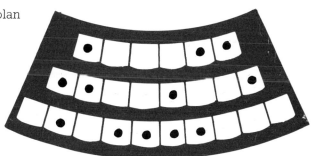

EQUAL FRACTIONS

Half the seats in this theatre balcony plan have been filled. Do you agree?

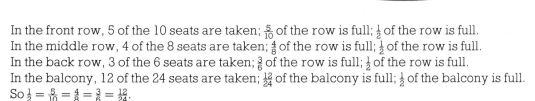

In the front row, 5 of the 10 seats are taken; $\frac{5}{10}$ of the row is full; $\frac{1}{2}$ of the row is full.
In the middle row, 4 of the 8 seats are taken; $\frac{4}{8}$ of the row is full; $\frac{1}{2}$ of the row is full.
In the back row, 3 of the 6 seats are taken; $\frac{3}{6}$ of the row is full; $\frac{1}{2}$ of the row is full.
In the balcony, 12 of the 24 seats are taken; $\frac{12}{24}$ of the balcony is full; $\frac{1}{2}$ of the balcony is full.
So $\frac{1}{2} = \frac{5}{10} = \frac{4}{8} = \frac{3}{6} = \frac{12}{24}$.

      $\frac{1}{2}$ is the simplest form of these equal fractions.

To get equal fractions, multiply the numerator and denominator by the same number or divide the numerator and denominator by the same number.

For example: (i) $\dfrac{1}{2} = \dfrac{1 \times 5}{2 \times 5} = \dfrac{5}{10}$ (ii) $\dfrac{12}{24} = \dfrac{12 \div 12}{24 \div 12} = \dfrac{1}{2}$

(ii) can be worked out like this: $\dfrac{\cancel{12}^{1}}{\cancel{24}_{2}} = \dfrac{1}{2}$

=========================== *Exercise 5A* ===========================

1 Copy and complete:

   a $\dfrac{1}{2} = \dfrac{1 \times 3}{2 \times 3} = \dfrac{}{}$ **b** $\dfrac{1}{3} = \dfrac{1 \times 2}{3 \times 2} = \dfrac{}{}$ **c** $\dfrac{3}{4} = \dfrac{3 \times 5}{4 \times 5} = \dfrac{}{}$

   d $\dfrac{1}{4} = \dfrac{}{8}$ **e** $\dfrac{1}{3} = \dfrac{5}{}$ **f** $\dfrac{1}{2} = \dfrac{}{6}$

2 Write down the simplest form of each of these fractions:

   a $\frac{2}{4}$ **b** $\frac{2}{6}$ **c** $\frac{2}{8}$ **d** $\frac{3}{6}$ **e** $\frac{3}{9}$ **f** $\frac{2}{10}$

   g $\frac{4}{6}$ **h** $\frac{4}{8}$ **i** $\frac{5}{10}$ **j** $\frac{6}{8}$ **k** $\frac{2}{8}$ **l** $\frac{9}{12}$

3 Find, in their simplest form, the fractions shaded in these shapes:

a    b   c    d   e

4 a How many months are there in a year?
   b How many begin with the letter A?
   c What fraction of the months in a year begin with A? (Simplest form.)
   d What fraction of the months in a year begin with J? (Simplest form.)

5 Copy and complete the following table, giving each answer in its simplest form.

Sum of money	50p	20p	25p	60p	75p	10p	5p
Fraction of £1	$\frac{1}{2}$						

6 Write as fractions of an hour, in their simplest form:
   a 30 minutes   **b** 15 minutes   **c** 20 minutes   **d** 45 minutes

7 What fraction of a 400 metre track is the 100 metre track?

8 What fractions of 90°, in their simplest form, are:
   a 10°   **b** 30°   **c** 45°   **d** 60°?

9 Which is the odd one out in these?

a 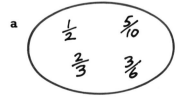   b    c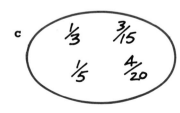

10 You should have the following teeth in both your upper and lower jaw:
4 incisors, 2 canines, 4 premolars and 6 molars.
  a Calculate the total number of teeth.
  b What fraction of this total is each of the
  four kinds of tooth?

=========================== *Exercise 5B* ===========================

1 Copy and complete:

  a $\frac{3}{4} = \frac{}{8}$ **b** $\frac{1}{5} = \frac{}{10}$ **c** $\frac{2}{3} = \frac{6}{}$ **d** $\frac{1}{8} = \frac{4}{}$

  e $\frac{1}{2} = \frac{}{4} = \frac{3}{} = \frac{}{8}$ **f** $\frac{3}{4} = \frac{12}{} = \frac{}{20} = \frac{30}{}$

2 Write down three fractions equal to:

  a $\frac{1}{4}$ **b** $\frac{3}{8}$ **c** $\frac{1}{10}$ **d** $\frac{2}{5}$

3 Ali is paying for his bicycle
in 16 weekly instalments.
What fraction has he paid
after 12 weeks?

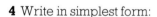

4 Write in simplest form:

  a $\frac{6}{9}$ **b** $\frac{4}{10}$ **c** $\frac{8}{12}$ **d** $\frac{6}{4}$ **e** $\frac{16}{12}$

5 a 16 out of 20 girls in a Ranger Guide company completed the Duke of Edinburgh gold
award. What fraction of the company was this?
  b 35 pupils in a school worked for the silver award, and 21 were successful. What fraction
  was this?

6 Sheila's school has 6 periods each day, Monday to Friday.
Calculate the fraction 1 period is of:
  a a school day   **b** a school week

7 A working week, Monday to Friday, is split into 10 equal shifts. What fraction of the week
is worked by someone who is employed for:
  a 2 days   **b** $2\frac{1}{2}$ days   **c** 3 days and 1 half-day.

8 In garages, the mechanics sometimes measure in thousandths of an inch ('thou'). Write down
the simplest form of 20 'thou'.

A game for two or more players

List all the halves, quarters, eighths and sixteenths which are equal to each of $\frac{1}{8}, \frac{2}{8}, \frac{3}{8}, \frac{4}{8}, \frac{5}{8}, \frac{6}{8}, \frac{7}{8}, \frac{8}{8}$.
For example, $\frac{2}{8} = \frac{1}{4} = \frac{4}{16}$. You should get 22 fractions altogether.
Put each fraction on a card, or a small rectangle of paper. Play 'Snap' like this. Share out the
cards. Take turns to place one, face up, on the desk. If the fraction is equal to the previous one,
call 'Snap', and take all the cards in the pile. Continue until one player has all 22 cards.

MIXED NUMBERS AND 'TOP HEAVY' FRACTIONS

(i)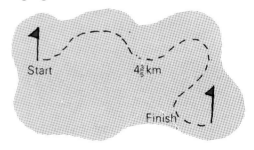

$$\frac{2}{2} + \frac{2}{2} + \frac{1}{2} = \frac{5}{2}$$

$$1 + 1 + \frac{1}{2} = 2\frac{1}{2}$$

$\frac{5}{2} = 5 \div 2 = 2\frac{1}{2}$ (a mixed number)

(ii)

$$\frac{3}{3} + \frac{2}{3} = \frac{5}{3}$$

$$1 + \frac{2}{3} = 1\frac{2}{3}$$

$\frac{5}{3} = 5 \div 3 = 1\frac{2}{3}$ (a mixed number)

(iii) $\frac{13}{8} = 13 \div 8 = 1\frac{5}{8}$

(iv) $2\frac{3}{4} = \frac{8}{4} + \frac{3}{4} = \frac{11}{4}$

Exercise 6

1 Write these as mixed numbers:

a $\frac{3}{2}$ **b** $\frac{5}{2}$ **c** $\frac{9}{4}$ **d** $\frac{9}{8}$ **e** $\frac{11}{8}$

f $\frac{11}{2}$ **g** $\frac{17}{16}$ **h** $\frac{4}{3}$ **i** $\frac{7}{3}$ **j** $\frac{15}{4}$

2 Change these to fractions:

a $3\frac{1}{2}$ **b** $4\frac{1}{2}$ **c** $1\frac{1}{4}$ **d** $1\frac{3}{4}$ **e** $3\frac{1}{4}$

f $1\frac{7}{8}$ **g** $1\frac{5}{8}$ **h** $2\frac{2}{3}$ **i** $3\frac{1}{3}$ **j** $1\frac{3}{16}$

3 In each pair, find which fraction is greater by changing them to mixed numbers:

a $\frac{3}{2}$ or $\frac{5}{4}$ **b** $\frac{4}{3}$ or $\frac{6}{5}$ **c** $\frac{13}{10}$ or $\frac{7}{5}$

4 Flags are placed every $\frac{1}{5}$km along the route of a 'fun run'. The course is $4\frac{3}{5}$km long. How many flags are there, including the ones at the start and finish of the race?

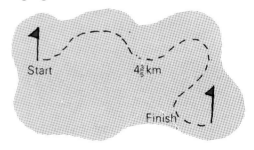

ADDING AND SUBTRACTING FRACTIONS

ONES FIRST!

(i)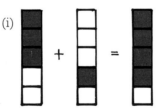

$$\frac{3}{5} + \frac{1}{5} = \frac{4}{5}$$

(ii)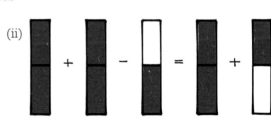

$$2 - \frac{1}{2} = 1\frac{1}{2}$$

(iii) $\quad 4\frac{1}{8} + 2\frac{3}{8}$

$= 4 + \frac{1}{8} + 2 + \frac{3}{8}$

$= 4 + 2 + \frac{1}{8} + \frac{3}{8}$

$= 6\frac{4}{8}$

$= 6\frac{1}{2}$

(iv) $\quad 4\frac{3}{8} - 2\frac{1}{8}$

$= 4 + \frac{3}{8} - 2 - \frac{1}{8}$

$= 4 - 2 + \frac{3}{8} - \frac{1}{8}$

$= 2\frac{2}{8}$

$= 2\frac{1}{4}$

Exercise 7

1 Simplify:

a $\frac{3}{8}+\frac{1}{8}$ **b** $\frac{1}{4}+\frac{1}{4}$ **c** $\frac{7}{8}-\frac{3}{8}$ **d** $\frac{3}{5}-\frac{2}{5}$

e $\frac{1}{2}+\frac{1}{2}$ **f** $\frac{1}{3}-\frac{1}{3}$ **g** $\frac{5}{8}+\frac{3}{8}$ **h** $\frac{7}{10}-\frac{2}{10}$

2 Simplify:

a $3+\frac{3}{8}$ **b** $1\frac{1}{3}+2\frac{1}{3}$ **c** $2\frac{3}{8}-1\frac{1}{8}$ **d** $4-\frac{1}{2}$

e $2-\frac{3}{4}$ **f** $3-1\frac{1}{2}$ **g** $2-1\frac{3}{8}$ **h** $2\frac{1}{8}+3\frac{3}{8}$

3 A car's petrol tank holds 9 gallons. $3\frac{1}{2}$ gallons are used. How much is left?

4 How far is it from:
  a the village to the coast
  b the village to the
  lighthouse
  c the coast to the
  lighthouse?

5 A video cassette lasts 3 hours. A programme lasting $\frac{3}{4}$ hour is recorded. How much time is left?

How much time is left after another $\frac{3}{4}$ hour programme is recorded?

Study

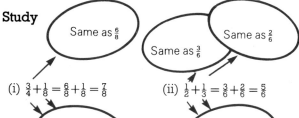

(i) $\frac{3}{4}+\frac{1}{8}=\frac{6}{8}+\frac{1}{8}=\frac{7}{8}$ (ii) $\frac{1}{2}+\frac{1}{3}=\frac{3}{6}+\frac{2}{6}=\frac{5}{6}$

lcm of 4 and 8

lcm of 2 and 3

NOW THE **HARDER** ONES!

(iii) $\frac{3}{4}+\frac{1}{16}=\frac{12}{16}+\frac{1}{16}=\frac{13}{16}$ (iv) $\frac{1}{4}+\frac{2}{3}=\frac{3}{12}+\frac{8}{12}=\frac{11}{12}$

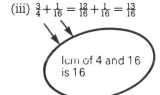

lcm of 4 and 16 is 16

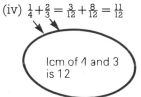

lcm of 4 and 3 is 12

Exercise 8A

1 Write down the least common multiples (lcms) of:
  a 2 and 4   **b** 4 and 8   **c** 2 and 8   **d** 8 and 16

2 Copy and complete:

a $\frac{1}{2}+\frac{1}{4}$ **b** $\frac{1}{4}-\frac{1}{8}$ **c** $\frac{1}{2}+\frac{5}{8}$

$=\frac{}{4}+\frac{1}{4}$ $=\frac{}{8}-\frac{1}{8}$ $=\frac{}{8}+\frac{5}{8}$

$=$ $=$ $=$

3 Copy and complete:

a $2\frac{1}{2}+1\frac{1}{4}$

$=2+1+\frac{1}{4}+\frac{1}{4}$

$=$

b $3\frac{7}{8}-1\frac{3}{4}$

$=3-1+\frac{7}{8}-\frac{6}{8}$

$=$

c $4\frac{3}{4}+2\frac{1}{2}$

$=4+2+\frac{3}{4}+\frac{2}{4}$

$=$

4 Calculate in their simplest form:

a $1\frac{1}{2}+1\frac{1}{2}$ **b** $3\frac{3}{4}-1\frac{1}{2}$ **c** $5\frac{5}{8}+1\frac{1}{2}$ **d** $4\frac{1}{2}-1\frac{1}{2}$

e $2\frac{3}{4}+\frac{1}{2}$ **f** $8\frac{3}{4}-1\frac{1}{2}$ **g** $\frac{7}{8}-\frac{1}{4}$ **h** $\frac{7}{16}-\frac{3}{8}$

5 Mrs Jenkins comes back from the butcher's with
$\frac{3}{4}$ lb mince, $1\frac{1}{2}$ lb steak and $1\frac{1}{4}$ lb chops.
Calculate the total weight of meat in her basket.

6 To make a strong join, the nail has to go $\frac{1}{2}$ inch into the second piece of wood.
How long does the nail have to be?

7 How much wider is a $\frac{7}{16}$ inch spanner than a $\frac{1}{4}$ inch one?

$\frac{5}{8}$ inch

Exercise 8B

1 Write down the lcm of 3 and 4. Now decide which is greater, $\frac{1}{3}$ or $\frac{1}{4}$.

2 Which is greater? **a** $\frac{3}{8}$ or $\frac{1}{4}$ **b** $\frac{4}{5}$ or $\frac{5}{6}$.

3 Put these spanners in order of size (smallest first):
$\frac{1}{2}$ inch, $\frac{3}{8}$ inch, $\frac{5}{16}$ inch, $\frac{3}{4}$ inch

4 Would you prefer $\frac{2}{3}$ or $\frac{3}{4}$ of a bar of chocolate? Why?

5 Calculate in their simplest form:

a $1\frac{3}{4}+1\frac{1}{2}$ **b** $2\frac{1}{4}+\frac{5}{8}$ **c** $1\frac{1}{2}-\frac{3}{4}$ **d** $5\frac{1}{8}-1\frac{1}{2}$

e $1\frac{1}{2}+1\frac{1}{4}+1\frac{3}{4}$ **f** $4-2\frac{3}{4}$ **g** $\frac{3}{5}+\frac{2}{3}$ **h** $\frac{3}{4}-\frac{1}{5}$

6

TOWN 3 ¾ KM
CHURCH ½ KM

FARM 2 KM
STABLES ¼ KM

How far is it from:
a the church to the stables
b the town to the farm
c the farm to the stables
d the town to the church?

7 The smallest of a set of spanners is $\frac{1}{4}$ inch, and each spanner is $\frac{1}{16}$ inch larger than the previous one.
If the $\frac{1}{2}$ inch one is just too small, which size should you try next?

8 A video tape lasts for 4 hours. Programmes lasting $1\frac{1}{2}$ hours, $\frac{3}{4}$ hour, $\frac{1}{2}$ hour and $\frac{3}{4}$ hour are recorded. How much time is left?

9 Nails $\frac{3}{4}$ inch and $\frac{7}{8}$ inch long are driven into a piece of wood $1\frac{1}{2}$ inches thick. How far is the point of each from the other side of the wood?

$1\frac{1}{2}$ inch

10 Put in order (shortest first) the camera speeds:

$$\frac{1}{500} \text{ second}, \quad \frac{1}{250} \text{ second}, \quad \frac{1}{1000} \text{ second}.$$

Puzzles

1 How many ways can you find to fold a rectangular piece of paper into quarters. Sketch your answers.

2 Copy these sequences, and add three more terms to each:

a $\frac{1}{8}, \frac{3}{8}, \frac{5}{8}, \dots$ **b** $2\frac{1}{2}, 3\frac{3}{4}, 5, \dots$ **c** $5\frac{5}{8}, 5\frac{2}{8}, 4\frac{7}{8}, \dots$

3 Find three pairs of replacements for x and y such that

$$\frac{x}{25} + \frac{y}{25} = \frac{1}{5}$$

4 How many terms of the sequence $1 + \frac{1}{2} + \frac{1}{4} + \frac{1}{8} + \frac{1}{16} + \dots$ would you have to add together to make:

a $1\frac{1}{2}$ **b** $1\frac{7}{8}$ **c** $1\frac{31}{32}$ **d** 2?

5

START $\frac{3}{4}$

$\frac{2}{3}$ $\frac{7}{8}$

$\frac{11}{16}$ $\frac{1}{2}$ $\frac{15}{32}$

$\frac{5}{2}$ $\frac{3}{5}$ $\frac{7}{16}$ $\frac{2}{3}$

$\frac{1}{5}$ $\frac{2}{5}$ $\frac{4}{9}$

$\frac{1}{3}$ $\frac{3}{7}$

$\frac{1}{4}$ FINISH

Stepping stones

You are only allowed to move from one stone to another named by a smaller fraction.

a Copy the diagram and colour your route.

b Can you find a different route? (Use a different colour.)

MULTIPLICATION

'of' and ' × '

(i) $4 \times \frac{2}{3} = \frac{2}{3} + \frac{2}{3} + \frac{2}{3} + \frac{2}{3} = \frac{8}{3} = 2\frac{2}{3}$

(ii) The area of this rectangle $= 6\,mm^2$

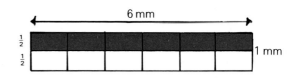

$\frac{1}{2}$ of $6\,mm^2 =$ the shaded area

$\qquad = \frac{1}{2} \times 6\,mm^2$

So $\frac{1}{2}$ of $6 = \frac{1}{2} \times 6 = 3$.

Examples

(i) $6 \times \frac{3}{8} = \frac{\overset{9}{\cancel{18}}}{\cancel{8}_4} = 2\frac{1}{4}$ 　　(ii) $\frac{1}{3}$ of £18 $= \frac{1}{3} \times £18 = £6$.

=============================== *Exercise 9A* ===============================

1 Calculate:

   a $8 \times \frac{1}{4}$ 　　**b** $6 \times \frac{1}{2}$ 　　**c** $4 \times \frac{2}{3}$ 　　**d** $3 \times \frac{1}{8}$ 　　**e** $2 \times \frac{3}{4}$

   f $8 \times \frac{3}{4}$ 　　**g** $10 \times \frac{1}{2}$ 　　**h** $12 \times \frac{1}{4}$ 　　**i** $15 \times \frac{2}{3}$ 　　**j** $6 \times \frac{2}{3}$

2 Calculate:

   a $\frac{1}{2}$ of 10 　　**b** $\frac{1}{3}$ of 18 　　**c** $\frac{1}{4}$ of 20 　　**d** $\frac{1}{8} \times 24$

   e $\frac{2}{5}$ of 25 　　**f** $\frac{3}{4}$ of 16 　　**g** $\frac{1}{8} \times 12$ 　　**h** $\frac{7}{8}$ of 32

3

   a A football match lasts 90 minutes. How long is the first half?

   b An American football match lasts 1 hour 20 minutes. How many minutes does the first quarter last?

4 Brian had 45p and he gave $\frac{1}{5}$ of it to Peter. How much did Peter get?

5 $\frac{3}{10}$ of a class of 30 pupils were absent. How many were present?

6 42 cars were in the car park, $\frac{1}{3}$ of them were blue. How many was this?

7 Calculate the area of a rectangular piece of carpet 8 m by $\frac{3}{4}$ m.

8 A shop window needed a new piece of glass 3 m by $1\frac{1}{2}$ m. What was the area of the glass?

9 Calculate in pence:

   a $\frac{1}{10}$ of £1 　　**b** $\frac{3}{10}$ of £2 　　**c** $\frac{3}{4}$ of £1 　　**d** $\frac{1}{2}$ of £5

10 In Petra's school, a period lasts for $\frac{3}{4}$ hour. How many minutes is this?

11 The oil storage tank, when full, holds 1600 litres. If it is $\frac{1}{4}$ full, how many litres of oil have been *used*?

12 Calculate the sale prices of these items:

a

½ PRICE SALE

EACH ITEM SOLD FOR
HALF THE MARKED PRICE

3 PIECE SUITE · · · · · **£570**

WARDROBE · · · · · · · **£234**

DRESSING TABLE · · · · **£198**

CHEST OF · · · · · · · **£76**
DRAWERS

b

CLOSING DOWN SALE

⅔ OFF LISTED PRICES

WALLPAPER · · · · · · · **£4·20**
A ROLL

CARPETS FROM · · · · **£99**

2½ LITRES PAINT · · · **£10·80**

CURTAINS FROM · · · · **£2·70**

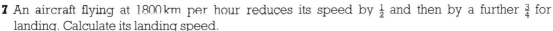

Exercise 9B

1 How many degrees are in: **a** $\frac{2}{3}$ of a right angle **b** $\frac{3}{4}$ of a straight angle?

2 $\frac{2}{3}$ of a person's weight is water. Jean weighs 63 kg. How much of this is water?

3 On the moon things weigh $\frac{1}{6}$ of their weight on the earth. How much will a 72 kg astronaut weigh on the moon?

4 Calculate the length of tape needed to record six TV programmes each lasting $\frac{3}{4}$ hour.

5 2 cups of oats and 5 cups of water will make enough porridge for 4 people. What amounts would you need for 1 person?

6 a $4\frac{1}{2}$ litres to the gallon. How many litres in 3 gallons?
b $2\frac{1}{2}$ cm to the inch. How many centimetres in 9 inches?
c $2\frac{1}{4}$ lb to the kilogram. How many lb in 6 kg?

7 An aircraft flying at 1800 km per hour reduces its speed by $\frac{1}{2}$ and then by a further $\frac{3}{4}$ for landing. Calculate its landing speed.

Fraction × fraction

This square has side of length 1 m.
(i) It is divided into 8 congruent rectangles.
      Check that the area of the shaded rectangle

$$= \tfrac{3}{8} \text{ of the area of the square}$$

$$= \tfrac{3}{8}\,\text{m}^2$$

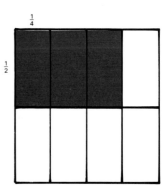

Now the area of the shaded rectangle = length × breadth $= \tfrac{3}{4} \times \tfrac{1}{2}\,\text{m}^2$.

So $\boxed{\tfrac{3}{4} \times \tfrac{1}{2} = \tfrac{3}{8}}$

(ii) This time the shaded rectangle's area $= \tfrac{6}{15}\,\text{m}^2$.

Also the shaded rectangle's area $= \tfrac{3}{5} \times \tfrac{2}{3}\,\text{m}^2$.

So $\boxed{\tfrac{3}{5} \times \tfrac{2}{3} = \tfrac{6}{15}}$

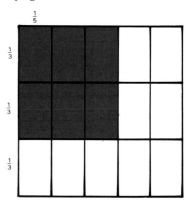

To multiply fractions, multiply their numerators and their denominators.

Examples

(i) $\tfrac{5}{6} \times \tfrac{3}{4}$ or

$$= \tfrac{15}{24}$$

$$= \tfrac{5}{8}$$

$$\frac{\cancel{5}}{\cancel{6}_2} \times \frac{\cancel{3}}{\cancel{4}} = \tfrac{5}{8}$$

(ii) $4 \times 1\tfrac{1}{3}$

$$= \tfrac{4}{1} \times \tfrac{4}{3}$$

$$= \tfrac{16}{3}$$

$$= 5\tfrac{1}{3}$$

(iii) $1\tfrac{1}{2} \times 2\tfrac{1}{4}$

$$= \tfrac{3}{2} \times \tfrac{9}{4}$$

$$= \tfrac{27}{8}$$

$$= 3\tfrac{3}{8}$$

====================== *Exercise 10A* ======================

1 Calculate:

  a $\tfrac{1}{2} \times \tfrac{1}{4}$ **b** $\tfrac{1}{2} \times \tfrac{3}{4}$ **c** $\tfrac{1}{4} \times \tfrac{3}{4}$ **d** $\tfrac{1}{3} \times \tfrac{3}{4}$

  e $\tfrac{1}{8} \times \tfrac{3}{4}$ **f** $\tfrac{1}{2} \times \tfrac{1}{2}$ **g** $\tfrac{3}{4} \times \tfrac{2}{3}$ **h** $\tfrac{1}{2} \times \tfrac{4}{5}$

2 Calculate:

  a $\tfrac{1}{4}$ of $\tfrac{4}{5}$ **b** $\tfrac{1}{2}$ of $\tfrac{3}{8}$ **c** $\tfrac{3}{10}$ of $\tfrac{5}{6}$ **d** $\tfrac{2}{3}$ of $\tfrac{3}{8}$

3 30 metres of carpet are needed for a stair $\tfrac{3}{4}$ m wide.
  a Calculate the area of carpet needed.
  b The carpet comes in a 1 metre width.
      Calculate the area of carpet which would have to be trimmed off.

4 Here is a recipe for Steak and Kidney Hotpot for 4:

$1\frac{1}{2}$ lb steak   1 medium onion
$\frac{1}{2}$ lb kidney   1 tablespoon flour
$1\frac{1}{2}$ lb potatoes   1 tablespoon dripping
$1\frac{1}{4}$ oz butter $\frac{3}{4}$ pint stock
$\frac{1}{4}$ lb mushrooms   Salt and pepper

What quantities would you need for sixteen people?

5 Copy these sequences, and then add three more terms to each one.

   a $1, \frac{1}{2}, \frac{1}{4}, \frac{1}{8}, \ldots$　　　**b** $27, 9, 3, 1, \ldots$　　　**c** $1000, 100, 10, 1, \ldots$

6 Calculate in their simplest form:

   a $\frac{3}{4} \times \frac{2}{3}$　　　**b** $\frac{5}{8} \times \frac{2}{5}$　　　**c** $\frac{7}{8} \times \frac{8}{7}$　　　**d** $4\frac{1}{2} \times 4\frac{1}{2}$

7 $\frac{2}{5} \times \frac{5}{8} = \frac{1}{x}$　　　$x = ?$

=========================== *Exercise 10B* ===========================

1 Calculate in their simplest form:

   a $3\frac{1}{2} \times 2\frac{1}{4}$　　　**b** $6\frac{1}{3} \times 2\frac{1}{4}$　　　**c** $1\frac{1}{2} \times 2\frac{1}{2}$　　　**d** $\frac{3}{4}$ of $\frac{11}{12}$

2 1 mile is about $1\frac{3}{5}$ kilometres. Estimate 15 miles in kilometres.

3 Four men pay equal shares for a football pools coupon. One week they have a winning entry. James gives a half of his share to his wife, Monica. What fraction of the winnings does Monica get?

4 Mrs Samson chose a patterned material to make a dress for herself and a skirt for each of her twin daughters. She bought $6\frac{3}{4}$ m at £6·40 a metre, and used $\frac{2}{3}$ of it for her dress and the rest for her daughters' skirts.
How much did the dress and each skirt cost?

5 Calculate the area of a rectangular floor 12 m by $4\frac{1}{3}$ m.

DIVISION

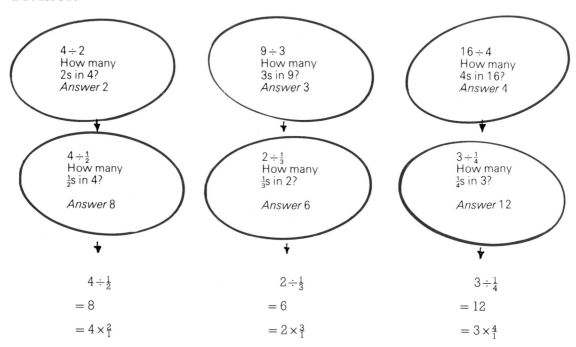

$4 \div 2$
How many
2s in 4?
Answer 2

$9 \div 3$
How many
3s in 9?
Answer 3

$16 \div 4$
How many
4s in 16?
Answer 4

$4 \div \frac{1}{2}$
How many
$\frac{1}{2}$s in 4?

Answer 8

$2 \div \frac{1}{3}$
How many
$\frac{1}{3}$s in 2?

Answer 6

$3 \div \frac{1}{4}$
How many
$\frac{1}{4}$s in 3?

Answer 12

$4 \div \frac{1}{2}$

$= 8$

$= 4 \times \frac{2}{1}$

$2 \div \frac{1}{3}$

$= 6$

$= 2 \times \frac{3}{1}$

$3 \div \frac{1}{4}$

$= 12$

$= 3 \times \frac{4}{1}$

To divide by a fraction, turn it upside down and multiply.

Examples

(i) $6 \div \frac{3}{4}$

$= 6 \times \frac{4}{3}$

$= \frac{24}{3}$

$= 8$

OR $\frac{\cancel{6}^2}{1} \times \frac{4}{\cancel{3}_1}$

$= 8$

(ii) $1\frac{1}{2} \div \frac{3}{8}$

$= \frac{3}{2} \times \frac{8}{3}$

$= \frac{24}{6}$

$= 4$

OR $\frac{\cancel{3}^1}{\cancel{2}_1} \times \frac{\cancel{8}^4}{\cancel{3}_1}$

$= 4$

=================== *Exercise 11A* ===================

1 Calculate:

a $\frac{1}{2} \div \frac{1}{4}$ **b** $\frac{1}{2} \div \frac{1}{8}$ **c** $\frac{3}{4} \div \frac{1}{2}$ **d** $\frac{1}{2} \div \frac{1}{2}$

e $2\frac{1}{8} \div \frac{1}{8}$ **f** $2 \div \frac{1}{4}$ **g** $3 \div \frac{3}{4}$ **h** $1\frac{3}{4} \div \frac{1}{4}$

i $5\frac{1}{2} \div \frac{1}{2}$ **j** $2\frac{5}{8} \div \frac{3}{4}$ **k** $3 \div \frac{2}{3}$ **l** $3\frac{1}{5} \div \frac{3}{4}$

2 Henry, the cat, eats a $\frac{1}{2}$ tin of Catto each day. How many days would a pack of 24 tins last him?

3 How many $\frac{1}{4}$ litre cartons of juice can be filled from a 48 litre tank?

4 How many $\frac{3}{4}$ hour programmes could be recorded on:
    a a 3 hour tape   **b** a $1\frac{1}{2}$ hour tape   **c** a 4 hour tape?

1 Calculate:

  a $4\frac{1}{2} \div 1\frac{1}{2}$ **b** $15 \div 2\frac{1}{2}$ **c** $10 \div 2\frac{1}{4}$ **d** $3\frac{3}{4} \div 2\frac{1}{2}$

  e $2\frac{4}{5} \div 1\frac{3}{5}$ **f** $24 \div 1\frac{1}{2}$ **g** $5\frac{1}{3} \div 2\frac{2}{3}$ **h** $1 \div \frac{1}{100}$

2 Isobel has a weekly piano lesson of $1\frac{1}{4}$ hours. She sat her first examination after a total of 25 hours piano lessons.
How many lessons did she need?

3 In music the lengths of sounds are shown by notes of different shapes.
These notes, with their shapes and lengths, are shown compared to the length of a semibreve.
How many semiquavers are there in each of the notes shown below?

Note	Shape	Value in terms of a semibreve
Semibreve	𝆕	1
Minim	𝅗𝅥	$\frac{1}{2}$
Crotchet	♩	$\frac{1}{4}$
Quaver	♪	$\frac{1}{8}$
Semi-quaver	♬	$\frac{1}{16}$
Demi-semi -quaver	𝅘𝅥𝅰	$\frac{1}{32}$

4 Jasmine works a $31\frac{1}{2}$ hour week, spread evenly over $4\frac{1}{2}$ days. How many hours does she work each full day, and how many on the half-day?

5 These three wheels have 20, 5 and 10 teeth. What happens to:
  a B, if A is given a clockwise quarter turn?
  b C, if A is given a clockwise quarter turn?
  c B, if C is given $1\frac{1}{2}$ turns anti-clockwise?
  d A, if C is given $2\frac{1}{2}$ turns anti-clockwise?

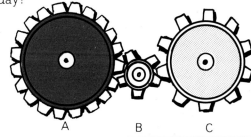

A wealthy merchant died, leaving seventeen valuable paintings to his three sons. The eldest son was to have one half of the paintings, the middle son one third, and the youngest son one ninth. The three sons were in despair. How could they divide out the seventeen paintings?
They explained their problem to a rich uncle, who said that there was an easy answer to their problem. He added a valuable painting of his own to the seventeen others. The eldest son took half of the eighteen paintings, the middle son took his third, and the youngest his ninth. The uncle then took back his own painting, and everyone was happy—or were they?

CHECK-UP ON **FRACTIONS IN ACTION**

Finding fractions

1A What fraction of these figures are
  a triangles   **b** rectangles   **c** circles?

2A

> Can you write a fraction in simplest form?

a Write $\frac{6}{12}$ and $\frac{10}{16}$ in their simplest form.

b There are 20 boys in a class of 30. What fraction of the pupils, in its simplest form, are girls?

c Copy and complete: $\frac{3}{4} = \frac{6}{} = \frac{15}{} = \frac{}{16}$

> Can you write equal fractions?

3A

> Mixed numbers
> ↕
> Fractions

a Change to mixed numbers: $\frac{5}{2}$ and $\frac{17}{4}$.

b Change to fractions: $2\frac{1}{2}$ and $3\frac{3}{8}$.

c $1\frac{1}{2}$ litres of water is added to $8\frac{1}{2}$ litres in a jar. Write down the volume of water in the jar.

4A, B

> Can you compare fractions?

a Write the greater first: $\frac{3}{4}, \frac{5}{8}$.

b Write the smaller first: $\frac{3}{4}, \frac{2}{3}$.

5A, B

> Can you add and subtract fractions?

Calculate in simplest form:

a $\frac{3}{8} + \frac{1}{8}$ **b** $1\frac{1}{4} + 2\frac{1}{4}$

c $3\frac{5}{8} - 1\frac{3}{8}$ **d** $\frac{5}{8} + \frac{1}{4}$

e $1\frac{1}{3} + 1\frac{1}{6}$ **f** $2\frac{2}{3} - 1\frac{1}{4}$

6A, B

> Can you multiply and divide fractions?

Calculate:

a $\frac{1}{4} \times \frac{3}{4}$ **b** $6 \times \frac{3}{4}$ **c** $\frac{3}{4}$ of 20

d $1\frac{1}{2} \times 2\frac{1}{4}$ **e** $4 \div \frac{1}{4}$ **f** $1\frac{1}{8} \div 1\frac{1}{4}$

7A, B

> Can you use fractions?

a How many $\frac{1}{4}$ kg bags of sugar can be made up from 40 kg?

b 4 programmes each last $1\frac{1}{3}$ hours. Calculate the total time.

c $\frac{1}{2}$ the class liked French, $\frac{1}{4}$ didn't. What fraction gave no opinion?

d What size of spanner is half-way between a $\frac{3}{4}$ inch and a $\frac{7}{8}$ inch one?

TILING PATTERNS

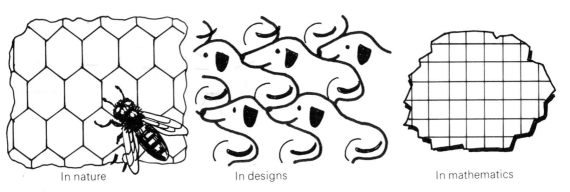

In nature   In designs   In mathematics

These tiling patterns are made of congruent shapes which fit together to cover the plane, without leaving any gaps.

Exercise 1

1A Trace the outline of this envelope.
By moving your tracing paper over and over again, use the envelope shape to draw a tiling pattern on it.

2A Draw tilings by tracing the *outlines* of these shapes over and over again:

  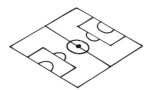

3A On squared paper draw a tiling of each of the following rectangular shapes. In each case use the same number of squares as in the drawing—eg the domino is 2 squares long and 1 square broad.

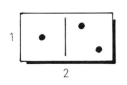

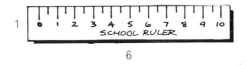

We will assume that:
congruent rectangles can make a tiling like this.

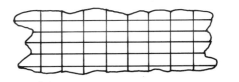

51

4A Use the rectangles in question **3A** to draw different tilings on squared paper. Think of patterns of brick walls, paved paths, wooden floors, Venetian blinds and so on.

5A Here is a sheet of postage stamps.
   a Why is this pattern better for stamps than a brick wall one?
   b Why would hexagonal stamps (like a bee's honeycomb) not be printed and arranged like this?

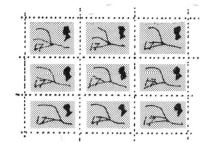

6A Sketch the following to show their tiling patterns:
   a A draughts or chess board   **b** Slates or tiles on a roof
   c A floor of lino tiles   **d** A tiled kitchen wall
   e A brick wall   **f** A patchwork quilt of squares

Trace the shaded tile. Slide it along a row, and up and down a column.
You can do this because its opposite sides stay the same distance apart. So they must be parallel.

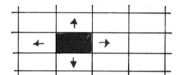

The opposite sides of a rectangle are parallel.

They can be marked like this:

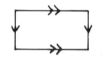

7A a Measure the width of your notebook page in 3 places.
   b Why does this suggest that the opposite edges are parallel?

8A Copy the rectangle ABCD in your notebook and mark in pairs of parallel sides.

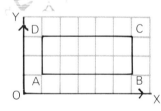

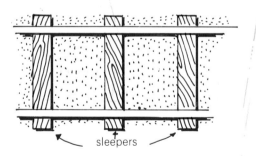

sleepers

9A a Why must railway lines always be the same distance apart?
   b Are railway lines parallel?
   c Are the railway sleepers parallel?

10B Write down some other examples of parallel lines.

Draw some tiling patterns based on these two rectangular tiles—or you can design and use your own pair of tiles, if you prefer.

PUTTING SHAPES IN THEIR PLACES

=== *Exercise 2* ===

1A

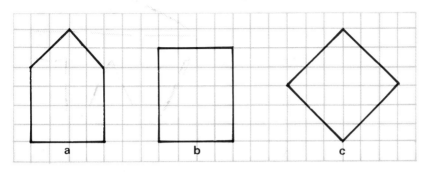

Draw these three window pane shapes on squared paper and cut them out, or trace them. In how many ways can you fit each shape back into its space? Remember that you can turn the shape round, or turn it over.

Put your results in a table:

Shape	**a**	**b**	**c**
Number of ways			

2A Find the number of ways in which each picture below can fit into its outline. Trace them if you need to.
Put your results in a table again.

a   b   c   d   e

3A In how many ways can each of these rectangular pictures fit into its outline? Remember that you can turn them round, or turn them over.

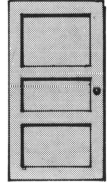

We will assume that:

a rectangle fits its outline in 4 ways.

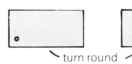

turn round   turn over   turn round

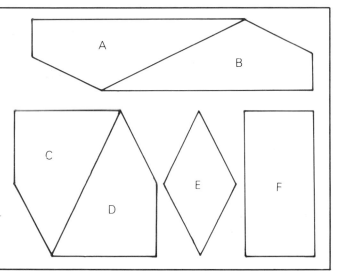

Trace these shapes, and mark the letters on them.
Cut them out of your tracing paper, or transfer them to card.

1 Fit parts A, B, C, D and E together to form a rectangle, with the diamond E in the middle.

2 Fit parts A, B, C, D and F together to form a diamond, with the rectangle F in the middle.

Class discussion/activity—Fitting a window

These men have been sent to fit a new rectangular pane of glass in a hotel window. The foreman has labelled the corners of the frame and the pane of glass to help them.

Draw the window frame in your notebook, with a 3 cm by 2 cm opening for the window. Trace the pane of glass, and write A, B, C, D and HOTEL on it.

First of all they try to fit the window like this. Fit your tracing into its frame in the same way.

A went to D's place: A→D
B went to C's place: B→C

So edge AB went where
edge DC should have been: AB→DC

The glass fits exactly, so AB = DC

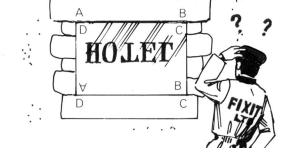

'Won't do', said the foreman. 'Turn it round.'
Do this with your tracing.
Copy and complete: A→___
                     D→___
                    AD→___
                    AD =___

Using the 4 way fitting property of a rectangle, we have found that:

the opposite sides of a rectangle are equal.

They can be marked like this:

Exercise 3

1A The cover of this book is a rectangle.
What are the lengths of the top and left-hand sides of the cover (PQ and PS)?

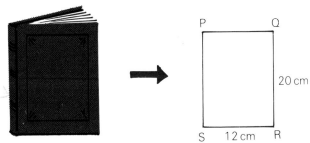

2A

ABCD is a rectangle:
AB = 5 cm and BC = 2 cm.
Copy and complete:
CD = ... cm, AD = ... cm.

3A The lengths of two sides of these rectangles are marked on the diagrams. Write down the names and lengths of the other sides.

a
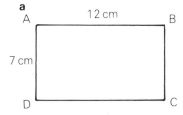

b
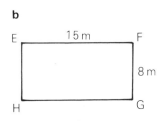

c
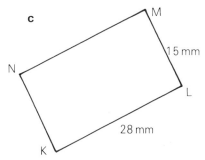

55

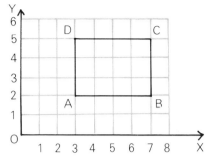

4A a Write down the names and lengths of the sides of this rectangle.

b Copy the rectangle in your notebook and mark the equal pairs of sides.

c Mark the parallel sides with arrows.

5A On squared paper draw the rectangle PQRS with P(2, 1), Q(5, 1) and R(5, 7).

a What are the coordinates of S?

b Which pairs of sides are equal?

c What are the lengths of the sides?

6A Repeat question **5A** for the rectangle OQRS, where O is the origin, Q is the point (6, 0) and R is (6, 5).

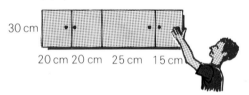

30 cm

20 cm 20 cm 25 cm 15 cm

8A Some builders have to find out the length of the top of this wall before they can repair it, but it is covered with barbed wire.

What is the length of the top, do you think, and the height of the far end of the wall?

2·5 m

7·5 m

7A Wayne can't reach the top of this row of kitchen cupboards. But he can calculate the length of the top. Can you?

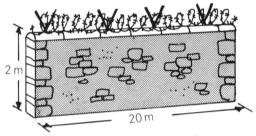

2 m

20 m

9A Draw this goalmouth.

a What shape is the goalmouth?

b How long is the crossbar (at the top)?

c What height is the right-hand post?

d What size should the goalmouth at the other end of the pitch be?

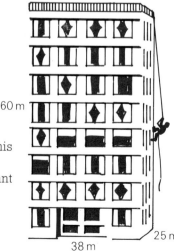

60 m

38 m

25 m

10B Roy has to find the length of the railings round the top of this high-rise block of flats.

Unfortunately there is no door to the roof, and he does not want to climb up the wall.

Can you help him to find the answer to his problem?

11B EFGH is a rectangle, with its sides parallel
to the x and y-axes.
E is the point (3, 3) and G is (8, 5).
Draw the rectangle on squared paper. Write down:
  a The coordinates of F and H.
  b The names of the equal sides.
  c The names of the parallel sides.
  d The lengths of the sides and the area of the rectangle.

12B Repeat question **11B** for points E(0, 2) and G(4, 6).

13C There is a fourth way of fitting the hotel window on page 54.
Draw it, then copy and complete:

    A→ _ _ _   A→ _ _ _
    B→ _ _ _   D→ _ _ _
    AB→ _ _ _   AD→ _ _ _
    AB = _ _ _   AD = _ _ _

Eventually the workmen got it right—or did they?

The playing pitches for football, hockey and rugby, and the courts for tennis and badminton, are all marked out in rectangles. Sketch one of them on squared paper. Explain what all the rectangles and lines mean.

In a corner

=========================== *Exercise 4* ===========================

1A Take a rectangular sheet of paper, and mark its angles A, B, C and D like this.
  a By folding, match angle A with angle B. Unfold. Then match angle A with angle D.
  b Which angles can you match angle C with by folding?
  c What does this suggest about all the angles?
  d Tear off the four corners, like this.
    Mark a point on your page, and try to fit the corners round it, without leaving any gaps.
    What can you say about the size of each angle?

2A From the workmen's attempts to fit the hotel window, you saw that angle A on the pane of glass fitted the window frame at every corner.

at B · at C · at D

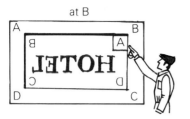 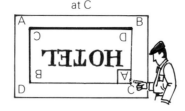 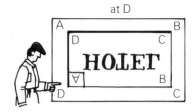

Using each diagram above, in turn, copy and complete:
angle A→angle___, angle A→angle___, angle A→angle___.
So angle A = angle___ = angle___ = angle___.

3A What does this tell you about all the angles of the pane of glass?

4A Every rectangle fits its outline like the window pane. What can you say about all the angles of a rectangle?

5A From the tiling of congruent rectangles you can see that there are equal angles at each of the four corners.
  a What is the sum of the angles round a point?
  b What is the size of each angle?

From the above:

all the angles of a rectangle are right angles.

These can be marked like this:

6A Copy rectangle PQRS, and fill in the size of every angle, in degrees.

7A Copy rectangle STUV and fill in the size of every angle, in degrees.

8A Draw a rectangle ABCD. Mark in:
  a the opposite sides equal
  b the opposite sides parallel
  c all the right angles.

9A What do the four angles of a rectangle add up to, in degrees?

10B a How many right angles are there on this side view of a brick wall?
  b How many rectangles can you see? (There are more than seven!)

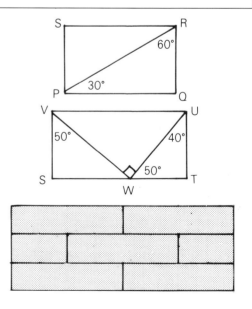

Exercise 5

1A Measure the lengths of the diagonals of:
    a this page   **b** a page of your notebook.
    What do you find?

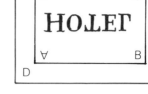

2A Back to the hotel window!
    Copy and complete:
    For the fitting shown,   A→___
                       C→___
           So AC→___
             AC = ___
    What does this tell you about the diagonals of a rectangle?

The diagonals of a rectangle are equal:
AC = BD

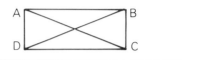

3A ABCD is a rectangle.
    a If BD = 75 mm, what is the length of AC?
    b If AC = 6·5 cm, what is the length of BD?

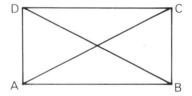

4A Draw a rectangle PQRS, and join PR and QS.
    Mark PQ = 8 cm, QR = 6 cm and PR = 10 cm.
    Write down the lengths of QS, SP and SR.

5A A(1, 1) and C(5, 3) are opposite corners of a rectangle ABCD which
    has its sides parallel to the x and y-axes.
    Draw the rectangle and its two diagonals.
    Write down three pairs of equal lines.

6A Repeat question **5A** for opposite corners E(6, 0) and G(8, 6) of a rectangle EFGH.

7A a What is meant by a '22 inch' screen?
    b What other common sizes are there?

8B The groundsman has to measure the length of the track along the diagonal of this rectangular field. There is some equipment in the way.

 a How can he find the length without moving the equipment?

 b What is the length of the track?

 c Draw a rectangle ABCD and its diagonals to represent the field.
 A jogging circuit is laid out like this:
 A→B→C→D→A→C→D→B→A.
 Calculate the length of the circuit.

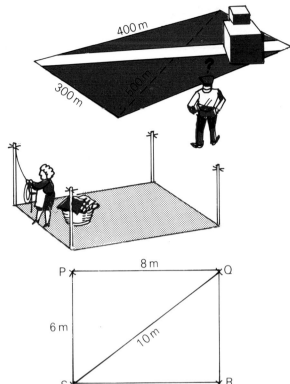

9B Mrs Jones needs a new washing line. Her husband has put up four poles, one at each corner of their lawn.
 The washing line has to be long enough to go round all four sides and across both diagonals in one piece.

 a What is the least number of lengths Mrs Jones has to measure?

 b Copy the rectangle PQRS and mark in all the lengths. How much rope is needed, allowing 1 metre for loops and knots?

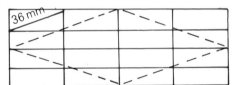

10B

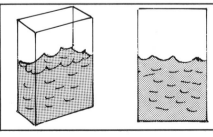

An engineering company has to cut diamond shapes from metal sheets which have rectangular grids on them. Calculate:

 a the perimeter of one of the diamond shapes

 b the fraction of each metal sheet that is used.

11C The second Union Jack flag is upside down.
 How would you put it the right way up?
 Use arrows (P→S, etc) to show that PR = SQ.

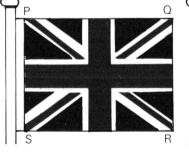 

The sides and base of this clear plastic tank are rectangles.
Without measuring, how could you pour out some of the water, to leave the tank half full? Would the same method work for a cylindrical jar?

================= *Exercise 6* =================

1A What shape is this tiling made from?
Trace the tile below.
Turn it over about the dotted line.
Does it fit its outline?
The dotted line is an
axis of symmetry.

2A Trace the outlines of the shapes below. Mark the axis of symmetry in each one.

3A a Cut out a rectangle from squared paper.
 b Fold it so that the two parts match exactly.
 c Open it out, and fold it in a different way to match.
 d Do the parts match when you fold it along a diagonal?
 e How many axes of symmetry have you found?

4A The workmen would have found that the hotel window still fitted its frame if they had *turned it over* in either of the ways shown below. Check this with your tracing paper window.

From the 4 way fitting property:

a rectangle has two axes of symmetry

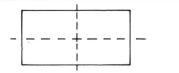

5A Here is a sign you might see spinning outside a garage.

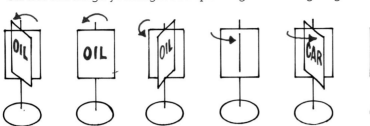

How does it spin without jamming?

6A Copy rectangle ABCD and its axis of symmetry XY. Fill in the lengths of as many lines and the sizes of as many angles as you can.

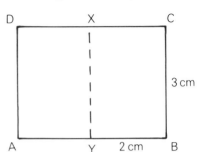

7A a Try to keep folding a rectangular piece of paper, so that the parts match each time.
b Unfold it, and look at the pattern. Where have you seen this before?
c Copy and complete this table:

Number of folds	0	1	2	3	...
Number of rectangles	1				...

How many rectangles would there be after: (i) 7 folds (ii) 10 folds (iii) n folds?

8B ABCD is a rectangle. Copy and complete:
Under reflection in the axis of symmetry,   D→___
                                            E→___
                                            DE→___
                                            DE =___
In the same way, show that AF = BF.

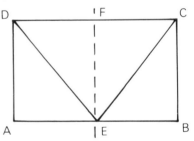

9B PQRS is a rectangle. An axis of symmetry is shown by the dotted line. Show that TR = TQ.

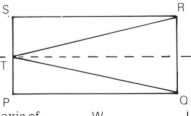

10C TUVW is a rectangle. The dotted line is an axis of symmetry, and X is any point on this line.
a Show that: WX = VX and TX = UX.
b Name a pair of congruent triangles.

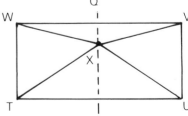

1 Cut out a rectangle in card.

2 Draw the diagonal joining A to C on both sides.

3 Draw an axis of symmetry.

4 Thread a loop of thin string or strong thread through pairs of holes close to the axis of symmetry.

5 Hold the loops, and spin the card.

6 Write a sentence about what you see.

7 Draw a canary in the middle of one side, and a cage on the other side of the card. What happens when you spin the card now?

Criss cross

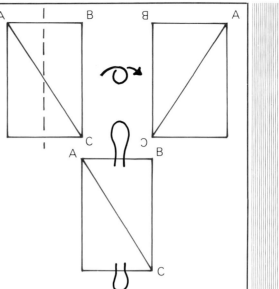

======================= *Exercise 7* =======================

1A a Draw a rectangle ABCD on squared paper. Mark the point O where its diagonals cross.

b Trace the rectangle, and join OA on the tracing.

c Place the tracing over ABCD, and give it a half turn about O. What do you find?

d Join OB, and give it a half turn about O. What do you find?

e What does this suggest about the diagonals of a rectangle?

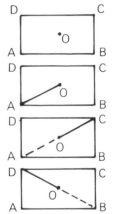

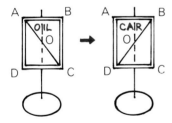

Copy and complete:

a Under reflection in axis of symmetry PQ,

$$AO \rightarrow \_\_\_ \qquad DO \rightarrow \_\_\_$$
$$So\ AO = \_\_\_ \qquad So\ DO = \_\_\_$$

b Under reflection in axis of symmetry RS,

$$AO \rightarrow \_\_\_ \qquad BO \rightarrow \_\_\_$$
$$So\ AO = \_\_\_ \qquad So\ BO = \_\_\_$$

It follows that AO = ___ = ___ = ___

2B The garage sign spins about an axis of symmetry, AC→BD.

BD is the image of AC under reflection in this axis of symmetry

So BD and AC meet on the axis, at O.

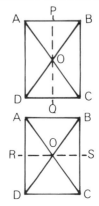

63

The diagonals of a rectangle bisect each other.

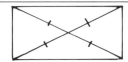

3A EFGH is a rectangle.
  a If HK = 5 cm, what are the lengths of KF, KG and KE?
  b If EG = 30 mm, what are the lengths of HF, HK and EK?

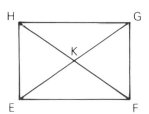

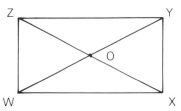

4A In rectangle WXYZ, WX = 40 mm, XY = 30 mm and WY = 50 mm.
What are the lengths of WZ, ZY, ZX, OW and OX?

5A a How long is this football pitch? (The measurements are shown to the nearest metre.)
  b The width should be between 45 m and 90 m. Would this pitch be all right?
  c How long is a diagonal of the pitch?
  d How far is it from the centre to a corner flag?
  e How far is it from the centre to the goalmouth?

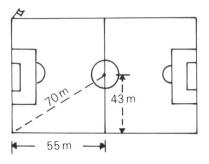

6A Use the axes of symmetry to help you to write down the sizes of the angles marked $x°$ and $y°$ in these rectangles:

a 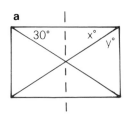 **b** 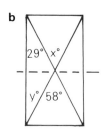 **c** **d**

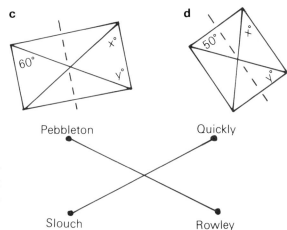

Pebbleton   Quickly

Slouch   Rowley

7B Four villages lie at the corners of a rectangle. They are connected by two straight roads. The distance from Pebbleton to the cross-roads is 2·6 miles.

  a How far is it from Pebbleton to Rowley?
  b A man walks from Pebbleton to Rowley in 72 minutes. How long would he take from Quickly to Rowley at the same speed?
  c Which village is nearest Slouch by road?

8C In this question, think about the symmetry of the rectangle. Draw the axes only if you have to.

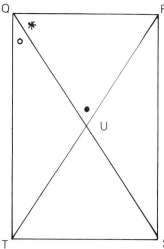

a Name three other angles equal to ∠RQS. Draw the diagram and mark all these angles with a ✳ .

b Name three other angles equal to ∠SQT.
Mark these with a ⊙ .

c What other angle equals ∠QUR? Mark both with a ●.

d Name two angles which make up a right angle.

e Name two angles which make up a straight angle.

f Name three angles which add up to 180°.

g Name two pairs of congruent triangles.

Imagine you are an archaeologist in the year 3000. You have dug up these two fragments. How would you reconstruct them? Explain what you assume about each one. Then trace them, and reconstruct them accurately.

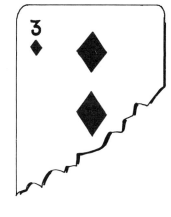

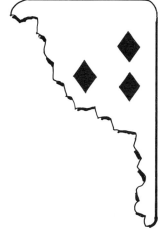

---

1 Windows open in many different ways. Draw sketches to help you to explain all the different ways you can think of.

2 These rectangles measure 1 cm by 2 cm.
They are arranged in rows as shown.
Copy and continue this table:

Number of 2 cm by 1 cm rectangles in *n*th row	1	2	3	4	...
Total number of 2 cm by 1 cm rectangles in first *n* rows	1	3			...

Find a systematic way to count the rectangles.
Then calculate the number of rectangles in the first 7, 10 and *n* rows.

Computer graphics

Laura is using her computer to draw on the screen. There is a square grid on the screen, and a flashing dot which tells her where she is at any time.

When she types MOVE (2, 1), the dot moves to the point (2, 1).

When she types DRAW (2, 4), the dot draws a line from (2, 1) to (2, 4).

============ *Exercise 8* ============

1A Use a computer and screen, or pretend you are the computer and obey the instructions on squared paper.

MOVE (2, 1) ⎤
DRAW (2, 4) ⎥ These are shown on the diagram.
DRAW (7, 4) ⎦
DRAW (7, 1)
DRAW (2, 1)

What shape have you drawn?

2A On squared paper draw the rectangle with corners (2, 2), (2, 8), (6, 8) and (6, 2). List instructions for drawing the rectangle by computer.

3A Repeat question **2A** for the rectangle with corners (0, 0), (5, 0), (5, 2) and (0, 2).

4A Duncan decided to try drawing on the screen. He began by drawing the diagonals of his rectangle, which he had worked out on squared paper. Follow his instructions on computer or on squared paper.

MOVE (3, 3)
DRAW (5, 9)
MOVE (1, 5)
DRAW (7, 7)

Write out the list of instructions needed to draw his rectangle.

5A Laura typed in these instructions:
MOVE (1, 1)   DRAW (1, 5)   DRAW (7, 5)
a Follow these instructions on computer or on squared paper.
b Laura was trying to draw a rectangle. Complete the instructions, and draw the rectangle.

6A To draw one of the diagonals Laura typed MOVE (1, 1) DRAW (7, 5).
a Give instructions for drawing the other diagonal.
b What instruction would move the dot to the point where the diagonals cross?

7A a On the same diagram as question **5A**, draw rectangles congruent to Laura's, with bottom left-hand corners (7, 1), (1, 5) and (7, 5).
b List computer instructions for the first one.
c Join the four points where the diagonals intersect in each rectangle.
d What is special about the shape you've drawn?

8B Pamela made a sketch of the rectangle she wanted to draw on the screen.

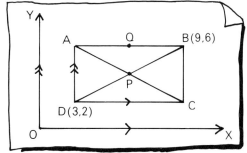

a What are the coordinates of A, C and P?

b She wanted to draw rectangles which formed a brick wall tiling. List the instructions for drawing the rectangle which has its bottom left-hand corner at Q.

9C Jan wants to draw a rectangle with sides 6 and 8 units long. She wants the sides to be parallel to the edges of the screen, and one corner to be at (3, 2).

a How many different rectangles can she draw on the screen?

b Draw them, and write down the coordinates of the corners of each one.

10C Paul listed his instructions, but then spilled coffee on them.

His instructions were for drawing a rectangle with its sides parallel to the axes. Can you find his rectangle and draw it?

Draw a sports pitch or court on a 16 by 16 squared grid. List instructions for drawing all the lines by computer.

Making sure

1 Congruent rectangles can make a tiling.

2 A rectangle fits its outline in 4 ways, and has 2 axes of symmetry.

3 All of its angles are right angles.

4 Its opposite sides are equal and parallel.

5 Its diagonals are equal, and bisect each other.

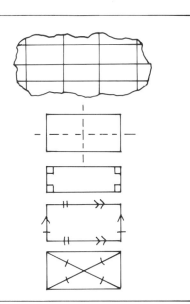

ALL ABOUT RECTANGLES

1A Draw a rectangle ABCD, with its diagonals crossing at O.
  a Name a line equal in length to: (i) AB (ii) BC (iii) AC.
  b Name three lines equal in length to OA.

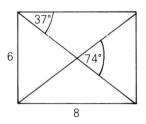

2A Copy this rectangle, and fill in:
  a the lengths of as many lines as you can
  b the sizes of as many angles as you can.

3A Draw rectangle OPQR on squared paper. O is the origin, P is the
  point (5, 0) and Q is (5, 8). Write down:
  a the coordinates of R   **b** the length, breadth and area of the rectangle.

4A a Draw a rectangle, and mark in its axes of symmetry.
  b In how many ways does a rectangle fit its outline?

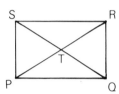

5A In rectangle PQRS, name:
  a two pairs of parallel lines
  b two pairs of congruent triangles.

6A The diagram shows two rectangles which
  overlap at right angles.
  a How many right angles can you see?
  b How many rectangles can you see?

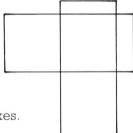

7B Rectangle EFGH has its sides parallel to the *x*- and *y*-axes.
  E is the point (2, 4), and the diagonals cross at (4, 5).
  Find the coordinates of F, G and H.

8B Which of the following are true and which are false?
  a Each angle of a rectangle is 90°.
  b All the sides of a rectangle are equal.
  c The diagonals bisect each other.
  d The diagonals are axes of symmetry.
  e The sides of a rectangle form four pairs of perpendicular lines.

9C ABCD is a rectangle. E lies on an axis
  of symmetry. Show that:
  a DE = CE   **b** AE = BE.

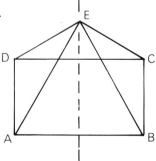

Class discussion

You can often see graphs on television and in newspapers and magazines. Which of the ones below are line graphs, bar graphs, pie charts or pictographs? Why do they have these names? It would be a good idea to make a class collection of graphs from newspapers, etc.

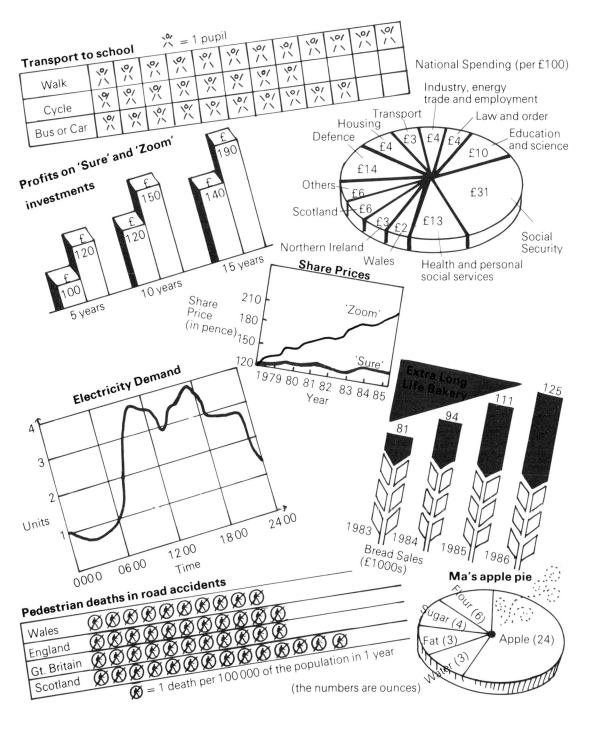

Transport to school

$\overset{\backslash 0/}{/\backslash}$ = 1 pupil

Walk										
Cycle										
Bus or Car										

National Spending (per £100)

Industry, energy trade and employment
Transport £3
Housing £4
Defence £14
Law and order £4
Education and science £10
Others £6
Scotland £6
Northern Ireland £3
Wales £2
Health and personal social services £13
Social Security £31

Profits on 'Sure' and 'Zoom' investments

£100 — 5 years
£120 — 10 years
£120, £150 —
£140, £190 — 15 years

Share Prices

Share Price (in pence)
210
180
150
120
'Zoom'
'Sure'
1979 80 81 82 83 84 85
Year

Electricity Demand

Units
4
3
2
1
0000 0600 1200 1800 2400
Time

Extra Long Life Bakery

81 — 1983
94 — 1984
111 — 1985
125 — 1986
Bread Sales (£1000s)

Pedestrian deaths in road accidents

Wales	
England	
Gt. Britain	
Scotland	

= 1 death per 100 000 of the population in 1 year

Ma's apple pie

Flour (6)
Sugar (4)
Fat (3)
Water (3)
Apple (24)

(the numbers are ounces)

SLICING PIE CHARTS

1 Each of these pie charts gives you a different piece of information about Carbo High School. What is it, in each one?

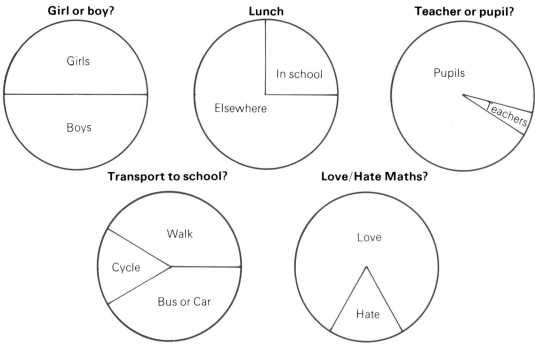

Girl or boy?

Girls

Boys

Lunch

In school

Elsewhere

Teacher or pupil?

Pupils

Teachers

Transport to school?

Walk

Cycle

Bus or Car

Love/Hate Maths?

Love

Hate

Fizzo

Hot chocolate

Tea

Coffee

2 Look at this pie chart. It shows the sales in Carbo High's drinks vending machine during the Christmas term. What fraction of the sales were for:
a coffee   **b** tea
c hot chocolate   **d** Fizzo?

3 Estimate the fraction of the earth's surface covered by:
a land   **b** water.

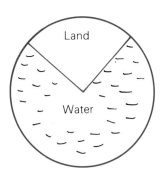

Land

Water

4 Class 2C voted on four pop groups.
List the groups in order, starting with the
most popular.

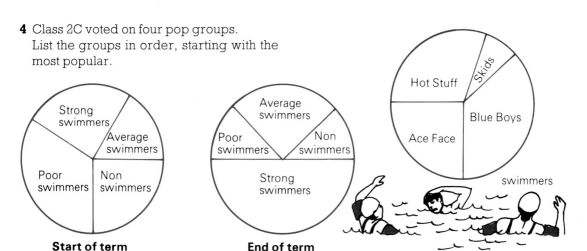

Start of term　　　**End of term**

5 Mr Armstrong gave class 2A swimming tests at the beginning and end of term. Why do you
think he was pleased with the results? Give several reasons.

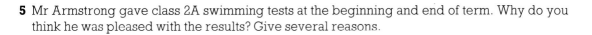

This is what Jane found

a Was Jane right?
b What does she mean by 'others'?
c List her results in order, from the most
popular to the least popular.
d What fraction of the total was British?

7 Angie works in a hairdresser's salon.
This pie chart shows how she divides up
her wage each week.
　a List the items in order from largest to
　smallest.
　b Estimate the fraction of her money that
　she spends on:
　(i) food　　(ii) clothes　　(iii) bus fares.
　c Her take-home pay is £96 a week.
　Estimate how much she spends each
　week on food, clothes and bus fares.

8 a Why do you think pie charts are good for showing some kinds of information?
　b Can you suggest a disadvantage pie charts might have?

DRAWING PIE CHARTS

1 The 30 pupils in class 2B were asked which country in the United Kingdom they would like to have a holiday in. The results were:
England—10; Scotland—10; Wales—5; Ireland—5.
They calculated the angles for the slices of a pie chart like this:

England's slice $= \frac{10}{30} \times 360° = 120°$

Scotland's slice $= \frac{10}{30} \times 360° = 120°$

Wales' slice $\quad = \frac{5}{30} \times 360° = 60°$

Ireland's slice $\quad = \frac{5}{30} \times 360° = 60°$

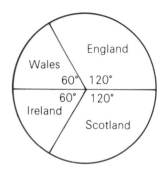

Use your protractor to help you to draw the pie chart.

2 Claire calculated the number of hours of 'repeats' on television in one week.

Channel	1	2	3	4
Hours of repeats	7	6	8	3

TOTAL HOURS = 24

She calculated the angle of the first slice in a pie chart like this:

Channel 1: $\frac{7}{24} \times 360° = 105°$.

Calculate the other angles, and draw the pie chart.

3 A large crowd turned out for the City v. United football match. It was estimated that half of them were City supporters, one third United supporters, and the rest were neither.
a Draw a pie chart to show this.
b Mark the fractions opposite the slices.

4 Suzanne asked her class to vote on the television programmes they liked best. Their votes were:

Sport—6   Cartoons—3   Films—9   Quizzes—3   Plays—1   Other—8
a How many votes were there?
b How many degrees on the pie chart should she give for each vote?
c Draw the pie chart. Mark in the programmes, and write the vote opposite each one.

5 Draw a pie chart to illustrate the ingredients in this recipe for Date Delight:
200 g plain chocolate
100 g margarine
75 g brown sugar
175 g dates
50 g rice flakes.

6 The chemical name for chalk is calcium carbonate ($CaCO_3$). One molecule of chalk is made of 1 atom of calcium (Ca), 1 atom of carbon (C) and 3 atoms of oxygen (O).
Draw a pie chart to show how chalk is made up.

7 In a mock election in school, candidates got the following votes:
Candidate A (Longer school holidays)......100
Candidate B (Longer school hours)............10
Candidate C (Abolish school rules) 260
Candidate D (Abolish teachers)...............270
Candidate E (Abolish schools)................360
Illustrate the voting in a pie chart.

8 Donald collects stamps from six countries. He drew this pie chart to show the proportions of stamps in his collection. He estimates that he has about 3000 stamps altogether. How many has he from each country?

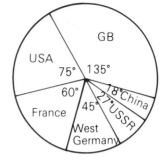

Collecting statistics and constructing pie charts

Statistics can be collected by:

1 Asking questions.

2 Looking at newspapers, books, magazines and advertisements.

3 Making observations, for example by counting or measuring.

════════════════════ *Exercise 3   (Practical)* ════════════════════

On your own, or with a partner, collect statistics for one part of each of the following two questions. Then illustrate them by pie charts.

1 a Methods of travelling to school (walking, cycling, bus, car).
 b Favourite pop groups.
 c Favourite sport.
 d Number of children in the family.

2 a Number of heads and tails obtained by tossing a coin 50 times.
 b Scores obtained (1, 2, 3, 4, 5 or 6) by throwing a dice 50 times.
 c Number of goals scored by English or Scottish football teams one Saturday.
 d Swimmers: (i) strong (ii) average (iii) weak (iv) non-swimmers.

USING LINE GRAPHS

Katie kept a record of the number of Christmas cards she got.

Each day she marked a point on her graph to show the **total number of cards to date.**

By 23rd December she had received 28 cards.

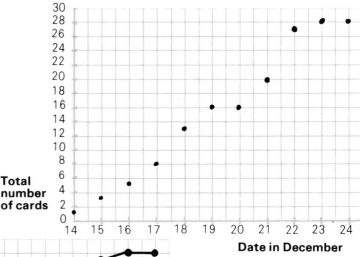

Total number of cards / **Date in December**

Her friend Sonya said that if she joined up the points she would get a **line graph**.

They agreed that this gave a good quick picture of the number of cards received.

Total number of cards / **Date in December**

═══════════════ *Exercise 4A* ═══════════════

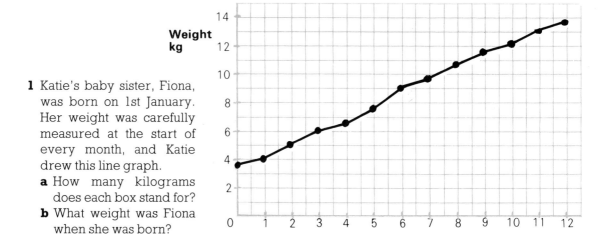

Weight kg / **Fiona's age (months)**

1 Katie's baby sister, Fiona, was born on 1st January. Her weight was carefully measured at the start of every month, and Katie drew this line graph.

  a How many kilograms does each box stand for?

  b What weight was Fiona when she was born?

  c What weight was she at: (i) 3 months (ii) 6 months?

  d When did she first weigh 12 kg?

  e During which month did she gain most weight (where the graph is steepest)?

2 Sonya came across this line graph of the number of babies born in Scotland from 1975–1984.
She found it interesting because it showed the trend of the number of births—
falling between 1975 and 1977,
rising between 1977 and 1981.

a Describe the trend in the number of births from 1981 to 1984.

b 2 boxes stand for 1000 births. What does 1 box stand for?

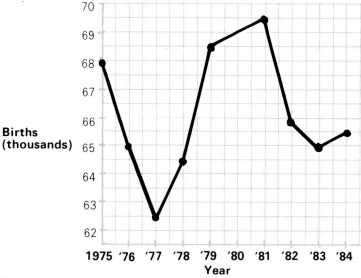

Births (thousands)

Year

c Copy and complete this table:

Year	1975	1976	1977	
Number of births				69 500

d In which year were: (i) most babies born (ii) fewest babies born?

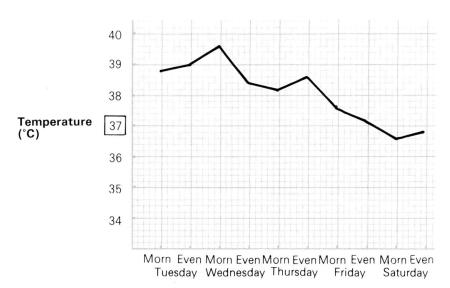

Temperature (°C)

Morn Even Morn Even Morn Even Morn Even Morn Even
Tuesday   Wednesday Thursday   Friday   Saturday

Time of taking temperature

3 Every morning and evening the nurses took Mr Lowe's temperature, and then made up the chart hanging at the foot of his bed.

a What was Mr Lowe's highest temperature? When was this?

b What happened to his temperature during Thursday?

c His temperature started to fall on two occasions. Can you find these?

d What was his temperature on Friday evening?

e When did his temperature return to normal (37°C)?

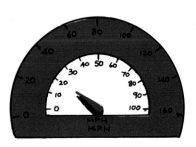

4 Here's a useful line graph for changing miles per hour to and from kilometres per hour.
Use it to change—
a to km/h (follow the arrows):
   (i) 50 mph (ii) 60 mph
   (iii) 100 mph
b to mph (follow the arrows):
   (i) 10 km/h (ii) 45 km/h
   (iii) 90 km/h.
Do you think the graph could be continued for speeds over 70 mph? Give a reason.

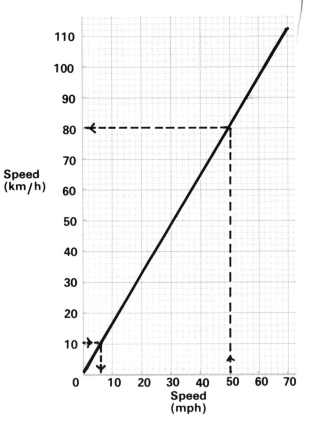

Speed (km/h)

Speed (mph)

5 Jim cycled from Brighton to Worthing to deliver a parcel to his aunt, then home again. He drew this graph of his journey.

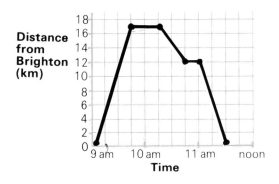

Distance from Brighton (km)

Time

a How many minutes does 1 box stand for on the **Time** axis?
b How long did Jim take to cycle from Brighton to Worthing?
c How far is this?
d How long did he stay at his aunt's?
e He had a puncture on the way home. How long did he take to mend it?
f How long did the return journey take?

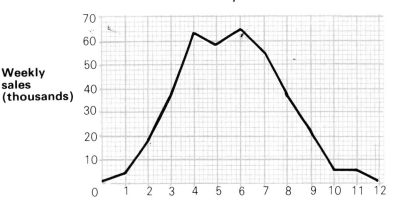

Weekly
sales
(thousands)

Weeks released

1 The agent of the group, 'The Three Decays' drew a graph of the sales of their hit record 'Toothache'.
  a In which week were most records sold? How many?
  b For how many weeks were more than 50 000 records sold?
  c Calculate the total number of records sold in the first (i) 2 weeks (ii) 3 weeks (iii) 4 weeks.
  d Describe the trend of the sales during these 12 weeks.

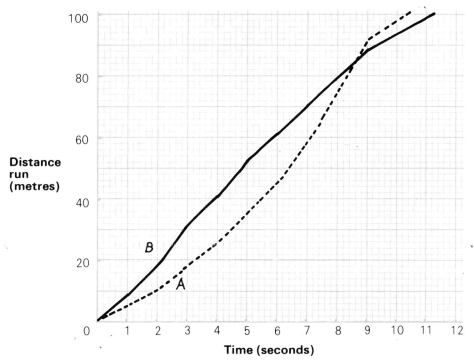

Distance
run
(metres)

Time (seconds)

2 Allan (A) and Brian (B) had their distance measured every second in a 100 metre race.
  a Who had the better start?
  b Who led at the half-way stage?
  c After what time were they level?
  d Who won? By how many metres and by what fraction of a second?
  e Describe the race in one or two sentences.

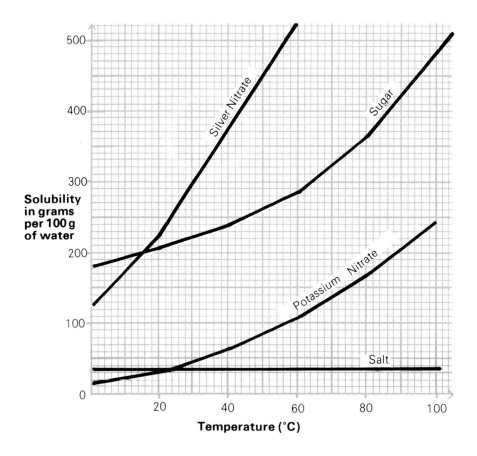

Solubility
in grams
per 100 g
of water

Temperature (°C)

THE SUGAR CUBES DISAPPEAR
BECAUSE THE SUGAR DISSOLVES
IN THE HOT TEA.
EVENTUALLY NO MORE WILL
DISSOLVE SINCE THE TEA WILL
BECOME SATURATED WITH SUGAR.

THE GRAPH SHOWS THE
GREATEST WEIGHT OF FOUR
DIFFERENT SUBSTANCES THAT
CAN DISSOLVE IN 100g OF
WATER AT DIFFERENT
TEMPERATURES.

3 a At 40°C, which substance is the most soluble, and which is least soluble? Is this true at all temperatures?
  b Which substance's solubility increases fastest as the temperature rises?
  c How does the solubility of salt differ from that of the other substances?
  d What is the temperature of 100 g of water for the following to dissolve in it?
    (i) Twice as much salt as potassium nitrate.
    (ii) Twice as much potassium nitrate as salt.
    (iii) Ten times as much sugar as salt.
  e A cup contains 100 g of water. A sugar cube contains 8 g of sugar. How many sugar cubes could be dissolved in water at: (i) 80°C (ii) 20°C?

DRAWING LINE GRAPHS

Exercise 5

1 Tony kept a note of his ice cream sales each day, to the nearest £5.

Day	Mon	Tue	Wed	Thu	Fri	Sat	Sun
Sales (£)	40	55	60	45	60	75	65

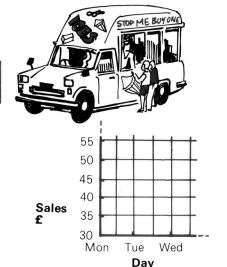

a On squared paper draw these axes and scales. Plot the points, and draw a line graph of his daily sales.

b On which day was most ice cream sold? Why do you think this was?

c Write a sentence about the trend of the sales—up or down during the week.

2 Alison's height was measured each year at the school medical inspection.

Age	8	9	10	11	12	13	14	15	16
Height (cm)	135	137	140	145	148	155	158	160	161

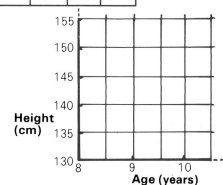

a On squared paper draw these axes and scales. Plot the points, and draw a line graph of her height.

b Did Alison grow by the same amount each year?

c Estimate her height at the age of 10½. Why can you use the graph to do this?

3 This table shows the average monthly temperatures in Glasgow.

Month	Jan	Feb	Mar	Apr	May	June	July	Aug	Sep	Oct	Nov	Dec
Temperature (°C)	4	4	6	8	11	13	15	15	13	10	7	5

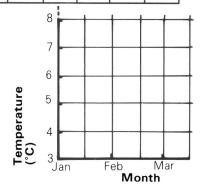

a On squared paper draw these axes and scales. Plot the temperatures, and draw a line graph

b What months have the highest average temperature?

c Look at your graph. Write a sentence or two about how the temperature changes over the year.

4 The pop group Metal Image, had a hit record with 'I think I'm great'. The table shows the record's position in the Top Thirty over several weeks.

Week	1	2	3	4	5	6	7	8	9	10	11
Position in the charts	28	21	17	9	3	3	4	10	16	25	30

a Draw a line graph of the record's progress. Choose the scales carefully, and remember to name the axes.
b For how many weeks was the record in the Top Ten?
c Use your graph to explain in a sentence or two how the record's popularity changed over the weeks.

=== *Exercise 5B/C* ===

1 A traffic census was started at 8 am. Every hour, a note was taken of the total number of vehicles which had passed so far.

Time	09 00	10 00	11 00	12 00	13 00	14 00	15 00	16 00	17 00	18 00
Total number of vehicles	250	400	500	550	700	850	950	1000	1250	1550

a Draw a line graph on 2 mm squared paper. Take 1 cm to represent 100 vehicles on the vertical axis.
b By what time had 1500 vehicles passed the census point?
c Did more vehicles per hour arrive before noon or after noon?
d Describe any trend you see in the number of vehicles passing the census point.

2 Alaska, Northern Canada, Greenland and Northern Russia are thinly populated lands inside the Arctic Circle. This area is called the Tundra. The average temperature and average rainfall each month in the Tundra are shown in the table. Draw 2 separate line graphs showing how the temperature and rainfall change throughout the year.

Month	Jan	Feb	Mar	Apr	May	June	July	Aug	Sep	Oct	Nov	Dec
Temperature (°C)	−22	−27	−23	−18	−6	2	5	3	−3	−9	−15	−23
Rainfall (mm)	2	2	3	3	3	5	13	13	10	3	2	5

a Between which two months is the greatest temperature (i) increase (ii) decrease?
b Describe in a sentence or two the trend over the year of:
  (i) the temperature   (ii) the rainfall.
c Calculate the average monthly rainfall, and the average monthly temperature.

3 A manufacturer wanted to design a new cup which would keep tea hot for as long as possible. Two designs were tested by filling both cups with the same volume of hot tea and measuring both temperatures as the tea cooled.

Cup A

Cup B

Time (minutes)		1	2	3	4	5	6	7	8
Temperature (°C)	Cup A	78	67	58	51	45	40	36	33
	Cup B	73	60	49	39	33	29	27	26

  a Draw two graphs on the same sheet of 2 mm squared paper.
  b Which cup was chosen?
  c Why did the tea in one cool more quickly than in the other?
  d How long did each cup take to cool to 60°C?
  e (i) Why is it reasonable to use your graph to estimate the temperatures of the tea after $5\frac{1}{2}$ minutes?
     (ii) Do this for both cups.

COLLECTING STATISTICS AGAIN, AND CONSTRUCTING LINE GRAPHS

======= *Exercise 6 (Practical)* =======

Choose one part of question **1** and one part of question **2**. When you have collected the statistics, draw a line graph for your two choices.

1 a Choose a record in the Top 40. Record its position week by week.
  b Look at the weather section in a newspaper. Choose one of the towns listed there, and record its daily temperature for two weeks.
  c Look at the financial section in a newspaper. Choose one of the shares, and record its daily price for two weeks.

2 a Each day for two weeks, before you leave for school or just when you get home, record the reading on the gas or electricity meter.
  b Take some strenuous exercise, like running or jumping. Then record your pulse rate every $\frac{1}{2}$ minute for 5 minutes.
  c Choose several squares with different lengths of sides. Calculate their areas. Plot length of side against area of square.

A 10 foot ladder leans against a wall. Its foot is placed at different distances from the foot of the wall. The distance it reaches up the wall is measured.
a Make scale drawings and record the pairs of distances in a table.
b Draw a line graph.
c Describe in a few sentences your investigation and your graph.

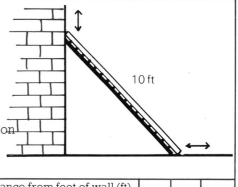
10 ft

Distance from foot of wall (ft)			
Distance up wall (ft)			

Don't be fooled

Advertisers, newspapers, television, politicians have all been known to tell the wrong story—sometimes this is by mistake, but sometimes it's because they want to.

===================== *Exercise 7* =====================

1 'We have halved unemployment since coming to power.'
One square is half the length of the other, but why is the picture misleading?

2 'Since advertising in our newspaper, Sky-Hi's profits have doubled.'
One cube is twice the length of the other, but . . . what's wrong here?

3 'Since we took over the company in 1980, profits have soared.'
Have they? What is wrong with the graph?

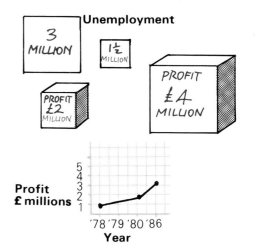

4 'More people pass their driving test with us than with any other company.'

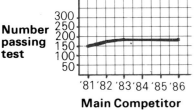

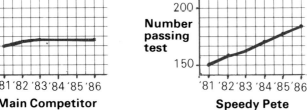

Why are these graphs misleading?

5 'Prices slashed!'
What have you to say about this claim?

6

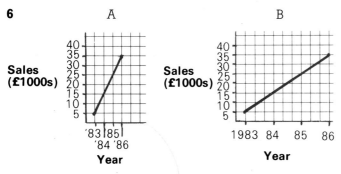

At first sight, which company is doing better? Look carefully! Have you changed your mind?

So study graphs carefully before you believe what they are telling you.

CHECK-UP ON **STATISTICS AND GRAPHS**

1 Pie charts

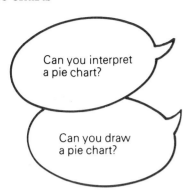

a

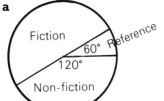

The pie chart shows the three types of book in a school library.
(i) Find the fraction of each type of book in the library.

(ii) There are 2400 books altogether. How many non-fiction books are there?

b In a class of 30 pupils, 15 have blue eyes, 5 have brown eyes and 10 have grey eyes.
Draw a pie chart to show this information.

2 Line graphs

a

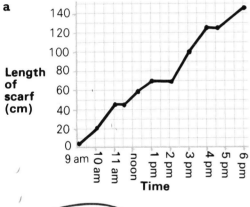

Rosie promised her brother she would knit him a football scarf for his birthday. She knitted it all in one day.
(i) How many centimetres had Rosie knitted by: 10 am, 1 pm, 3 pm and 6 pm?
(ii) How many times did she stop for a rest?
(iii) How long did she stop each time?
(iv) What time was it when she reached 130 cm?

b This table shows the sales of the school newspaper.

Month	Sep	Oct	Nov	Dec	Jan	Feb	Mar
Number sold	220	240	210	230	360	350	320

(i) Draw a line graph of the monthly sales.
(ii) Describe the trend of the sales in a sentence or two.

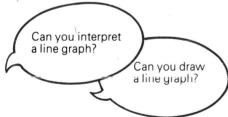

3 Don't be fooled

Others

Roadroar

'ROADROAR now sell twice as many tyres as any other company.'

Comment on this advertisement.

4 Choose several circles with different diameters. Calculate their circumferences. Put your results in a table, and show them in a line graph.

LETTERS FOR NUMBERS

1A Copy these notes, and fill in the parts that have been torn off.

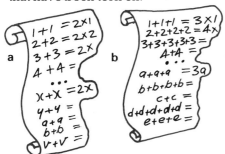

2A Write in shorter form:
a $m+m$
b $n+n+n$
c $k+k+k+k$
d $p+p+p$
e $q+q$
f $d+d+d+d$
g $y+y+y$
h $x+x+x+x$
i $t+t+t+t+t+t+t$

3A Copy and complete all the missing parts of these torn notes:

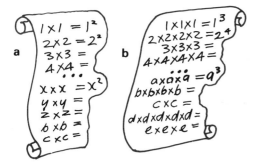

4A Write in shorter form:
a $g\times g$
b $h\times h\times h$
c $y\times y\times y\times y$
d $x\times x$
e $t\times t\times t$
f $d\times d$
g $k\times k\times k$
h $z\times z\times z\times z$
i $n\times n\times n\times n\times n\times n$

5A Copy and complete the parts that are missing from these notes:

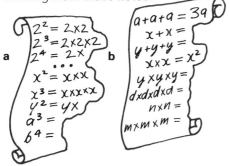

6A Write out in full:
a 3^2
b 4^2
c 3^3
d 5^2
e x^2
f y^3
g m^4
h n^2
i 10^2

7A Write in shorter form:
a $a+a$
b $a\times a$
c $b+b+b$
d $b\times b\times b$
e $c+c+c+c$
f $c\times c\times c\times c$

8A Copy and complete:

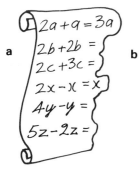

9A Write in shorter form:
a $x+x$
b $2x+x$
c $3x+2x$
d $3a+a$
e $b+4b$
f $5c+5c$
g $5a-2a$
h $6c-c$
i $2b-2b$
j $2a-a$
k $6y-4y$
l $3n-n$

10A Write in shorter form:
a $y\times y$
b $2y\times 2y$
c $4y\times y$
d $3a\times 3a$
e $2b\times 3b$
f $5c\times 2c$
g $4\times 2x$
k $5\times 3m$
i $6\times n$

11B

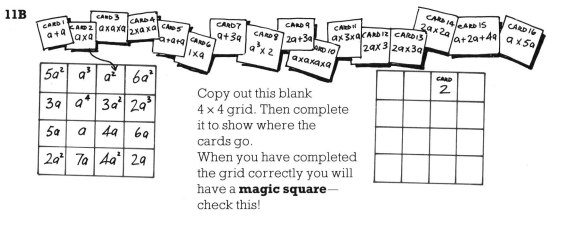

$5a^2$	a^3	a^2	$6a^2$
$3a$	a^4	$3a^2$	$2a^3$
$5a$	a	$4a$	$6a$
$2a^2$	$7a$	$4a^2$	$2a$

Copy out this blank
4 × 4 grid. Then complete
it to show where the
cards go.
When you have completed
the grid correctly you will
have a **magic square**—
check this!

			CARD 2

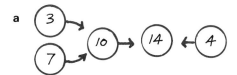

═══════════════════ *Exercise 2   Adding in circles* ═══════════════════

1A Look at these diagrams:

a

Where do the 10 and 14 come from?

b

Why should 6 go in the
empty circle?

c

Why should 2 go in the empty circle?

d

Why should 6x go in the
empty circle?

2A Write down the numbers and letters that should go in the empty circles. All the diagrams
deal with adding.

a   **b**   **c**   **d**

e   **f** 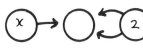   **g**

h   **i**   **j** 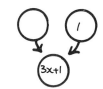   **k**

85

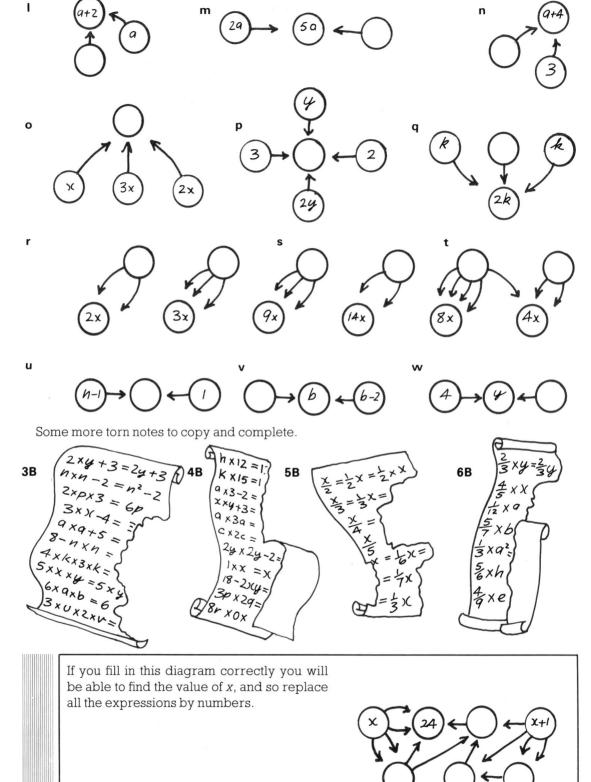

Some more torn notes to copy and complete.

If you fill in this diagram correctly you will be able to find the value of x, and so replace all the expressions by numbers.

Exercise 3 Snakes and ladders and crocodiles

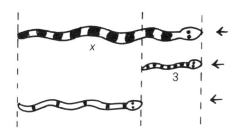

This snake has length x metres,

and this snake has length 3 metres.

So this snake must have length $x - 3$ metres.

Find expressions for the lengths of the unmarked snakes and ladders and crocodiles below. The lengths are in metres.

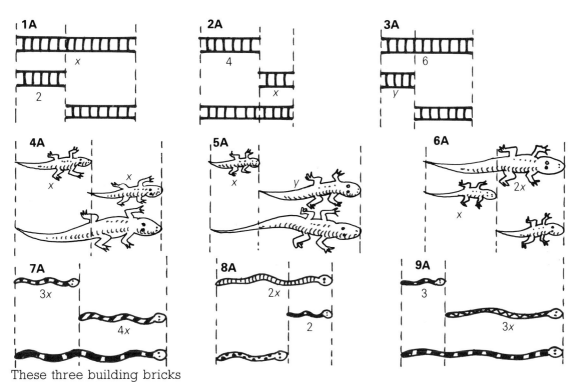

1A x / 2

2A 4 / x

3A 6 / y

4A x / x

5A x / y

6A $2x$ / x

7A $3x$ / $4x$

8A $2x$ / 2

9A 3 / $3x$

These three building bricks can be fitted together in various ways:

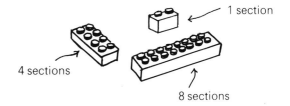

1 section

4 sections

8 sections

10A

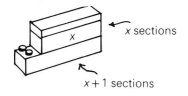

x sections

x

$x + 1$ sections

a Explain why the bottom brick has $x + 1$ sections if the top brick has x sections.

b If the bottom brick had y sections, how many would the top one have?

11A Write down expressions for the lengths of the shaded bricks in terms of x. Lengths are measured in sections.

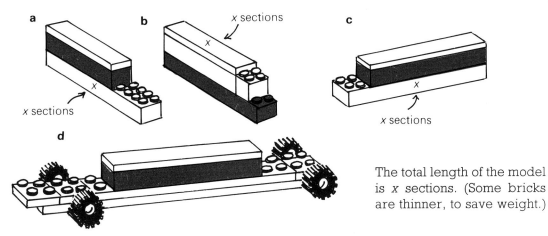

a

b x sections

c

x sections

x sections

d

The total length of the model is x sections. (Some bricks are thinner, to save weight.)

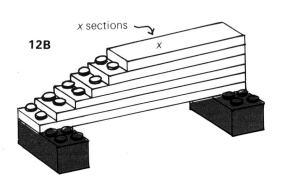

x sections

12B

a Find expressions for the lengths of all the thin bricks in this diagram.
b What is the length of the gap underneath?
c The largest brick in the diagram has a length of 14 sections. Find:
(i) x (ii) the length of the gap underneath.

13B a Find expressions for the lengths of all the bricks in the diagram.

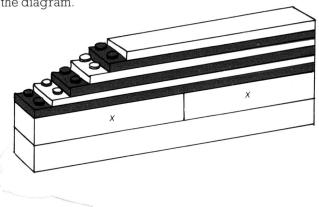

b The longest brick in the diagram has a length of 18 sections. Find:
(i) x (ii) the length of the shortest brick.

Find expressions for the lengths of the unmarked straws. All the lengths are in centimetres.

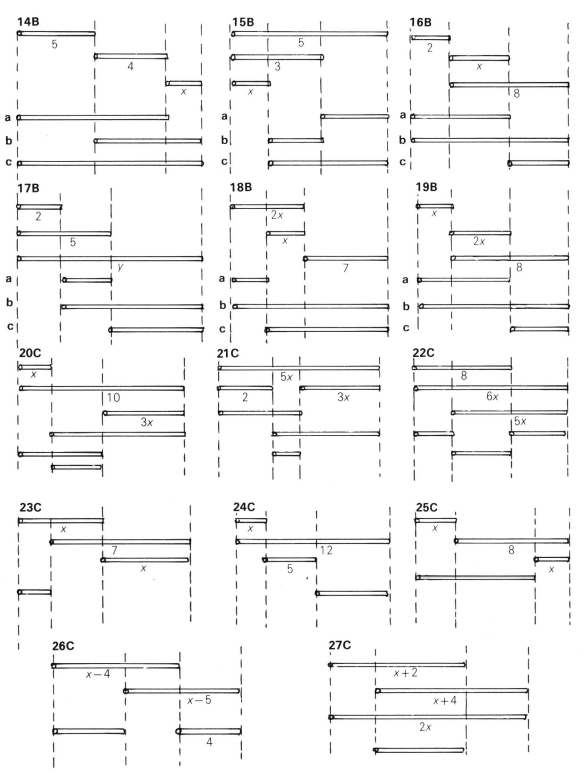

14B

5
4
x
a
b
c

15B

5
3
x
a
b
c

16B

2
x
8
a
b
c

17B

2
5
y
a
b
c

18B

2x
x
7
a
b
c

19B

x
2x
8
a
b
c

20C

x
10
3x

21C

5x
2
3x

22C

8
6x
5x

23C

x
7
x

24C

x
12
5

25C

x
8
x

26C

x − 4
x − 5
4

27C

x + 2
x + 4
2x

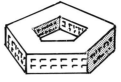

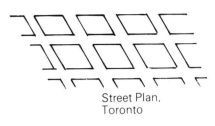

George Square,
Glasgow

The Pentagon,
Washington

Street Plan,
Toronto

LETTERS FOR NUMBERS

Calculate the perimeters of the following shapes:

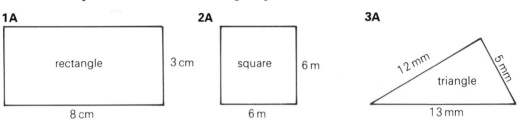

1A rectangle 3 cm 8 cm

2A square 6 m 6 m

3A triangle 12 mm 5 mm 13 mm

Make a formula for the perimeter (P) of each shape below; for example, $P = 2x + 2y$. All the lengths are in centimetres.

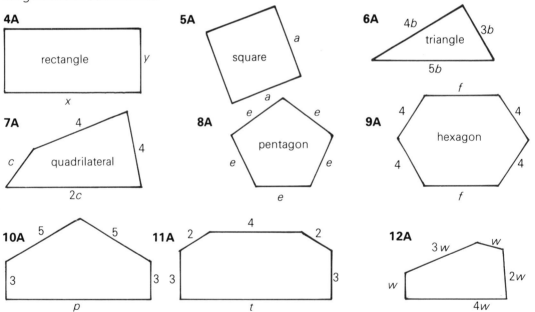

4A rectangle y x

5A square a a

6A triangle $4b$ $3b$ $5b$

7A quadrilateral 4 4 c $2c$

8A pentagon e e e e e

9A hexagon f 4 4 4 4 f

10A 5 5 3 p

11A 4 2 2 3 3 t

12A $3w$ w w $2w$ $4w$

Make a formula for the total length (L) of wire in these grids. The lengths are in metres.

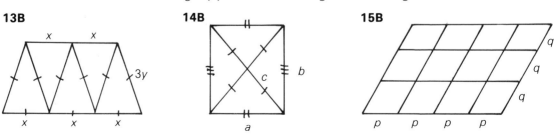

13B x x $3y$ x x x

14B c b a

15B q q q p p p p

===== *Exercise 5   Areas* =====

Calculate the areas of these shapes:

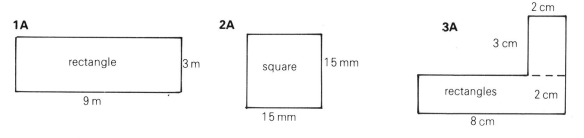

1A

rectangle

3 m

9 m

2A

square

15 mm

15 mm

3A

2 cm

3 cm

rectangles

2 cm

8 cm

Make a formula for the area (A) of the shapes below, which consist of rectangles and squares. All the lengths are in centimetres.

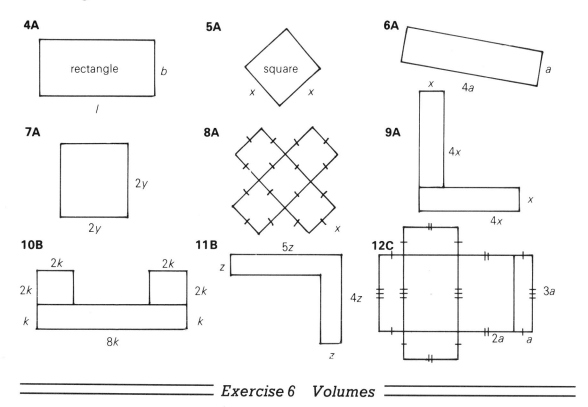

4A

rectangle

b

l

5A

square

x x

6A

a

x $4a$

7A

$2y$

$2y$

8A

x

9A

$4x$

x

$4x$

10B

$2k$ $2k$

$2k$ $2k$

k k

$8k$

11B

$5z$

z

$4z$

z

12C

$3a$

$2a$ a

===== *Exercise 6   Volumes* =====

Calculate the volumes of these solids:

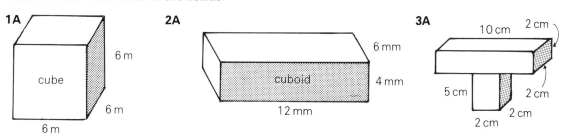

1A

cube

6 m

6 m

6 m

2A

6 mm

cuboid

4 mm

12 mm

3A

10 cm   2 cm

5 cm   2 cm

2 cm   2 cm

Make a formula for the volume (*V*) of each of the solids below, which are based on cubes and cuboids. All the lengths are in centimetres.

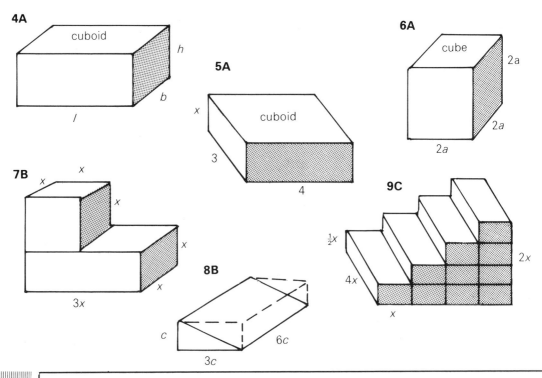

4A cuboid — *h*, *b*, *l*

5A cuboid — *x*, 3, 4

6A cube — 2*a*, 2*a*, 2*a*

7B — *x*, *x*, *x*, *x*, 3*x*

8B — *c*, 3*c*, 6*c*

9C — $\frac{1}{2}x$, 4*x*, *x*, 2*x*

LETTERS FOR NUMBERS

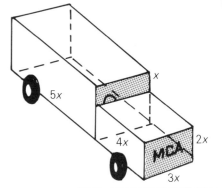

A wire frame is made for the shape of a model truck. Find an expression for the length of wire needed. The lengths are in centimetres.
The truck is then made in solid wood. Find expressions for the total area and volume of the model wooden truck.

(truck labels: 5*x*, 4*x*, 3*x*, 2*x*, *x*, MCA)

CHECK-UP ON **LETTERS FOR NUMBERS**

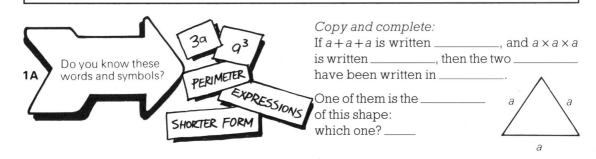

1A Do you know these words and symbols?

3*a*   *q*³   PERIMETER   EXPRESSIONS   SHORTER FORM

Copy and complete:
If *a*+*a*+*a* is written _____, and *a* × *a* × *a* is written _____, then the two _____ have been written in _____.

One of them is the _____ of this shape: which one? _____

(triangle labelled *a*, *a*, *a*)

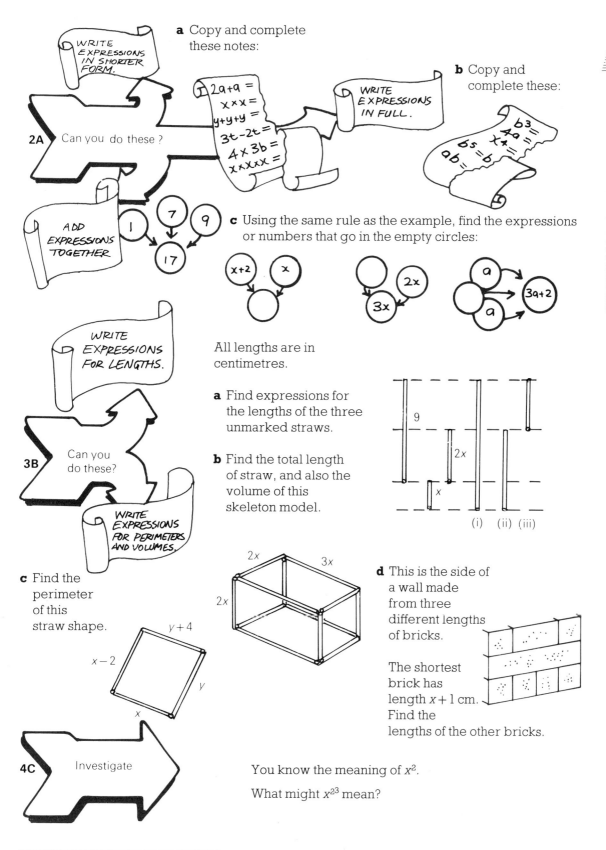

a Copy and complete these notes:

WRITE EXPRESSIONS IN SHORTER FORM.

2A Can you do these ?

$2a + a =$
$x \times x =$
$y + y + y =$
$3t - 2t =$
$4 \times 3b =$
$x \times x \times x =$

WRITE EXPRESSIONS IN FULL.

b Copy and complete these:

$b3 =$
$4a =$
$b5 =$
$x4 =$
$ab =$

ADD EXPRESSIONS TOGETHER

1   7   9
17

c Using the same rule as the example, find the expressions or numbers that go in the empty circles:

$x+2$ x

$2x$
$3x$

a
$3a+2$
a

WRITE EXPRESSIONS FOR LENGTHS.

All lengths are in centimetres.

3B Can you do these?

a Find expressions for the lengths of the three unmarked straws.

b Find the total length of straw, and also the volume of this skeleton model.

9
$2x$
x
(i)   (ii) (iii)

WRITE EXPRESSIONS FOR PERIMETERS AND VOLUMES.

c Find the perimeter of this straw shape.

$2x$ $3x$
$2x$

$y+4$
$x-2$
y
x

d This is the side of a wall made from three different lengths of bricks.

The shortest brick has length $x+1$ cm. Find the lengths of the other bricks.

4C Investigate

You know the meaning of x^2.

What might x^{23} mean?

MESURING LENGTH

DECIMAL MEASURES

MESURING LENGTH

Class discussion—units of length

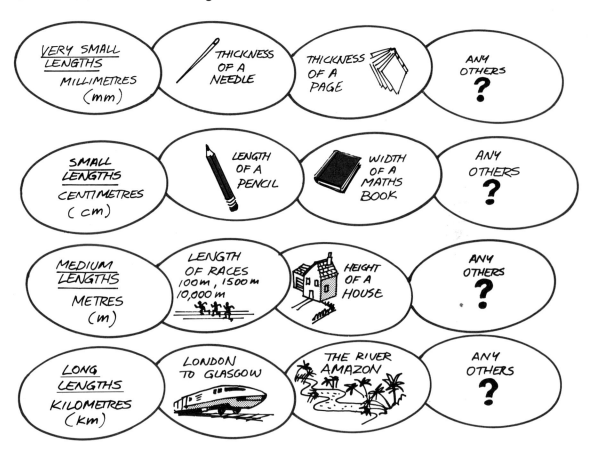

VERY SMALL LENGTHS
MILLIMETRES (mm)

THICKNESS OF A NEEDLE

THICKNESS OF A PAGE

ANY OTHERS ?

SMALL LENGTHS
CENTIMETRES (cm)

LENGTH OF A PENCIL

WIDTH OF A MATHS BOOK

ANY OTHERS ?

MEDIUM LENGTHS
METRES (m)

LENGTH OF RACES 100m, 1500m 10,000m

HEIGHT OF A HOUSE

ANY OTHERS ?

LONG LENGTHS
KILOMETRES (km)

LONDON TO GLASGOW

THE RIVER AMAZON

ANY OTHERS ?

=============== *Exercise 1* ===============

1 Which units of length would you use to measure these?
   a The distance from York to Edinburgh.
   b The length of one of your fingers.
   c The length of a football pitch.
   d The thickness of your notebook.
   e The breadth of the classroom.
   f The distance from the earth to the moon.

2 Estimate:
   a The height of a double-decker bus.
   b The distance to London.
   c The thickness of a pane of glass in the window.
   d The height of a prizewinning high jump.
   e The thickness and the diameter of an LP record.
   f The distance across the Atlantic Ocean.

YORK 245 MILES

3 Tom was always making up stories. Here is one of them:

'On my way home I passed a boy 170 centimetres tall. He was standing beside a car 100 metres long. Then I saw a man jump from a building 3 kilometres high. He gave me such a fright that I jumped 1 millimetre into the air.'

Which parts of his story are hard to believe?

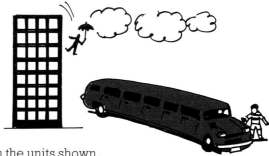

4 Estimate these lengths. Then measure them in the units shown.
  a The length of your middle finger (to the nearest cm).
  b The width of your thumb (in mm).
  c The width of your pen or pencil (in mm).
  d The length of this book (in cm, correct to 1 decimal place).
  e The diameter of a 10p coin (in mm).
  f The length, breadth and height of your desk (to the nearest cm).
  g The height and width of the classroom door (in m, correct to 2 decimal places).
  h The length and breadth of the classroom (in m, correct to 2 decimal places).
  i Your height (to the nearest cm). Add up your height and some of your friends' heights, and calculate the average height of the group.

All change

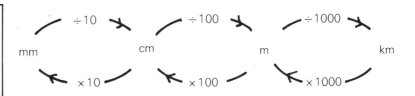

| 10 mm = 1 cm |
| 100 cm = 1 m |
| 1000 m = 1 km |

Remember!

Changing to a larger unit→fewer of them→divide by 10, 100 or 1000.
Changing to a smaller unit→more of them → multiply by 10, 100 or 1000.

Examples

(i) Change 50 mm to cm. A larger unit, fewer of them, divide by 10.
$$50 \text{ mm} = 50 \div 10 \text{ cm} = 5 \text{ cm}$$

(ii) Change 1·6 km to m. A smaller unit, more of them, multiply by 1000.
$$1 \cdot 6 \text{ km} = 1 \cdot 6 \times 1000 \text{ m} = 1600 \text{ m}$$

===== *Exercise 2A* =====

1 Change to millimetres:
  a 5 cm   **b** 12 cm   **c** 4·8 cm   **d** 0·4 cm

2 Change to centimetres:
  a 400 mm   **b** 60 mm   **c** 72 mm   **d** 4 mm

3 Change to centimetres:
  a 4 m   **b** 14 m   **c** 5·2 m   **d** 0·42 m

4 Change to metres:
  a 800 cm   **b** 480 cm   **c** 90 cm   **d** 52 cm

5 Change to metres:
  a 5 km   **b** 2·6 km   **c** 14·2 km   **d** 0·65 km

6 Change to kilometres:
  a 6000 m   **b** 8400 m   **c** 9420 m   **d** 870 m

7 On squared paper draw the following rectangles. Then measure the length of a diagonal in each one.
ABCD, with AB = 12 cm and BC = 5 cm.
PQRS, with PQ = 60 mm and QR = 45 mm.

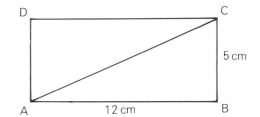

8 Measure the length and breadth of both these stamps in millimetres.
Then calculate their perimeters (the distances right round their edges.)

9 Measure the distances in millimetres from the point A on this ivy leaf to each of the other points named. Change the lengths to centimetres.

10 Sandy boasted that he could cover 1 km with four drives on the golf course. His first three shots went 205 m, 217 m and 196 m towards the hole. How far would he need to hit his fourth shot? Do you think he will do this?

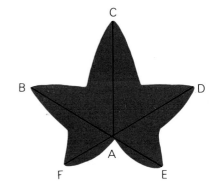

11 A piece of elastic is 47 cm long. How far has it to be stretched to be 1 m long?

12 A pile of 12 tiles is 6 cm high. Calculate the thickness of each tile, in millimetres.

13 A swimming pool is 50 m long. How many lengths would be swum:
  a in the men's 1500 m freestyle race
  b in the 4 by 100 m medley event?

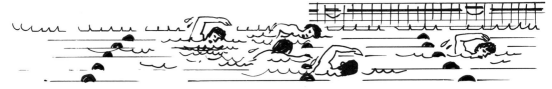

1 Change the following measurements to the units in brackets:
   a 12 mm (cm)   **b** 3 m (cm)   **c** 7 cm (mm)   **d** 6·5 km (m)
   e 189 cm (m)   **f** 96 mm (cm)   **g** 1200 m (km)   **h** 1·5 m (cm)

2 Copy and complete:
   a 4 km + 200 m = ... m   **b** 1 km − 400 m = ... m
   c 5 cm + 20 mm = ... mm   **d** 8 cm − 30 mm = ... mm
   e 2 m + 40 cm = ... cm   **f** 4 m − 20 cm = ... cm

3 Calculate the perimeters of these shapes:

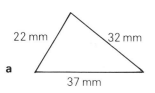
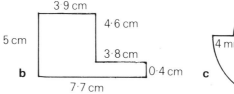
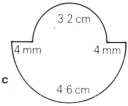

4 Taking 1 mile to be the same as 1·6 km, calculate the speed limits of 30 mph and 70 mph in km/h.

5 How many blocks of wood 40 cm long can be cut from the length shown?

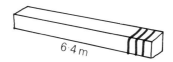

6 Five encyclopedias in the library are each 4·8 cm thick.
   a What length of shelf is needed for them?
   b How many could be put on a shelf 20 cm long?
   c A bookworm eats its way from the front cover of volume 1 to the end cover of volume 5. What distance does it travel?

7 Lorna walks to school each day, a distance of 2 km 250 m. How far does she walk in a week?

8 In a roll of photographic film, each frame is 35 mm long. There is a 2 mm gap between each frame. 5 cm is provided at each end of the film for loading.
   What is the length of a film with: **a** 10 frames   **b** 24 frames?

9 The longest track event at the Olympic Games is the 10 000 metres race.
   a How many kilometres is this?
   b How many laps of a 400 m track would have to be run?

DECIMAL MEASURES

10 The table lists the lengths and breadths in metres of some popular cars of the 1980s.

Car	Length	Breadth
Metro	3·40	1·55
Maestro	4·05	1·69
Fiesta	3·65	1·57
Sierra	4·41	1·73
Nova	3·63	1·54
Astra	4·00	1·67
Volvo	4·80	1·71
Panda	3·38	1·45
Rover	4·74	1·77
Renault	3·99	1·66

What is the difference in length, in metres, between the longest and shortest cars?

What is the difference in width, in centimetres, between the widest and narrowest cars?

Miss Allen has decided to buy a new car. The space in her garage for a car is 3·50 m by 1·60 m. Which of the cars could she choose?

═══════════ *Exercise 2C* ═══════════

Did you know?

1 The speed of sound at sea level is 341 metres per second:
   a How many kilometres will sound travel in one minute?
   b How long, to the nearest second, will sound take to travel 1 km?

2 The speed of light is 299 800 kilometres per second:
   a How long, to the nearest second, does light take to travel from the sun, which is 149 675 000 km from the earth?
   b How long would lightning take to travel 1 km?

3 You hear the thunder after you see the lightning:
   a Do you think this is true? Explain your answer.
   b Jim heard the thunder 10 seconds after seeing the lightning. How far was he from the thunderstorm, to the nearest tenth of a kilometre?

Investigate ways of finding the thickness of a page of this book.

MEASURING AREA

Class discussion—units of area

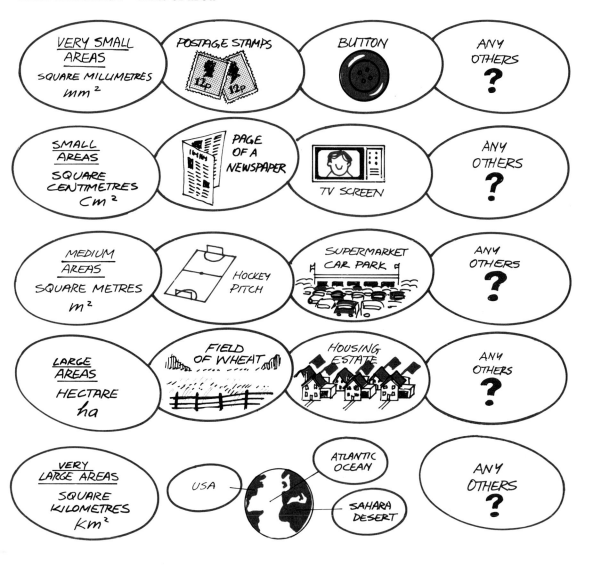

═══════════════════ *Exercise 3* ═══════════════════

1 Which units would you use to measure the areas of:
   a the classroom floor   **b** the cover of your book
   c the top of your desk   **d** one of your finger nails
   e a farmer's field   **f** Wales?

2 Estimate the areas of:
   a the classroom door   **b** a 10p coin   **c** the top of your pen or pencil
   d the blackboard   **e** your thumbnail   **f** this page

3 Check your estimates for questions **2a**, **d** and **f** by measurement and calculation.

4 Tom had another story to tell.

'I painted the garage door. It took all day because its area was 100 square centimetres. Next day I cut the grass, which covered 10 hectares. After that I washed the windows which each had 2 square metres of glass, and I swept the garage floor which had an area of 900 square millimetres.'

Which parts of his story can you not believe?

All change

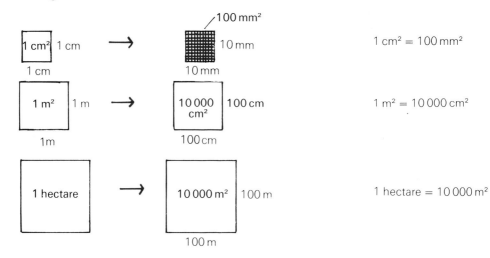

$1 \text{ cm}^2 = 100 \text{ mm}^2$

$1 \text{ m}^2 = 10\,000 \text{ cm}^2$

$1 \text{ hectare} = 10\,000 \text{ m}^2$

Reminder

Area of rectangle = length × breadth

$A = lb$

(The length and breadth must be in the same unit.)

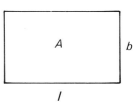

═══════════════════════ *Exercise 4A* ═══════════════════════

1 Find the areas of these shapes by counting the number of squares inside them. Count squares that are half-squares or more—don't count smaller parts.

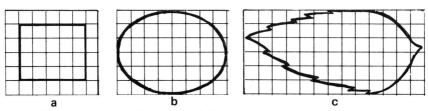

a   b   c

2 How could you calculate the area of the rectangle in question **1a** without adding up the squares? Could you do this for the other shapes?

3 Calculate the areas of these rectangles and squares:

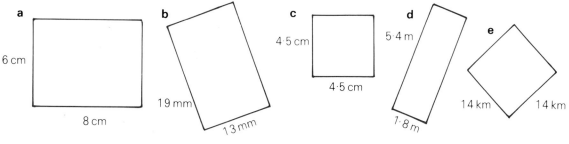

a 6 cm, 8 cm

b 19 mm, 13 mm

c 4·5 cm, 4·5 cm

d 5·4 m, 1·8 m

e 14 km, 14 km

4 Daniel's small sister Lucy was playing with two wooden rectangles, making different shapes. An edge of one rectangle was always wholly or partly in contact with an edge of the other.

Sketch six different shapes she could make.

What can you say about the area of each shape?

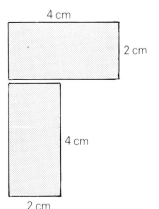

4 cm

2 cm

4 cm

2 cm

5 a A toyshop window had been broken at the weekend, so a man was sent to mend it. He measured the window, and found that it was 4 m by 3 m. Calculate the area of glass he would need.

b Change the units of the length and breadth to centimetres. Calculate the area in cm². Why is the number in your answer much greater?

6 The runway at an airport has to be resurfaced. It is 2 km long and 20 m wide. Calculate its area in square metres. Divide your answer by 10 000 to find the area in hectares.

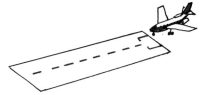

7 Calculate the area of this **L**-shape in three different ways. The dotted lines show you how to do this, by adding or subtracting areas.

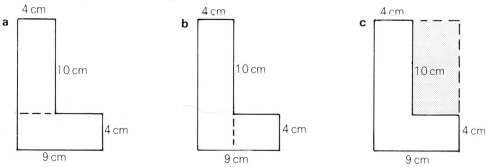

a 4 cm, 10 cm, 4 cm, 9 cm

b 4 cm, 10 cm, 4 cm, 9 cm

c 4 cm, 10 cm, 4 cm, 9 cm

Which way do you like best? Why?

8 A park is laid out for four football pitches. It is in the shape of a rectangle 400 m long and 150 m broad. Calculate the area of the park in square metres, and in hectares.

DECIMAL MEASURES

1 Calculate the areas of these rectangular shapes:

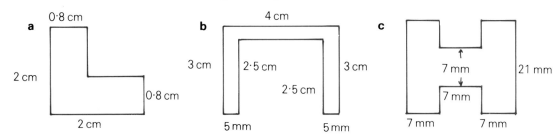

a 0·8 cm, 2 cm, 0·8 cm, 2 cm

b 4 cm, 3 cm, 2·5 cm, 3 cm, 2·5 cm, 5 mm, 5 mm

c 7 mm, 21 mm, 7 mm, 7 mm, 7 mm

2 A maths classroom measures 8 m by 6 m. There is a school rule which says that before a class can use a room, there must be at least 1·5 m² of floor space for each pupil.
   a What is the largest number of pupils allowed in the classroom?
   b What floor area would your class need, using this rule?

3 An estate agent advertises a rectangular plot of ground for sale. It measures 250 m by 180 m. What is the area of the plot in hectares?

4 An office floor is 4 m by 3 m. It has a fixed cupboard with a square base 50 cm long at each corner. What area of floor is left to be carpeted?

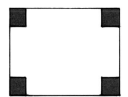

5

35, 10, 100, 30, 11, 35, 40

The diagram shows a metal plate at the side of a door. The shaded slot is cut out of the metal for the door lock. Calculate the area of the metal plate. All the measurements are in millimetres.

6 How many: **a** mm in 1 cm   **b** mm² in 1 cm²   **c** mm² in 5 cm²?

7 How many: **a** cm in 1 m   **b** cm² in 1 m²   **c** cm² in 8 m²?

8 Harry decided to make a tunnel for his model railway. He drew a sketch of it, like this.
   a Make scale drawings of the entry and exit sides, of the left and right sides, and of the roof. Take 1 cm on your drawing for 4 cm on the tunnel.
   b Calculate the total area of plywood he would need.

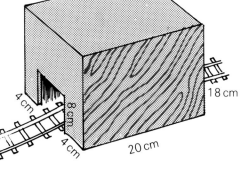

16 cm, 18 cm, 20 cm, 4 cm, 8 cm, 4 cm

The Anderson family have decided to make some improvements to their house and garden.
They make a list.

1 The hall. New stair carpet. 15 m of carpet 120 cm wide.
Calculate: **a** the area of the carpet in m²
b the cost at £15·50 a square metre.

2 The lounge. New hardwood floor. The floor is 6 m by 4 m.
The strips of hardwood are 2 m by 8 cm.
Calculate: **a** the number of strips needed
b the cost of this number at £2·75 each.

3 The kitchen. To be tiled to a height of 1·5 m. The kitchen is 4 m by 2 m. A 3 m width of the wall does not have to be tiled, because of a door and a window. Tiles are squares of side 150 mm.
Calculate: **a** the number of tiles required
b the cost at £8 per pack of 10.

4 The garden. A new rose-bed with a single width paved path all round it. The outside edges of the path will be 6 m and 3 m long. The paving slabs are squares of side 600 mm.
a How many slabs are needed?
b What is the area of the rose-bed?

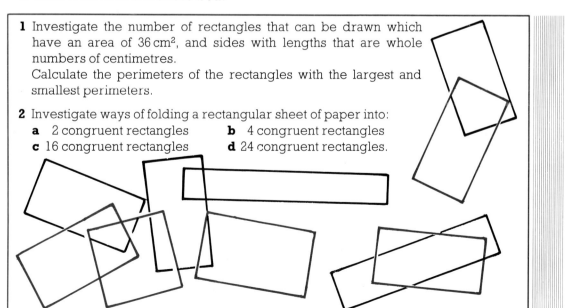

1 Investigate the number of rectangles that can be drawn which have an area of 36 cm², and sides with lengths that are whole numbers of centimetres.
Calculate the perimeters of the rectangles with the largest and smallest perimeters.

2 Investigate ways of folding a rectangular sheet of paper into:
a 2 congruent rectangles **b** 4 congruent rectangles
c 16 congruent rectangles **d** 24 congruent rectangles.

MEASURING VOLUME

Class discussion—units of volume

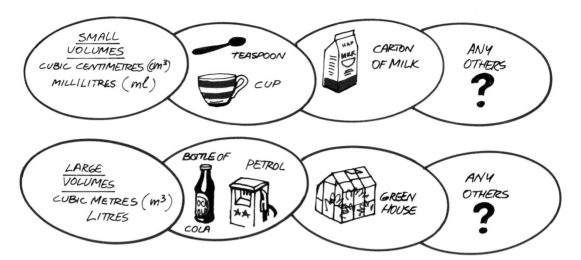

All change

1 litre = 1000 ml
$\quad\quad\quad$ = 1000 cm³
1 litre = 100 centilitres

$÷1000$
$÷100$
millilitres $\quad$ centilitres $\quad$ litres
$×100$
$×1000$

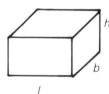

The litre is used for measuring volumes of liquids and gases, and for the capacity of containers.

Reminder

Volume of cuboid = length × breadth × height
$$V = lbh$$

(The length, breadth and height must be in the same unit.)

═══════════════════ *Exercise 5A* ═══════════════════

1 Which units would you use to measure the volume, or capacity, of:
   a a carton of fruit juice   **b** a thimble   **c** a classroom
   d a bottle of perfume   **e** this book   **f** a car's petrol tank?

2 A large packing box is in the shape of a cube. Each inside edge is 1 metre long.
   a Write down its volume in cubic metres.
   b What is the length of each edge in centimetres? Calculate the volume of the box in cubic centimetres.
   c How many dice with edge 1 cm long could be packed into the box? Does this number surprise you?

3 Write down the volume of water in each measuring jar:

4 Change to litres:
  a 7000 millilitres   **b** 12 000 millilitres   **c** 4500 millilitres

5 Change to millilitres:
  a 5 litres   **b** 25 litres   **c** 1·8 litres   **d** 0·2 litre

6 Calculate the capacity of each of the following in millilitres.

  a 50 litres   **b** 0·8 litre   **c** 10 litres   **d** 12 litres   **e** 0·45 litre.

7 Calculate the volume of each box of breakfast cereal in cm³; the measurements are in cm.

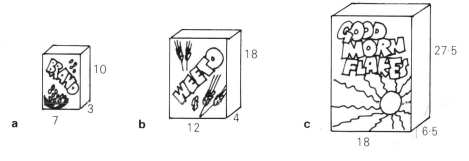

8 a Calculate the volume of this packet of Fruitos.
  b The packet contains 12 sweets. What is the volume of each one?

9 Explain the meaning of each of these:
  a The capacity of the football ground is 23 000.
  b The seating capacity of the minibus is 12.
  c The capacity of the spin drier is 4 kilograms.
  d The capacity of the petrol tank is 40 litres.

DECIMAL MEASURES

1 Calculate the volumes of these solids; all angles are right angles.

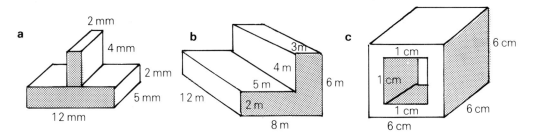

2 The tank in Mr Thomas' car measures 58 cm by 50 cm by 12 cm.
How much does a tankful of petrol cost at 54p a litre?

3 The school fish tank is 2 metres long, 1·5 metres broad and 50 cm
high. How many litres of water does it hold?

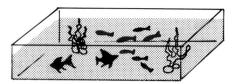

4 Ian got a 250 millilitre bottle of medicine from the chemist, and with it a 5 ml spoon. The label
said 'one spoonful, 3 times a day'. How long will the bottle last?

5 Sandra was planning a party for 24 friends.
   a 'A glass of juice holds 150 millilitres. How many millilitres will I need—not forgetting
   myself—for one glass each?'
   b 'Say each person drinks 2 glasses. How many millilitres now?'
   c 'The juice comes in 2-litre bottles. How many will I need?'
   d At the party her friend Mark is very thirsty. Would there be enough juice for him to have
   another glass?

1 A rectangular tank is 2 m long, 1 m broad and 50 cm high. It is open at the top to collect
rainwater.
   a How many litres of rainwater can it hold?
   b If the tank is quarter full of rainwater, what is the depth of water in it?

2 Beef stock cubes of edge 2 cm have to be packed in cubical boxes, each holding 27 cubes.
   a What is the volume of the box?
   b What are the dimensions of the box?

3 Tissues are sold in boxes measuring 25 cm by 15 cm by 5 cm. Find the dimensions of packing
boxes that could hold 20 boxes.

4 A central heating tank is being designed to hold 1250 litres of oil. It has to be fitted into a
space 1·8 m long and 1·5 m broad. What height should the tank be?

5 A manufacturer has to decide which of these shapes of box to use for his chocolates.

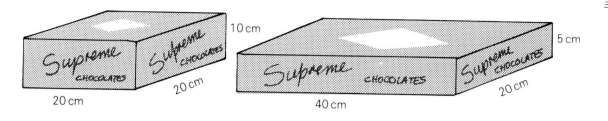

10 cm
20 cm
20 cm

5 cm
40 cm
20 cm

a Which box has the greater volume?
b Which box uses more card?
c Which box do you think the manufacturer should choose?

Copy and complete this table for cubes with lengths of edge 1 cm, 2 cm, 3 cm, ...

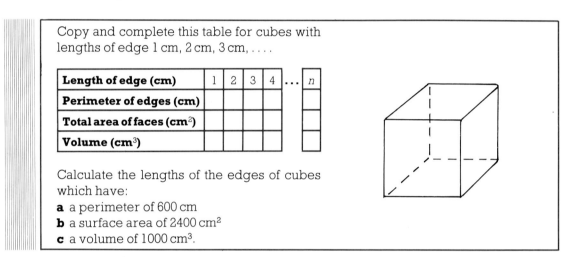

Length of edge (cm)	1	2	3	4	. . .	n
Perimeter of edges (cm)						
Total area of faces (cm²)						
Volume (cm³)						

Calculate the lengths of the edges of cubes which have:
a a perimeter of 600 cm
b a surface area of 2400 cm²
c a volume of 1000 cm³.

MEASURING WEIGHT

Class discussion—units of weight

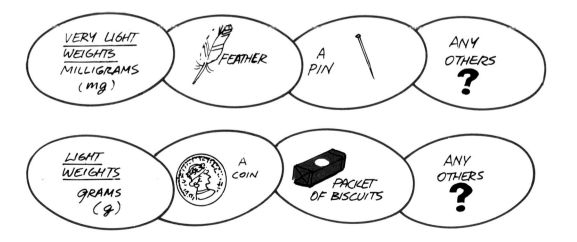

VERY LIGHT WEIGHTS
MILLIGRAMS
(mg)

FEATHER

A PIN

ANY OTHERS ?

LIGHT WEIGHTS
GRAMS
(g)

A COIN

PACKET OF BISCUITS

ANY OTHERS ?

====== *Exercise 6* ======

1 Which units would you use to measure the weights of:
   a a bag of sugar   **b** a key   **c** a bus
   d a sheet of paper   **e** a letter for posting   **f** a baby
   g a chestnut leaf   **h** an aeroplane   **i** a heavy suitcase?

2 Estimate the weights of:
   a this book   **b** a sack of coal   **c** a stamp

3 Here's Tom again!
'I put my 2 kilogram pencil in my pocket, and on my way to school I stopped to weigh myself. I was glad to see I only weighed 5 tonnes. I posted a letter weighing 100 grams, and bought a 5 milligram box of chocolates for my Mum.'
Which parts of his story can you not believe?

4 Measure:
   a the weight of this book. Then calculate the weight of 1 page, counting 6 pages for the front cover, 6 pages for the back cover, and two for the spine.
   b your own weight. Then calculate the average weight of some friends and yourself.

All change

1000 mg = 1 g
1000 g = 1 kg
1000 kg = 1 tonne

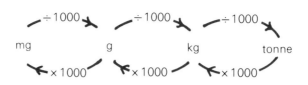

=================== *Exercise 7A* ===================

1 Change to grams:
   a 7000 mg   **b** 15 000 mg   **c** 800 mg   **d** 55 mg

2 Change to grams:
   a 1 kg   **b** 6 kg   **c** 2·3 kg   **d** 1·74 kg

3 Change to kilograms:
   a 3000 g   **b** 300 g   **c** 10 000 g   **d** 75 g

4 Change to kilograms:
   a 1 tonne   **b** 5 tonnes   **c** 6·4 tonnes   **d** 2·85 tonnes

5 A recipe for blackberry crumble lists these ingredients:
   750 g blackberries
   225 g brown sugar
    75 g butter
   175 g self-raising flour
    50 g granulated sugar
   What is the total weight of the ingredients?

6 An empty lorry weighs 8750 kg. When it is filled with sand it weighs 13 320 kg. What is the weight of the sand?

7 Which is heavier, a tonne of bricks or a tonne of feathers?

8 An empty box weighing 300 g is filled with 50 packets of crisps, each weighing 25 g. What is the total weight of the box and crisps: **a** in grams   **b** in kilograms?

9 Before going on holiday Angela weighed herself. Her weight was 48·7 kg. When she came back, her weight was 50 kg. Calculate the increase in her weight, in kilograms, and also in grams.
She decided to diet, and after a month had lost 2·8 kg. What was her weight now?

10 Mohammed lost weight while training for a marathon. His starting weight was 65·3 kg, and he lost 1500 g. What was his new weight?

ROOFING FELT
1 m × 10 m ROLLS
24 kg
£8·99 EACH

11 Mr Johnson laid 4 rolls of this felt. Calculate:
   a the total length of felt he laid
   b the total weight of felt he laid
   c the total cost of the felt.

Exercise 7B

1 Change to grams:
   a 6600 mg   **b** 305 mg   **c** 1·75 kg   **d** 0·09 kg

2 Change to kilograms:
   a 9200 g   **b** 2·65 tonnes   **c** 910 g   **d** 0·16 tonnes

3 Calculate the following, giving your answers in kilograms:
   a 1·2 kg + 800 g   **b** 1100 g + 900 g   **c** 4 tonnes + 500 kg

4 a 1 litre of water weighs 1 kilogram. Calculate the weight of 1 cm³ of water.
   b 20 cm³ of material weighs 60 g. Why will this material sink in water?
   c 20 cm³ of another material weighs 15 g. Will it sink or float?
      Explain your answer. What might these two materials be?

5 A sugar refinery is packing 6·5 tonnes of sugar in 1 kg bags.
How many bags will be filled?

6 The postman is struggling with a big load
of mail. In his bag there are 75 letters
weighing 50 g each, 43 weighing 120 g
each, and 18 weighing 175 g each. How
much does the mail weigh, in kg?

7 The inland letter postal rates were:

	\multicolumn{4}{c}{**Weights up to—**}			
	60 g	100 g	150 g	200 g
1st class	24p	31p	38p	45p
2nd class	18p	22p	28p	34p

For the postman's load in question **6**, calculate:
   a the least possible total postage paid   **b** the greatest possible total postage paid.

Exercise 7C

The Royal Mint brochure lists these weights of UK coins:

Coin	Weight
£1	9·50 g
50p	13·50 g
20p	5·00 g
10p	11·31 g
5p	5·65 g
2p	7·12 g
1p	3·56 g

1 How much does a £5 bag of 10p coins
weigh?

2 Mrs Gordon's handbag was rather heavy
because of all the coins in her purse.
She had six £1 coins, nine 50p coins, eight
10p coins and six 2p coins.
What did all these coins weigh?

3 Calculate the weight of £1's worth of 'copper' coins.

A SPECIAL RECTANGLE

═══════════════ *Exercise 1* ═══════════════

1A Here is a collection of rectangles.
They all have the same length, but one of them is special. Which one?

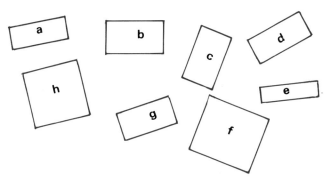

2A

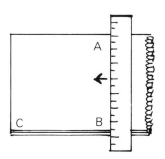

Turn your notebook crosswise like this. Slide your ruler across from one side to the other, keeping it parallel to the left-hand side. Among all the rectangles you have made by moving your ruler in this way there is a special one. Move your ruler back to this one. Draw AB. Measure the lengths of AB and BC.

3A Two strips of Meccano are bolted together at the middle, and elastic is threaded through holes at the ends. (Do this if you can.)

a As the strips are opened out the elastic makes rectangles.

b Among the rectangles there is a special one. Draw it on squared paper.

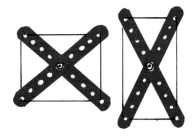

4A

Tony is getting ready for business. He slides open the window ABCD. EF is a fixed bar.
As the window slides, among the possible rectangles AEFD there is a special one. Draw it in your notebook.

The special rectangle is a square—

So all the properties of a rectangle are true for a square.

5A What can you remember about:
  a all the angles of a rectangle
  b the opposite sides of a rectangle (2 properties)
  c the diagonals of a rectangle (2 properties)?
These are all true for a square too, since it is a special rectangle.

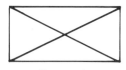

Rectangle

6A

The chequered flag is a tiling of congruent squares.
Can you think of two more examples of square tilings in real life?

7B

This sliding puzzle works because the opposite sides of a square are parallel.
  a Can you see how to get the 8 to:
    (i) the 1 place   (ii) the 15 place?
  b Can you think of other examples of sliding squares?

QUARTER-TURNS

========================= *Exercise 2* =========================

1A

Can you see what Ron Rabbit and Don Duck share? No?
Try turning Don Duck through a clockwise quarter-turn. Still no ideas?
Think about their frames.

2A Use tracing paper to find out which of the figures below have quarter-turn symmetry.

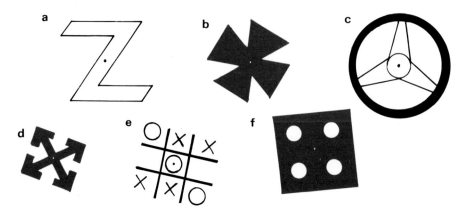

a

b

c

d

e

f

 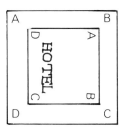 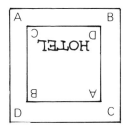 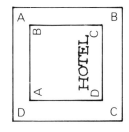

They never give up! This time the men have to fit a square window.

a Trace the glass in the first picture.

b By giving it quarter-turns check that the window fits its outline in all four ways. **It has quarter-turn symmetry.**

c Turn the tracing over. Now check that it fits its outline in four more ways.

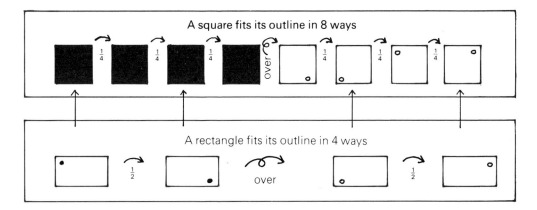

4A Quarter-turns in action: the Rubik cube (all faces square).

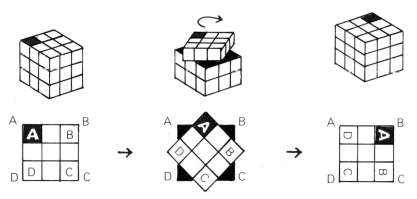

Copy and complete:

After one quarter-turn, AB→BC, so AB = ...

After two quarter-turns, AB→CD, so AB = ...

After three quarter-turns, AB→.............., so AB = ...

So AB = ... = ... = ...

The sides of a square are all equal.

5A A cycle race is to be held on a track laid out round some squares in a city centre. Each square is 75 m long. Calculate the length of each lap, from A back to A.

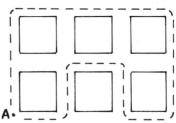

6A

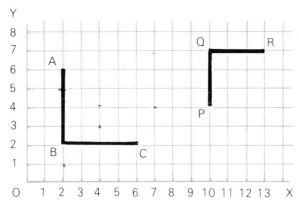

a Copy this diagram on squared paper.

b Complete square ABCD, and write down the coordinates of A, B, C and D.

c Complete square PQRS, and write down the coordinates of P, Q, R and S.

7B E(2, 1), F(4, 3), G(2, 5) and H are corners of a square. Find the coordinates of H.

8B K is the point (4, 4) and L is (7, 4). KLMN is a square. Find the coordinates of the two possible positions of M and N.

9C

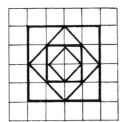

a Copy this 'nest' of squares on squared paper.

b If the side of each small square in the grid is x cm long, calculate the perimeter of the largest square.

c If the diagonal of each small square is y cm long, calculate the perimeter of the second largest square.

d Calculate the sum of the perimeters of all four squares in the nest, in its simplest form.

AXES OF SYMMETRY

=== *Exercise 3* ===

1A a Cut out a large square from squared paper.

b Fold it in different ways to discover all the axes of symmetry. (You know two of them already. Why?)

c Draw the lines of symmetry as dotted lines.

A square has four axes of symmetry.

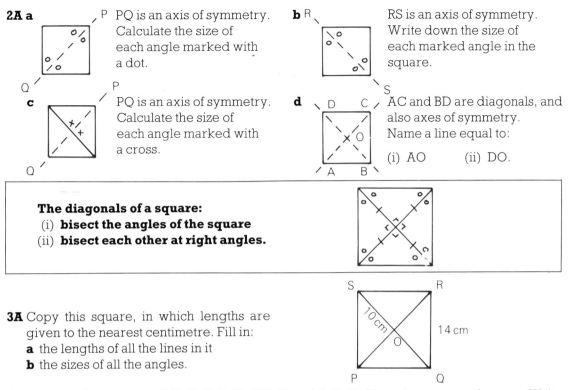

2A a P PQ is an axis of symmetry. Calculate the size of each angle marked with a dot.

b R RS is an axis of symmetry. Write down the size of each marked angle in the square.

c PQ is an axis of symmetry. Calculate the size of each angle marked with a cross.

d AC and BD are diagonals, and also axes of symmetry. Name a line equal to:
(i) AO   (ii) DO.

The diagonals of a square:
(i) **bisect the angles of the square**
(ii) **bisect each other at right angles.**

3A Copy this square, in which lengths are given to the nearest centimetre. Fill in:
a the lengths of all the lines in it
b the sizes of all the angles.

4A A square has corners A(3, 0), B(6, 3), C(3, 6) and D(0, 3). Draw it on squared paper. Write down the lengths of the diagonals and the coordinates of the point where they cross.

5B The movement, or transformation, of the square from position (i), direct to position (viii), is explained by the vertical axis of symmetry.

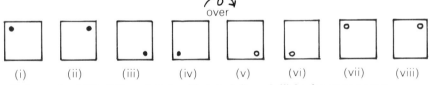

over

(i)   (ii)   (iii)   (iv)   (v)   (vi)   (vii)   (viii)

a Pair each of (ii), (iii) and (iv) with (v), (vi) or (vii) in the same way.
b Write down four pairs of positions which are explained by the horizontal axis of symmetry.
c Write down four pairs which are explained by one of the diagonal axes of symmetry.
d Repeat for the other diagonal axis of symmetry.

6B Check some properties of the diagonals of a square by copying and completing:
a Under reflection in AC, ∠ACD→∠ACB
So ∠ACD = ∠ACB
And ∠CAD→∠_____
So ∠CAD = ∠_____
b Under reflection in AC,   DO→BO
So   DO = _____

And ∠DOC→∠_____
So ∠DOC = ∠_____

What size must each of these angles be?

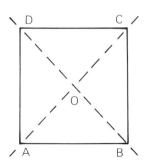

THE STORY OF THE SQUARE

Copy and complete the following in your notebook:

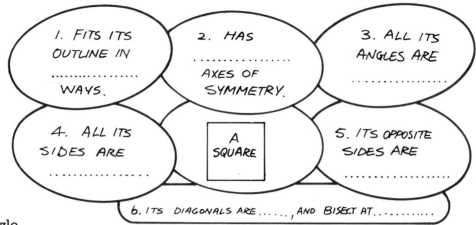

1. FITS ITS OUTLINE IN .... WAYS.

2. HAS .... AXES OF SYMMETRY.

3. ALL ITS ANGLES ARE ....

4. ALL ITS SIDES ARE ....

A SQUARE

5. ITS OPPOSITE SIDES ARE ....

6. ITS DIAGONALS ARE ......, AND BISECT AT.............

Puzzle

Explain, with the help of drawings, how you could balance a square sheet of wood horizontally on:

a a compass point **b** the edge of a ruler.

=========== *Exercise 4* ===========

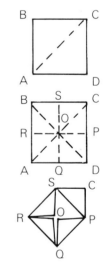

Fold a square, and make yourself a 'fortune teller'.

1A Start by folding a square sheet of paper along a diagonal.

1B Fill in the sizes of all the angles.

2A Fold the square along the dotted lines.

2B (i) How many angles of 45° have you made?
(ii) What is the size of ∠ AOC?

3A Fold the corners A, B and D into the middle to make the shape PQRSC.

3B PQ = 10 cm. Calculate the area of:
(i) PQRS (ii) SOPC (iii) the original square.

4A Fold the corner C into the middle as well, and then 'flip' the paper over. Now fold the corner P into the middle.

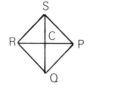

4C (i) What are the lengths of SR and TR?
   (ii) What is the area of the third shape?
   (iii) Copy this shape in your notebook, and draw any axes of symmetry.

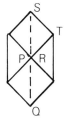

5A Fold corner R into the middle.

5C (i) What is the area of the new shape?
   (ii) How many axes of symmetry does it have?

6A Fold corners Q and S into the middle.

7A Now write in some 'fortunes' and tell your friends their future!

COMPUTER SQUARES

=============== *Exercise 5* ===============

1A Helen was working at the computer, and started to draw a square.
MOVE (1, 1). This plots the point (1, 1).
DRAW (1, 8). This draws a straight line from (1, 1) to (1, 8).
DRAW (8, 8).
a On squared paper, or on the screen, complete the square.
b List the rest of the instructions for drawing the square on the screen.

2A a Draw the diagonals in Helen's square.
b List the instructions for drawing the diagonals on the screen.

3B Helen is trying to draw a picture frame. Its outside edge is the square she has already drawn. She wants the frame to be 1 unit wide all round.
a Draw the complete frame on squared paper or on a screen.
b List the instructions for drawing the inner square on the screen.

4B Sam is planning a square tiling on the screen, with the sides of the tiles parallel to the sides of the screen. Each tile is 3 units long, and the point (8, 9) is the bottom left-hand corner of one of the tiles.
a On squared paper, or on a screen, draw the four tiles around the point (8, 9).
b What larger shape is formed by these tiles?
c List instructions for drawing this larger shape on the screen.

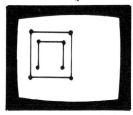

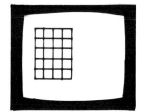

5C Sam plans another square tiling, with its diagonals parallel to the sides of the screen, and 4 units long. (8, 9) is still a point where four corners meet. Repeat questions **4a**, **b** and **c** for this tiling.

BRAINTEASERS

1   Move one of these matchsticks to make a square.

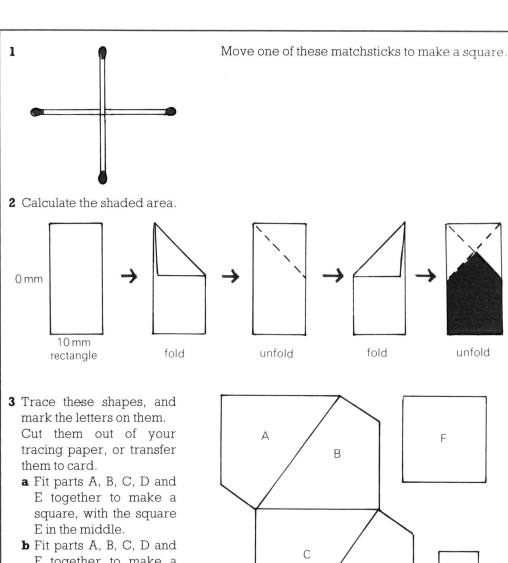

2 Calculate the shaded area.

0 mm

10 mm
rectangle

fold   unfold   fold   unfold

3 Trace these shapes, and mark the letters on them. Cut them out of your tracing paper, or transfer them to card.

   a Fit parts A, B, C, D and E together to make a square, with the square E in the middle.

   b Fit parts A, B, C, D and F together to make a square, with the square F in the middle.

A   B   F

C   D   E

1 On paper or card draw a square with sides 10 cm long.
Mark each side off in centimetres (1–10).
Draw and colour, or stitch in wool, patterns of straight lines like the ones shown.
Investigate other designs of your own.

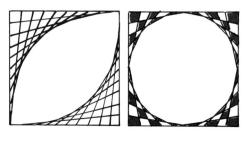

2 a You see rectangular shapes everywhere—windows, doors, books, newspapers, carpets, pictures . . . . Did you ever notice that some rectangular shapes looked better than others? Artists have agreed for many years that one particular rectangle pleases them more than any other. They call it the Golden Rectangle. Can you pick it out from these?

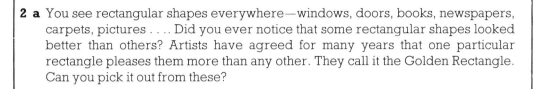

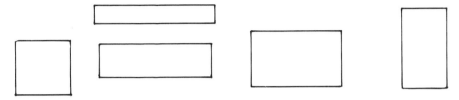

b Carry out these instructions for constructing a golden rectangle.

     (i) Draw a square ABCD of side 5 cm.

     (ii) Draw an axis of symmetry PQ.

     (iii) With centre Q, and radius QC, draw an arc to cut AB produced to a point S.

     (iv) Complete the golden rectangle ASTD. Was this the shape you chose?

     (v) Can you name a second golden rectangle in this diagram?

c An Italian mathematician, Fibonacci, who lived in the thirteenth century, discovered the sequence: 1, 1, 2, 3, 5, 8, 13, . . .

 (i) Write down four more terms of the sequence.

 (ii) There is a surprising connection between this sequence and the lengths of the sides of a golden rectangle. Can you find the connection?

CHECK-UP ON **THE SQUARE**

1A Copy these squares, and fill in the lengths of as many lines and the sizes of as many angles as you can:

a

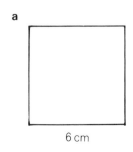

6 cm

b

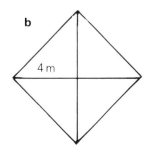

4 m

2A Sketch a square, and mark its axes of symmetry.

3A Plot the points A(6, 0) and B(6, 3). ABCD is a square. Write down two possible sets of coordinates for C and two for D.

4A Which of the following are true, and which are false?
    a A square fits its outline in 8 ways.
    b All the sides of a square, and all the angles, are equal.
    c Each diagonal bisects the angles of the square.
    d One diagonal is longer than the other.
    e A square has quarter-turn symmetry.
    f A square has half-turn symmetry.

5B This diagram shows a square and its image after turning about its centre O. How many of each of the following can you see:
    a right angles
    b sets of parallel lines
    c sets of congruent triangles.

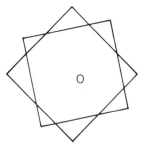

6B Calculate the areas of the two squares in question **1**.

7B P is the point (3, 4) and R is (3, 10). If PQRS is a square find the coordinates of Q and S.

8C A(2, 3), B(2, y), C(x, y) and D(x, 3) are corners of a square.
    a Write down the coordinates of three possible positions of C.
    b Find an equation connecting x and y.

9C Describe how to fold a rectangular piece of paper to make a square. Explain which properties of a square you have used.

BELOW ZERO

The temperature on this thermometer is 5 degrees above zero (0°C). It is +5°C, which means +5° Celsius.

+5 is a positive number, and is read 'positive 5'. Often the '+' is left out, and 5 is taken to mean +5.

This temperature is 5 degrees below zero. It is −5°C.

−5 is a negative number, and is read 'negative 5', or sometimes 'minus 5'.

Exercise 1

1A Draw a line to show a thermometer scale. Mark it every degree from 10 to −10.

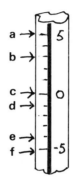

2A Here is part of a thermometer scale from −5°C to 5°C.
Write down the temperatures at the points marked **a** to **f**.

3A Using negative numbers, write down these temperatures. Watch the different scales.

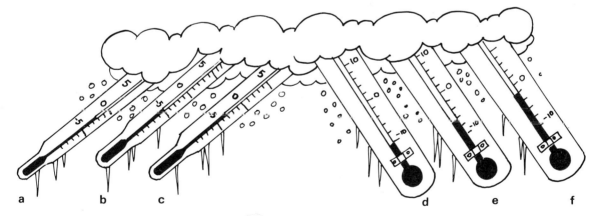

4A a Which temperature is colder: −7°C or −8°C?
   b Which temperature is warmer: −12°C or −11°C?
   c Which temperature is higher: 3°C or −3°C?
   d Which temperature is lower: 0°C or −1°C?

5A Write down the highest and lowest temperatures in each of these:
   a 0°C, −10°C, 5°C   **b** −3°C, −5°C, −4°C

6A In each of the following write down:
  a the temperatures in the glass and in the cup
  b the lower of the two temperatures.

 (i)  (ii) 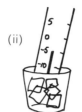 (iii)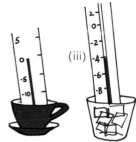

7A Using the thermometer you drew for question **1** if you wish, write down temperatures that are:
  a 4° lower than: (i) 6°C (ii) 4°C (iii) 0°C (iv) −3°C
  b 5° higher than: (i) 0°C (ii) −2°C (iii) −5°C (iv) −8°C.

8A Write these temperatures in order, from coldest to warmest:
  a 5°C, −3°C, 0°C, −1°C
  b −10°C, −20°C, 0°C, 10°C, 9°C
  c 100°C, −1°C, −19°C, 50°C, 0°C, −100°C.

9A The freezing point of water is 0°C. Use + or − to describe temperatures:
  a 18° above freezing point   **b** 12° below freezing point.

10B When a freezer is defrosted its temperature is 15°C. When set to 'freeze', its temperature drops by 25°. What is its temperature now?

11B Antifreeze is used in a car radiator so that it will not freeze unless the temperature drops down to −18°C. The temperature one evening is −5°C. How many degrees can it fall before the radiator will freeze?

12B The dotted lines on this map are called isotherms. These are lines joining points where the temperature is the same. All places on a dotted line have the same temperature.

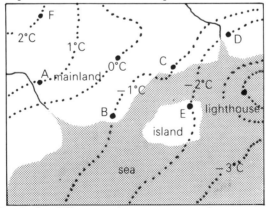

  a What is the temperature at town A?
  b Which town has the same temperature as town E?
  c Name two towns on the coast that have the same temperature.
  d Which two towns are colder than town C?

  e What is the difference in temperature between town A and town E?
  f Name a town which is 4° warmer than town D.
  g By how much must the temperature of town B rise to be the same as town A?
  h What are two possible temperatures for the lighthouse? Try to draw pictures to explain your answer.

POSITIVE AND NEGATIVE NUMBERS

13C On 22nd January 1943 the temperature rose an astonishing 27·2° in 2 minutes at Spearfish, South Dakota, in America. It rose to 7·3°C at 7.32 am. What was the temperature at 7.30 that morning?

=== *Exercise 2* ===

1A Copy the countdown, and continue it until 10 seconds after blast-off.

2A What number has the count reached after half a minute from blast-off?

3A A film crew started filming the launch when the count was 100. They filmed for 2 minutes. What was the count at the end of that time?

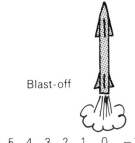

Blast-off

... 10 9 8 7 6 5 4 3 2 1 0 −1

4A Write down four more numbers for each of these sequences, and describe the rule you used in each case:

  a 6, 4, 2, ...   **b** −4, −3, −2, ...   **c** 10, 5, 0, ...

  d −8, −6, −4, ...   **e** 9, 7, 5, ...   **f** −50, −40, −30, ...

5A On this island, all places on the same dotted line (contour) are the same height above sea-level.

  a Make a sketch of the island.

  b What are the heights above sea-level of the tree, the cave and the jetty?

  c Estimate the height above sea-level of the cairn of stones at the top.

The sea level rises 10 metres.

  d What are the 'heights' above the new sea-level of the tree, cave, boat and jetty? (Use a negative number here.)

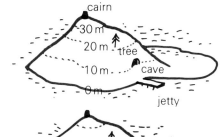

cairn
30 m
20 m tree
10 m cave
0 m
jetty

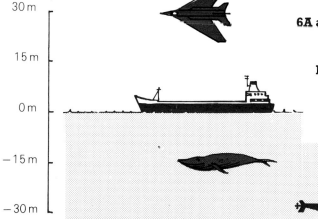

30 m

15 m

0 m

−15 m

−30 m

6A a Use negative numbers to give the positions of the whale and the submarine from sea-level.

  b The whale goes down 10 m, and the submarine rises 20 m.
Describe their new positions, using negative numbers again.

7B Over the centuries, as sea-level fell, raised beaches appeared like this.

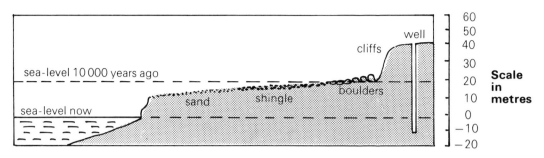

a Relative to sea-level now, what is the height of:
  (i) the top of the well   (ii) sea-level 10 000 years ago   (iii) the boulders
  (iv) the lowest part of the sand   (v) the bottom of the well?
b How deep is the well?
c Make a '10 000 year old' scale, and use it to answer part **a** again.

THE NUMBER LINE

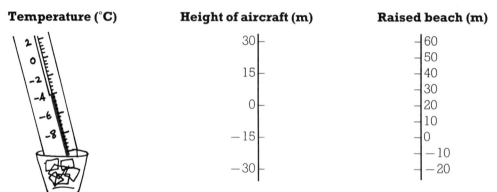

Above you can see some examples of **number lines**.

Here is the number linesman preparing for action!

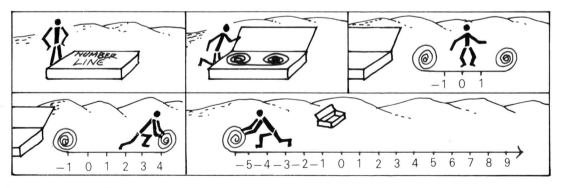

Steps on the number line are measured from 0. **Positive** numbers are marked to the right of 0, **negative** numbers to the left. Zero is neither positive nor negative.

The numbers are in order. If one number is greater than another then it lies to the right of the other, in the direction of the arrow.

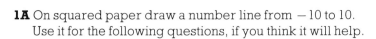

Exercise 3

1A On squared paper draw a number line from -10 to 10.
Use it for the following questions, if you think it will help.

2A Write down:
   a the first five positive whole numbers   **b** the first five negative whole numbers.

3A In each of these, write down the smaller number:
   a $10, 9$ **b** $-10, -9$ **c** $0, 1$ **d** $0, -1$ **e** $5, -5$
   f $9, 11$ **g** $9, -11$ **h** $-1, -2$ **i** $-2, 2$ **j** $-2, -3$

4A In each of these, write down the larger number:
   a $-1, 1$ **b** $-3, -4$ **c** $-2, 0$ **d** $1, 10$ **e** $1, -10$
   f $-9, 1$ **g** $-11, -8$ **h** $0, -1$ **i** $4, -5$ **j** $-1, -2$

Shorthand

For '5 is greater than 3', you can write $5 > 3$.
For '-2 is less than -1', you can write $-2 < -1$.

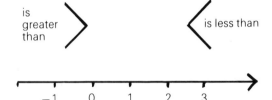

is greater than   >

<   is less than

Examples

   (i) For 3 and 2, $3 > 2$.
   (ii) For -1 and 1, $-1 < 1$.
   (iii) For 2, -1, 0, $-1 < 0 < 2$, or $2 > 0 > -1$.

5B Put the symbol $>$ (is greater than), or $<$ (is less than),
   between each pair of numbers as they are given.
   a 8 and 5   **b** 1 and 3   **c** 0 and 5   **d** 7 and 6
   e 6 and 7   **f** 2 and -2 **g** 10 and -10 **h** 10 and 9
   i -3 and 2   **j** 0 and -5 **k** -4 and -5 **l** -9 and 1

6C Arrange the following in order, using only the symbol $<$:
   a 7,   5, 0   **b** $1, -1, 6, -6$ **c** $9, -7, 0, -4, 2$

7C Arrange the following in order, using only the symbol $>$:
   a $-3, 6, 0$ **b** $4, -2, 0, -4$ **c** $-1, -6, 1, 8, 0$

8C Given $x > -3$, which of these numbers could x stand for?
   $-2, 0, 4, -1, -5, 3, -3$.

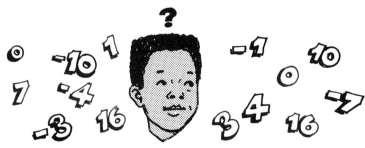

POSITIVE AND NEGATIVE NUMBERS

COORDINATES

In Book 1 this diagram showed you how to plot the point P(4, 2).

4 is the *x*-coordinate of P, and 2 is the *y*-coordinate of P. Using two number lines at right angles any point in their plane can be plotted. The horizontal line is the *x*-axis, and the vertical line is the *y*-axis.

Q is the point $(-5, 3)$.
R is the point $(-2, -4)$.
S is the point $(1, -3)$.
O is the point $(0, 0)$, and is called the **origin**.

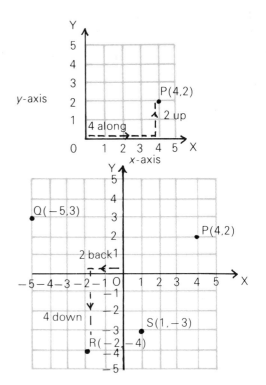

POSITIVE AND NEGATIVE NUMBERS

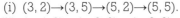

Exercise 4

1A Here is another treasure hunt. Copy and complete these guesses. For example, P(4, 2).
  a Adam guesses the point A(4, . . .).
  b Barry guesses the point B$(-3, . . .)$.
  c Carmen's guess is C(. . . , -1).
  d David's guess is D(. . . , . . .).
  e Emma's guess is E(. . . , . . .).
  f Farah's guess is F(. . . , . . .).

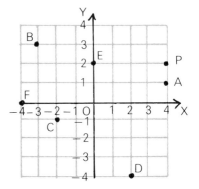

2A The sign-writer is at work again painting letters.
  a On squared paper draw *x* and *y*-axes from -5 to $+5$.
  b Plot each of these sets of points. Join them up as shown by the arrows to find the letters.

  (i) $(3, 2) \rightarrow (3, 5) \rightarrow (5, 2) \rightarrow (5, 5)$.
  (ii) $(-4, 3) \rightarrow (-3, 0) \rightarrow (-2, 3)$.
  (iii) $(-5, -2) \rightarrow (-5, -5) \rightarrow (-3, -5)$.
  (iv) $(1, 0) \rightarrow (2, -3) \rightarrow (3, -1) \rightarrow (4, -3) \rightarrow (5, 0)$.

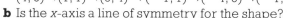

3A a Plot these points, and join each one to the next to make an interesting shape.
$(4, 0) \rightarrow (1, 1) \rightarrow (0, 4) \rightarrow (-1, 1) \rightarrow (-4, 0) \rightarrow (-1, -1) \rightarrow (0, -4) \rightarrow (1, -1) \rightarrow (4, 0)$.
b Is the x-axis a line of symmetry for the shape?
c Name another line of symmetry.
d Has the star-shape half-turn symmetry about O?
e Has it quarter-turn symmetry about O?

4A Repeat question **3A** for the points: $(0, 4) \rightarrow (1, 2) \rightarrow (3, 2) \rightarrow (2, 0) \rightarrow$
$(3, -2) \rightarrow (1, -2) \rightarrow (0, -4) \rightarrow (-1, -2) \rightarrow (-3, -2) \rightarrow (-2, 0) \rightarrow (-3, 2) \rightarrow (-1, 2) \rightarrow (0, 4)$.

5A For each of the diagrams below, list the coordinates of the points in the sequences A, B, C, ..., F and P, Q, R, ..., U.

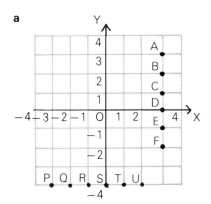

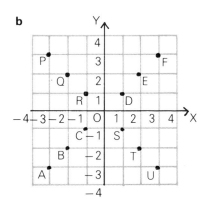

6A a Plot the following points:
$A(1, 3), B(-2, 2), C(3, -4), D(-1, -1), E(0, -6), F(-9, 0), G(1, -3)$.
b Write down the points that are: (i) on the x-axis (ii) below the x-axis
(iii) above the x-axis.

7A Write down three more sets of points in question **6A**:
(i) Those on the y-axis   (ii) Those to the right of the y-axis
(iii) Those to the left of the y-axis.

8B When $A(2, 3)$ is reflected in the x-axis
mirror, its image is $A'(2, -3)$.
When A is reflected in the y-axis mirror,
its image is $A''(-2, 3)$.
a On squared paper draw the x and y-axis mirrors.
b Plot the point $B(4, 4)$, and its images
B' in the x-axis and B'' in the y-axis.
c What do you notice about the co-ordinates of B' and B''?

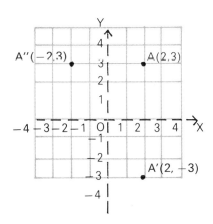

9B Repeat question **8B** for: **a** the point $C(-2, 1)$ **b** the point $D(-3, -4)$.

10C

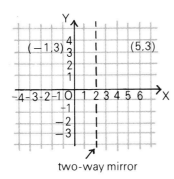

two-way mirror

The image of the point $(5, 3)$ in the two-way mirror is the point $(-1, 3)$.

Point	Image
$(3, -2)$	
$(5, -3)$	
$(-2, 1)$	
$(0, -3)$	
$(-1, -1)$	

a Plot the points on squared paper.

Reflect them in the mirror (the dotted line). Then copy and complete the table.

b Explain how to find the images of the points $(100, 2)$ and $(-100, -2)$ in the dotted line.

A picture to plot and colour

On squared paper, drawn an x-axis from -20 to 20, and a y-axis from -20 to 10.
Plot these points, joining them up in order in the five sets below.
$(-14, 6)$, $(-11, 7)$, $(-9, 9)$, $(-6, 10)$, $(-3, 9)$, $(0, 7)$, $(5, 5)$, $(8, 3)$, $(15, 5)$, $(20, 5)$, $(15, 3)$, $(10, 1)$, $(9, -2)$, $(4, -7)$, $(0, -7)$, $(-5, -5)$, $(-10, 0)$, $(-12, 5)$, $(-14, 6)$, $(-11, 7)$, $(-10, 6)$, $(-12, 5)$. Stop.
$(0, 5)$, $(5, 3)$, $(10, 0)$, $(12, -2)$, $(9, -2)$, $(3, -1)$, $(-1, 0)$. Stop.
$(0, -7)$, $(-5, -11)$, $(-8, -11)$, $(-5, -11)$, $(-8, -13)$, $(-5, -11)$, $(-6, -14)$, $(-5, -11)$, $(-1, -10)$. Stop.
$(4, -7)$, $(0, -12)$, $(-3, -12)$, $(0, -12)$, $(-3, -14)$, $(0, -12)$, $(-1, -15)$, $(0, -12)$, $(4, -11)$. Stop.
$(-9, 6)$, $(-8, 7)$, $(-7, 6)$, $(-8, 5)$, $(-9, 6)$. Stop.

ADDING AND SUBTRACTING POSITIVE AND NEGATIVE NUMBERS

The linesman goes for a walk to calculate $2 + 3 = 5$.

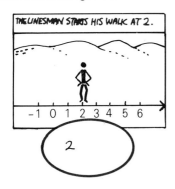

Here he is on another walk . . .

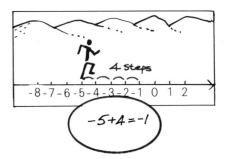

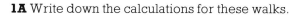
1A Write down the calculations for these walks.

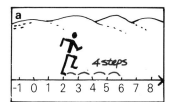
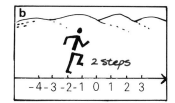
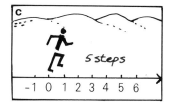

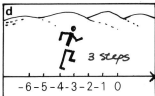

2A Write down the calculations for these walks:

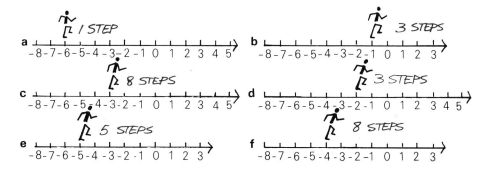

3A Draw the number line from -10 to 10. Use it to calculate:

    a $-6+4$ **b** $-2+6$ **c** $-4+4$ **d** $1+9$ **e** $-8+5$

    f $-10+1$ **g** $-1+1$ **h** $-1+11$ **i** $0+5$ **j** $-7+7$

4A Copy and complete this table, using the thermometer:

Temperature at 06 00 hours	6°C	0°C	−2°C	−4°C	−8°C	−3°C
Change in temperature	+2°	+4°	+4°	+2°	+10°	+7°
Temperature at 12 00 hours						

5B Try to calculate these without using the number line:

    a $-1+4$ **b** $-3+3$ **c** $-2+0$ **d** $-2+7$ **e** $-1+1$

    f $5+8$ **g** $-7+6$ **h** $-1+9$ **i** $-8+8$ **j** $-9+7$

    k $-1+0$ **l** $-1+8$ **m** $100+100$ **n** $-100+100$ **o** $-100+50$

6B Copy and complete these *crossadds*:

a → add across   b   c   d

↓ a d d d o w n

a

-2	1	-1
3	4	
1		

b

-5	2	
4	1	

c

-6	1	
2	1	

d

-21		-8
	17	
-12		

7C What number does x stand for in each of these equations?

  a $x+4 = 3$ **b** $-5+x = 0$ **c** $-6+x = 1$ **d** $x+1 - -2$

  e $-x+1 = -3$ **f** $-8+x = -8$ **g** $-7+x = -1$ **h** $-10+3x = -4$

The linesman takes a walk in the opposite direction to find $5-6$.

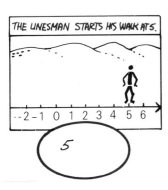

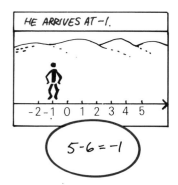

He starts at 5, and takes 6 steps in the negative direction.
We can describe this by $5-6$, or by $5+(-6)$.

$$5-6 = 5+(-6) = -1.$$

Subtracting 6 is the same as adding -6.

Here he is on another walk.
We can describe this by
$-2-3$, or by $-2+(-3)$.

$$-2-3 = -2+(-3) = -5.$$

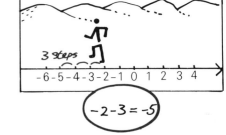

1A Describe each of these walks in two ways. For example, $5-6 = -1$,

$$5+(-6) = -1.$$

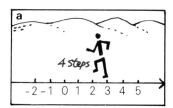

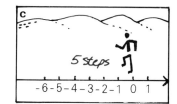

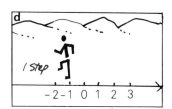

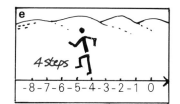

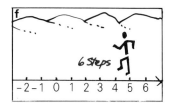

2A Describe each of these walks in two ways.

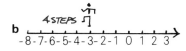

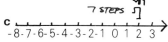

3A Copy and complete these calculations:

a $-1+(-4) =$

b $-3-6 =$

c $-2+4 =$

4A Draw the number line from -10 to $+10$. Use it to calculate:

a $8+(-2)$	**b** $4+(-4)$	**c** $1+(-3)$	**d** $-5+(-1)$	**e** $1+(-9)$
f $3-5$	**g** $0-2$	**h** $-1-4$	**i** $-2-8$	**j** $1-10$
k $6+(-4)$	**l** $-1+(-1)$	**m** $-2+5$	**n** $-6+(-4)$	**o** $0+(-5)$

5A Copy and complete this table:

Temperature at midday	15°C	6°C	7°C	−2°C	0°C	−5°C
Change in temperature	−5°	−6°	−9°	−3°	−10°	−1°
Temperature at midnight						−4

6A Here is a game for two players. Both you and your partner should have a pencil.

Draw your number line from -15 to $+15$, spacing the points 5 mm apart.

Place your pencils pointing to zero, then roll a dice.

If you score 2, 4 or 6, move your pencil 2, 4 or 6 to the *right* (*adding* to your total).

If you score 1, 3 or 5, move your pencil 1, 3 or 5 to the *left* (*subtracting* from your total).

Take turns. The first player to reach $+15$ is the winner. A player reaching -15 loses the game.

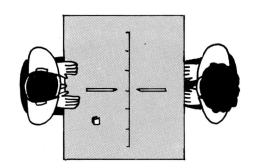

7B Copy and complete these additions.

Compare the last two lines of each with the answers you would obtain by using the number line.

a $5+2 \quad = 7$	**b** $-6+2 \quad = -4$	**c** $0+2 = \underline{\quad}$
$5+1 \quad = 6$	$-6+1 \quad = \underline{\quad}$	$0+1 = \underline{\quad}$
$5+0 \quad = \underline{\quad}$	$-6+0 \quad = \underline{\quad}$	$0+\underline{\ } = \underline{\quad}$
$5+(-1) = \underline{\quad}$	$-6+(-1) = \underline{\quad}$	$0+\underline{\ } = \underline{\quad}$
$5+(-2) = \underline{\quad}$	$-6+(\underline{\quad}) = \underline{\quad}$	$0+\underline{\ } = \underline{\quad}$

8B Try to calculate these without using the number line:

a $3+(-1)$	**b** $5+(-4)$	**c** $6+(-6)$	**d** $2+(-3)$	**e** $1+(-5)$
f $-2+(-2)$	**g** $-7+(-3)$	**h** $-3+(-5)$	**i** $0+(-6)$	**j** $-5+(-5)$

9B Calculate:

a $5-4$	**b** $5-5$	**c** $5-6$	**d** $3-8$	**e** $1-7$
f $-2-2$	**g** $-1-7$	**h** $9-6$	**i** $6-9$	**j** $1-1$

10B Copy and complete these *crossoffs* and *crossadds*:

a *crossoffs*

s↓ → *subtract* across

(i) subtract down

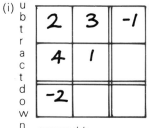 (ii) (iii) 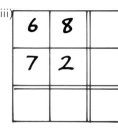 (iv)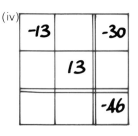

b *crossadds*

→ *add* across

(i) add down

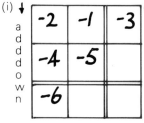 (ii) 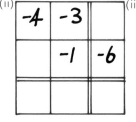 (iii) 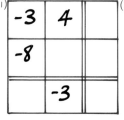 (iv)

11C Solve these equations:

   a $x+(-3)=0$ **b** $x+(-1)=-4$ **c** $x+(-2)=6$ **d** $x+(-5)=-1$

   e $2+x=-1$ **f** $-3+x=5$ **g** $x-4=-6$ **h** $x-2=7$

12C Copy and complete the following. Replace x by the number it stands for in each one.

a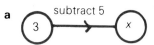

b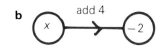

c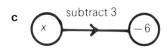

d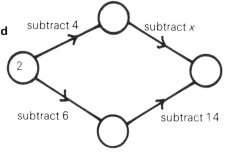

e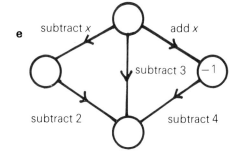

(both routes lead to the same number in the right-hand circle).

Now it's $5-(-1)$. **The linesman's work is done.**

Look at this subtraction table:

$$5 - 3 = 2$$
$$5 - 2 = 3$$
$$5 - 1 = 4$$
$$5 - 0 = 5$$
$$\downarrow \qquad \downarrow \qquad \downarrow$$
$$5-(-1)=6 \underline{\quad}\text{(i)}$$
$$5-(-2)=7 \underline{\quad}\text{(ii)}$$
$$5-(-3)=8$$
$$\underline{\quad}\;\underline{\quad}=\underline{\quad}$$

Line (i) suggests that *subtracting negative* 1 is the same as *adding* 1.
Line (ii) suggests that *subtracting negative* 2 is the same as *adding* 2, and so on.
We will assume that these are true. So $5-(-1)=5+1=6$
                    and $5-(-2)=5+2=7$.

Examples

(i) $8-(-3)$ (ii) $-2-(-4)$
    $= 8+3$ $= -2+4$
    $= 11$ $= 2$

POSITIVE AND NEGATIVE NUMBERS

1A Copy and complete these subtractions:

a $4-3 = 1$ **b** $6-2 = 4$ **c** $5-1 = \_\_$ **d** $2-0 = \_\_$
  $4-2 = 2$ $6-1 = \_\_$ $5-0 = \_\_$ $2-(-1) = \_\_$
  $4-1 = \_\_$ $6-0 = \_\_$ $5-(-1) = 6$ $2-(-2) = \_\_$
  $4-0 = \_\_$ $6-(-1) = 7$ $5-\_\_ = \_\_$ $2-(-3) = \_\_$
  $4-(-1) = \_\_$ $6-(-2) = \_\_$ $5-\_\_ = \_\_$ $2-(-4) = \_\_$
  $4-(-2) = \_\_$ $6-(-3) = \_\_$ $5-\_\_ = \_\_$ $2-(-5) = \_\_$
        $5-\_\_ = \_\_$ $2-(-6) = \_\_$

2A Calculate:

a $5-(-2)$ **b** $4-(-3)$ **c** $8-(-8)$ **d** $1-(-5)$ **e** $2-(-4)$
f $-1-(-2)$ **g** $-2-(-6)$ **h** $-8-(-3)$ **i** $1-(-1)$ **j** $-6-(-5)$
k $0-(-2)$ **l** $7-(-8)$ **m** $-7-(-8)$ **n** $5-(-5)$ **o** $-2-(-2)$
p $-1-(-1)$ **q** $11-(-1)$ **r** $-1-(-9)$ **s** $0-(-1)$ **t** $-9-(-1)$

3A Copy and complete this table:

First temperature	10°C	−1°C	8°C	3°C	−2°C	5°C	−3°C	−5°C
Second temperature	5°C	−4°C	2°C	−1°C	4°C	−1°C	3°C	−7°C
Change in temperature	$5°-10°$ $= -5°$	$-4°-(-1°)$ $= -4°+1°$ $= -3°$						

4A Another game for two players.
Make a pack of 11 cards, and write one of the numbers $-5, -4, -3, -2, -1, 0,$ $1, 2, 3, 4, 5$ on each card.
Draw a number line from -15 to $+15$, spacing the points 5 mm apart. Take a card from the pack, and, starting at 0, move a marker (eg your pencil point) when you add the number on the card.
Take turns. The winner is the player who finishes farther to the right.

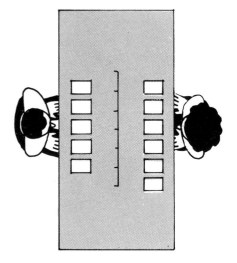

5B Copy these subtractions until you have five lines in each. Then rewrite the last two lines of each in the form of additions.

a $1-2 = -1$ **b** $-4-2 = -6$ **c** $0-2 = -2$
  $1-1 = \_\_$ $-4-1 = \_\_$ $0-1 = \_\_$
  $1-0 = \_\_$ $-4-0 = \_\_$ $0-0 = \_\_$
  $1-(-1) = \_\_$ _____ _____
  $1-(-2) = \_\_$ _____ _____

6B Some more *crossoffs*.

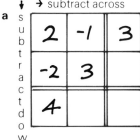

7C Solve these equations:

   a $2-x=5$ **b** $-3-x=2$ **c** $-7-x=-4$

   d $4-x=-3$ **e** $4-x=11$ **f** $-4-x=11$

Making sure

(i) $2+3=5$ (iii) $-2+3=1$ (v) $2+(-3)=-1$

(ii) $2-3=-1$ (iv) $-2-3=-5$ (vi) $2-(-3)=2+3=5$

====================== *Exercise 8* ======================

1A Calculate:

   a $6+5$ **b** $-2+5$ **c** $0+3$ **d** $-7+4$ **e** $-3+0$

2A Calculate:

   a $4+(-2)$ **b** $-3+(-2)$ **c** $0+(-2)$ **d** $-5+(-5)$ **e** $-1+(-6)$

3A Calculate:

   a $5-2$ **b** $2-5$ **c** $-4-1$ **d** $-4-4$ **e** $0-10$

4A Calculate:

   a $5-(-1)$ **b** $2-(-3)$ **c** $-1-(-6)$ **d** $-1-(-1)$ **e** $0-(-4)$

5A Calculate:

   a $8-5$ **b** $5-8$ **c** $4-(-1)$ **d** $-2+(-3)$ **e** $0-7$

   f $6+(-4)$ **g** $2-(-3)$ **h** $-1+(-4)$ **i** $-7-(-1)$ **j** $-9+6$

   k $-1-3$ **l** $7-(-4)$ **m** $-6-6$ **n** $-9-(-9)$ **o** $-(-1)$

   p $9-(-1)$ **q** $9-1$ **r** $-9-1$ **s** $-9+1$ **t** $-9-(-1)$

6A Try this version of the game in question **4A** of *Exercise 7*.

Add a separate pack of 10 cards, and mark 5 of them with a ' + ',
and 5 of them with a ' − '.

Each player takes a ' + '/' − ' card, followed by a number card.

Then, for example: a ' + ' card and a 3 card means 'Go forward 3'.

                    a ' + ' card and a −3 card means 'Go back 3'.

                    a ' − ' card and a 3 card means 'Go back 3'.

                    a ' − ' card and a −3 card means 'Go forward 3'.

The other rules are the same as before.

POSITIVE AND NEGATIVE NUMBERS

7B Calculate:
a $-12-8$　　**b** $17+(-9)$　　**c** $-15+7$　　**d** $14-(-6)$　　**e** $0-(-11)$
f $-(-11)$　　**g** $-11+9$　　**h** $-11-9$　　**i** $-11-(-9)$　　**j** $-9+11$

8B Calculate:
a $4+(-3)+(-1)$　　**b** $6-(-2)-(-1)$　　**c** $-2+3-4$　　**d** $1-(-1)-1$
e $-3-(-2)+(-5)$　　**f** $1+(-2)-(-4)$　　**g** $-5+(-2)-1$　　**h** $1-11-111$
i $6+(-3)+(-2)+(-1)$　　**j** $6-(-3)-(-2)-(-1)$　　**k** $1-1-(-1)+1$
l $-(-1)-(-1)$　　**m** $-8-5+7-(-6)$　　**n** $1-0-10-(-9)$

9C Copy and complete these:
　　a A *crossadd off*　　　　　　**b** A *crossoff add*　　　　　　**c** A *crossoff off*

-3	2	3	-4
4	1	-2	7
	-3	-3	
-1		4	

-3	-2	1	0
		-3	17
		-3	
-8	-7		15

5	5	-2	2
		2	8
-4	-6		5
3			

10C Copy and complete these magic squares (all rows, columns and the two diagonals add up to the same number).

a

-6		-1	3
7	-5	2	
		8	
0			5

b

8		4	-4
	6	10	2
-5		-1	3
1	-12		-3
7	-6	11	

11C a Copy and complete this pattern:

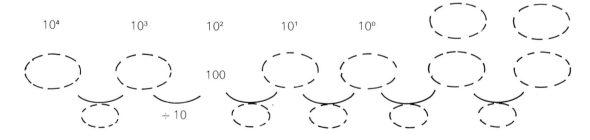

10^4　　　10^3　　　10^2　　　10^1　　　10^0

100　　　$\div 10$

b Suggest what these numbers might be: (i) 10^{-3} (ii) 10^{-6}.
c On your calculator, start with 2. Keep multiplying by 10, if you can. Explain what happens when the calculator display is full.
d Try part **c** again for repeated *division* by 10, if you can.

A conversation from 1986

Tom   : 'I can get 1 from all the digits of 1986.'

Sheena: 'How?'

Tom   : '$8 \div (9 + 1 - 6)$.'

Sheena: 'That's 2, not 1!'

Tom   : 'Sorry. Well, how about $9 + 8 - 16$?'

Sheena: 'Are you allowed to do that?'

Tom   : 'Why not?'

Sheena: 'I suppose it's all right, but I think the digits should be in order, as in 1986.'

Tom   : 'That's far too hard—it'll be impossible.'

Sheena: (5 minutes later) 'It's not impossible: how about $-1^9 + 8 - 6$?'

Tom   : 'I don't understand that.'

Sheena: 'Well 1^9 means $1 \times 1 \times 1 \times 1 \times 1 \times 1 \times 1 \times 1 \times 1$ which is 1.'

Tom   : 'Right, so 1^9 is really 1; I see.' Well, I bet you can't get 2.'

Sheena: 'But you've already got 2. It was $8 \div (9 + 1 - 6)$.'

Tom   : 'Yes, but the order 8, 9, 1, 6 was wrong.'

Sheena: (8 minutes later) 'No. I can't do it.'

Tom   : 'Well I can. 'It's $1 + \sqrt{9} - 8 + 6$.'

Sheena: 'What does $\sqrt{9}$ mean?'

Tom   : 'That's the square root of 9, which is 3, because $3 \times 3 = 9$.'

Sheena: 'Well, that's one each. Let's see who's first to get 3.'

Tom   : (3 minutes later) 'I've got it: $\cdot 1 + \cdot 9 + 8 - 6$.'

Sheena: 'I bet I'll get 4 before you do . . . .'

How far can you and your neighbour, or the whole class, get, using the digits of the present year in order? Can you make all the numbers from 1 to 20? From 1 to 100?

(handwritten scroll:)

$$1986$$
$$1 = 1^9 + 8 - 6$$
$$2 = 1 + \sqrt{9} - 8 + 6$$
$$3 = \cdot 1 + \cdot 9 + 8 - 6$$
$$4 = -1 - 9 + 8 + 6$$
$$5 = 19 - 8 - 6$$
$$6 = (1 \times 9 - 8) \times 6$$
$$7 = 1 \times 9 - 8 + 6$$
$$8 = 1 + 9 - 8 + 6$$
$$9 = 1 \times \sqrt{9} \cdot 8 - 6$$

CHECK-UP ON **POSITIVE AND NEGATIVE NUMBERS**

1A

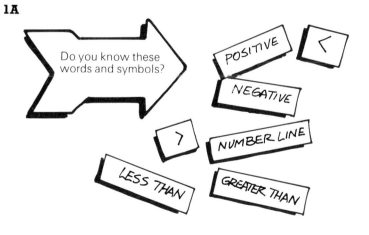

Do you know these words and symbols?

POSITIVE

NEGATIVE

NUMBER LINE

LESS THAN

GREATER THAN

<

>

(number line:) -3 -2 -1 0 1 2 3

Copy and complete:

The drawing above shows the _____ _____. Numbers that are _____ _____ 0 are _____ numbers. Numbers that are _____ _____ 0 are _____ numbers. We can shorten this and write 3_0, and -3_0.

2A, B

UNDERSTAND ORDER AMONG THE POSITIVE AND NEGATIVE NUMBERS.

Can you do these?

USE NEGATIVE NUMBERS IN DESCRIPTIONS.

USE NEGATIVE COORDINATES.

	°C
Geneva	−1
Gibraltar	13
Glasgow	1
Helsinki	−11
Hong Kong	22
Innsbruck	−2
Inverness	−5
Istanbul	15

a These were the temperatures at midday on Monday December 30th 1985 at the places shown. Arrange them in order from the coldest to the warmest.

b Measuring from low tide what are the heights of:
(i) Top of the Cliff (ii) Caves (iii) Boulders (iv) Sand (v) Mud (vi) Sea bed?
Answer these questions again relative to high tide.

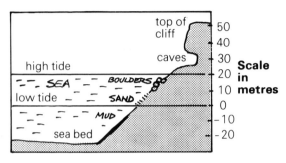

c On squared paper draw x and y-axes with scales from −10 to 10.

Plot these points joining them up as you go. Colour the finished design.
(−2, 6) (−8, 4) (−6, −2) (−2, 0) (−4, 4) (−6, 2) (−4, 0) (−2, 4) (−6, 6) (−8, 0) (−2, −2) (−2, 0) (−4, 0) (−2, −6) (4, −4) (2, 0) (−2, −2) (0, −4) (2, −2) (−2, 0) (−4, −4) (2, −6) (4, 0) (2, 0) (2, −2) (8, 0) (6, 6) (2, 4) (4, 0) (6, 2) (4, 4) (2, 0) (6, −2) (8, 4) (2, 6) (−2, 6).

3A

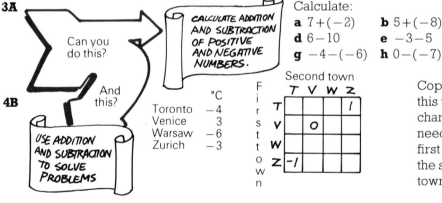

Can you do this?

CALCULATE ADDITION AND SUBTRACTION OF POSITIVE AND NEGATIVE NUMBERS.

And this?

4B

USE ADDITION AND SUBTRACTION TO SOLVE PROBLEMS

Calculate:
a $7 + (−2)$ **b** $5 + (−8)$ **c** $−3 + (−2)$
d $6 − 10$ **e** $−3 − 5$ **f** $5 − (−2)$
g $−4 − (−6)$ **h** $0 − (−7)$

	°C
Toronto	−4
Venice	3
Warsaw	−6
Zurich	−3

Second town

First town	T	V	W	Z
T				1
V		0		
W				
Z	−1			

Copy and complete this table. It shows the change in temperature needed to make the first town temperature the same as the second town temperature.

5C

Investigate:

∗ can be replaced by + or −. For example, 1 ∗ 2 could be 1 + 2 or 1 − 2. 1 ∗ 2 has two possible values, 3 and −1.
a Find all the possible values of:
(i) 1 ∗ 2 ∗ 3   (iii) 1 ∗ 2 ∗ 3 ∗ 4.

b Copy and complete this table:

	1∗2	1∗2∗3	1∗2∗3∗4
Number of possible values	2		

c What does this suggest for 1 ∗ 2 ∗ 3 ∗ 4 ∗ 5? Check your guess.
d 1 ∗ 2 ∗ 3 ∗ 4 ∗ 5 ∗ 6 can have a value of 3 in three different ways. Can you find them?

=== *Exercise 1* ===

Paul collects coins.

Jo collects stamps.

Paul's father has a
set of spanners.

Jo's mother has a set
of matching china.

THE LANGUAGE OF SETS

Collections often have special names-
a flock of sheep, a herd of cattle, a gaggle of geese, a pride of lions.

1 Can you think of any others?
Items in a collection often have something in common.
For example, 1, 2, 3 and 6 are all factors of 6.

2 What do the items in each of the four collections above have in common?
But collections might not have anything
in common, for example: hammer, hat,
football, egg.

3 Which is the odd one out in each of the
collections below? Say why.

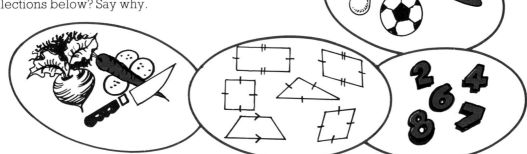

A collection of objects (usually all different) is called a **set**.
Marie made a list of the colours she needed to draw a rainbow.
She gave her list the name R, and wrote it out in **set notation**, using curly brackets and commas, like this:
$R = \{$red, orange, yellow, green, blue, indigo, violet$\}$.
She said 'My set has 7 members.

Orange is a member of R, which is written
Orange $\in R$, but black $\notin R$.'

What does she mean by $\notin$?

Exercise 2

1A
a

Shopping List
BREAD
JAM
FRUIT
VEG
MEAT
CHICKEN
EGGS
CEREAL

b
Morning Check
PENCIL
RULER
BOOKS
BUS PASS
SNACK
MONEY

c
TRAIN ARRIVALS

FROM	PLATFORM
LONDON	1
MANCHESTER	2
BIRMINGHAM	4
CARLISLE	6
EDINBURGH	5
ABERDEEN	3
BRISTOL	9

Use $\{\ldots\ldots\}$ to list the members of **a** and **b**. For **c**, list the platform numbers.

2A A table for one is set for a three-course meal. List the set of cutlery needed, using curly brackets.

3A List the set of:
  a natural numbers from 1 to 6 (including both 1 and 6)
  b even numbers from 2 to 10.

4A a List the set F of the first five letters of the English alphabet.
  b $a \in F$. Write down four more statements like this.

5A $P = \{$acute angles (between 0° and 90°)$\}$, $Q = \{$obtuse angles (between 90° and 180°)$\}$ and $R = \{$angles greater than 180°$\}$.
Use the symbol $\in$ to link each of following angles with its set:
30°, 300°, 125°, 89°, 98°, 360°, 60°.

6A

Frances arranged this set of coins and called it C. Which of the following statements are true and which are false?
  a $20p \in C$ **b** $1p \in C$ **c** $\frac{1}{2}p \notin C$
  d C has seven members.
  e The members of C have a total value of £1·88.

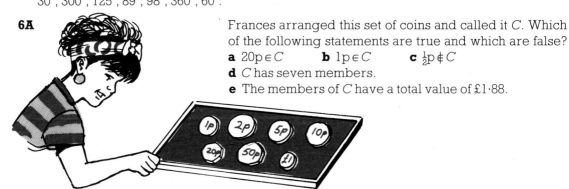

7A $B = \{2, 4, 6, 8\}$. List the new sets of numbers given by:
 a dividing each member of B by 2
 b adding 1 to each member of B
 c multiplying each member of B by 6
 d subtracting 4 from each member of B.

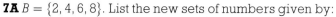

8A Choose the member of $\{1, 2, 3, 4, 5\}$ which is a solution of:
 a $3x = 3$ **b** $x + 2 = 5$ **c** $x - 2 = 2$ **d** $4x - 2 = 14$

 e $2x + 3 = 13$ **f** $16 - 3x = 1$ **g** $\dfrac{20}{x} = 4$ **h** $\dfrac{x}{3} = 1$

9B List the set of factors of:
 a 15 **b** 14 **c** 22 **d** 39 **e** 37

10B Which members of $\{2, 3, 4, 5, 7\}$ are factors of:
 a 27 **b** 24 **c** 18 **d** 49 **e** 55?

11B Andy said that if you wanted to find a factor of 24, any member of $\{1, 2, 3, 4, 6, 8, 12, 24\}$ would do. Do you agree?

12B Start with this set of temperatures in degrees Fahrenheit:
 $F = \{32, 95, 122, 212\}$. Then list:
 a the set A which is made by taking 32 from each member of F
 b the set B which is made by dividing each member of A by 9
 c the set C which is made by multiplying each member of B by 5.
 Describe set C in words.

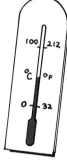

ORDER; EQUAL SETS

Janet phones her husband to ask him to collect some shopping on his way home.

Copying the list, George missed out the tomatoes. So he put them in at the end of his list. He had a different list from Janet . . . or had he?
Using his list, would he get all the things that Janet wanted?
Does the order of the members in a set matter?

Janet's set is equal to George's set.

Example 1
 =

Example 2 $\{A, E, L, Q, U\}$ = $\{E, Q, U, A, L\}$

1A Which of these sets are equal?
  a {1, 2}, {2, 3}, {2, 1}, {3, 1}, {3, 2}
  b {S, L, A, K, E}, {L, A, K, E, S}, {S, C, A, L, E}, {S, L, E, A, K}

2A Write down pairs of equal sets:
  a {a, b, c, d}, {a, c, b, d}, {a, b, c}
  b {0, 1, 2}, {0, 2, 1, 3}, {2, 0, 1}
  c {p, q, r}, {q, r, p, t}, {r, q, p}, {p, q, r, s}
  d {☆, △, □}, {△, ○, ◇}, {□, ☆, ◇}, {◇, □, ○}, {○, ◇, △}

Long lists

Marie is taking a holiday during the first fortnight of July. This set of dates is rather long to list, so, to make it shorter, she writes:

H = {July 1, July 2, July 3, . . . , July 14}.

The dots stand for all the missing dates.

Calendar

JULY

S		7	14	21	28
M	1	8	15	22	29
T	2	9	16	23	30
W	3	10	17	24	31
T	4	11	18	25	
F	5	12	19	26	
S	6	13	20	27	

3A Write out these long lists in the same way:
  a The months in a year.
  b The dates in February in a leap year.
  c The letters in the English alphabet.
  d The first 50 odd numbers.

Sets which never end

4B The set of whole numbers never comes to an end—it just goes on and on. So Marie writes W = {0, 1, 2, 3, . . .}.
Write these never-ending sets in the same way:
  a Natural numbers (starting with 1).
  b Even numbers (starting with 0).
  c Odd numbers (starting with 1).
  d Multiples of 5 (starting with 5).

5B List the set of:
  a whole numbers greater than 10
  b whole numbers greater than 100
  c multiples of 3 greater than 1000

6C The set of letters in the word LITTLE is {L, I, T, T, L, E}. It has four different members L, I, T, E. In mathematics, {L, I, T, T, L, E} and {L, I, T, E} are equal sets. Write two equal sets for the letters of the words:
  a MOON   **b** MADAM   **c** ADDITION   **d** ENGINEERING

THE LANGUAGE OF SETS

THE EMPTY SET

Old Mother Hubbard
went to the cupboard
to get her poor dog a bone,
But when she got there
The cupboard was empty (?)

Some sets have no members.
A set with no members is called **the empty set**. It is written { } or ∅.

=== Exercise 4 ===

1A Sometimes it can be very useful to know whether or not a set is empty.
The set of people with the same finger prints as Will Steel is empty. How does this help the police?

2A Which of the following are examples of the empty set?
  a Pupils in the class who are over 4 m tall.
  b Pupils in the class who are over 100 years old.
  c The set of cubes with 4 faces.
  d The set of numbers less than zero.
  e The set of whole numbers greater than 10 and less than 11.

3A Make up two more examples of the empty set.

4A Marie says that the solution set of the equation $2x + 1 = 15$ is $\{7\}$.
  Write down the solution sets of these equations in the same way:
  a $x - 2 = 10$ **b** $y + 5 = 11$ **c** $2n - 1 = 19$ **d** $20 - m = 10$
  e $2k = 12$ **f** $3a + 1 = 10$ **g** $4b + 1 = 13$ **h** $7x + 1 = 1$

5A Sometimes there is only a limited number of members to choose from.

Here are all the suspects at a murder trial; the evidence given by three different witnesses makes things very difficult for the judge and jury.
  a Witness 1 said the murderer was a man. List the possible solutions.
  b Witness 2 said the murderer wore glasses. List the possible solutions.
  c Witness 3 said the murderer was a gorilla. List the possible solutions.

6C In this question you can only choose the members of your solution set from $\{1, 2, 3, 4, 5, 6, 7\}$. Be careful; the solution set might be the empty set.

a $4x+5 = 25$ **b** $4x+5 = 35$ **c** $16-2x = 10$ **d** $y^2+1 = 1$

e $9x+2 = 20$ **f** $x^2+4 = 13$ **g** $1-x = 1$ **h** $x > 5$

i $x < 1$ **j** $2x < 7$ **k** $2x > 5$ **l** $x^2 > 10$

SUBSETS

Mrs Jones took her son Trevor to the shopping centre. She asked him to get the bacon, chicken and eggs at the butcher's. A list within a list, **a set within a set**!

Marie knows all about this too. She would call {bacon, chicken, eggs} a **subset** of {bread, jam, fruit, veg, bacon, chicken, eggs, cereal}.

THE LANGUAGE OF SETS

=============== *Exercise 5* ===============

1A List the subsets of items in Mrs Jones' shopping list that you might buy in:

a a fruit shop   **b** a baker's   **c** a supermarket   **d** a jeweller's

2A

This picture shows a set of British coins. List the subsets of:

a 'copper' coins   **b** 'silver' coins   **c** round coins   **d** coins worth more than £1

3A Marie has two dogs, Spot and Rover. When she goes for a walk she can take both dogs, or one of them, or neither of them. List these four subsets of her set of dogs.

4B Marie gave Kevin this set of cards, saying 'see how many subsets you can make from these'.

Kevin thought out this flowchart. Follow it through, and end up with:

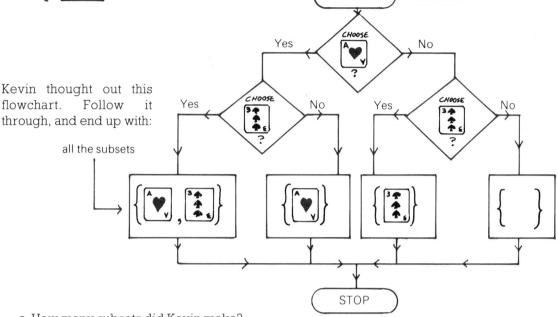

a How many subsets did Kevin make?
b Is one of them the empty set?
c Is one of them the set he started with, containing two cards?

5B List all the subsets of: **a** {Z} **b** {1, 2}

6B List all the subsets of {−1, 0, 1} which have exactly:
    a 3 members   **b** 2 members   **c** 1 member   **d** no members

7C Illustrate your answers to question **6B** by means of a flowchart.

8C List the set of whole numbers W, and the set of natural numbers N.
Which one is a subset of the other?

Another symbol
Marie explained that '{a, b} is a subset of {a, b, c}' can be
written '{a, b} $\subset$ {a, b, c}'.

=================== *Exercise 6* ===================

1B Which of the following are true and which are false?
    a {2, 3} $\subset$ {2, 3, 5}   **b** {1, 2, 3} $\subset$ {1, 2}   **c** {x, y} $\subset$ {y, x}
    d {A, C, T} $\subset$ {A, C, T, I, O, N}   **e** {a, b} $\subset$ {b, a, c}   **f** {4} $\subset$ {8}

2B In the following question link pairs of sets using the symbol $\subset$:
    a $A = \{c, a, t\}, B = \{m, o, u, s, e\}, C = \{m, e\}, D = \{c, a, s, t\}$
    b $E = \{m, e\}, F = \{m, e, a, n, t\}, G = \{a, t\}, H = \{m, e, a, t\}$
    c $P = \{$multiples of 2$\}, Q = \{$multiples of 3$\}, R = \{$multiples of 4$\}, S = \{$multiples of 6$\}$

10 INTERSECTION

=== **Exercise 7** ===

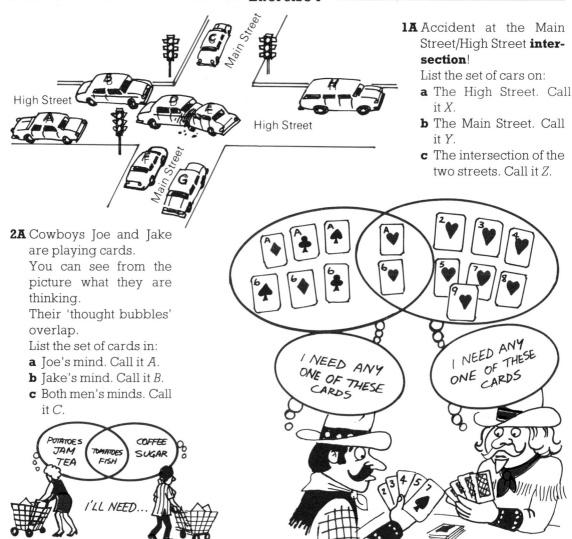

1A Accident at the Main Street/High Street **inter-section**!

List the set of cars on:

a The High Street. Call it X.

b The Main Street. Call it Y.

c The intersection of the two streets. Call it Z.

2A Cowboys Joe and Jake are playing cards.

You can see from the picture what they are thinking.

Their 'thought bubbles' overlap.

List the set of cards in:

a Joe's mind. Call it A.

b Jake's mind. Call it B.

c Both men's minds. Call it C.

3A The shoppers' 'thought bubbles' overlap. List the set of things needed by:

a Mrs Gray. Call it G.

b Mrs Whyte. Call it W.

c Both shoppers. Call it B.

4A Meg's thinking about some even numbers.

Beth's thinking about some multiples of 3.

a List the set P of numbers Meg's thinking about.

b List the set Q of numbers Beth's thinking about.

c List the set R of numbers both girls are thinking about.

In mathematics, the set whose members are common to two (or more) sets is called the intersection of these sets.

In question **4A**, R is the intersection of sets P and Q.
This can be written $R = P \cap Q$ ('P intersection Q').

5A a Check that in question **1A**, $X \cap Y = \{D, E\}$.
   b In question **2A**, list $A \cap B$.
   c In question **3A**, list $G \cap W$.
   d In question **4A**, list $P \cap Q$.

6A Stephen: 'I have Maths, French, English and Art today'.
   Jonathan: 'You're lucky. I have French, History, Geography and English'.
   Draw the boys' 'thought bubbles'. Do they intersect?
   Which subjects belong to the intersection?

7A $B = \{$letters in the word BLUE$\}$
   $R = \{$letters in the word RED$\}$
   $K = \{$letters in the word BLACK$\}$
   a List the set: (i) B (ii) R (iii) K (iv) $B \cap R$ (v) $B \cap K$ (vi) $R \cap K$.
   b Draw the intersection diagram for $B \cap K$.

8B a Write down the set of the first six multiples of 2, starting with 2. Call it T.
   b Write down the set of the first six multiples of 3, starting with 3. Call it H.
   c Write down the set $T \cap H$, and also its smallest member.
   d What is the name for the smallest member of $T \cap H$?
   e Draw a diagram for the sets T and H.

9B Repeat question **8B** for multiples of 4 and 6.

10B Three wise monkeys sat upon a log. One thought of SIGHT, one of HEARING and one of SPEECH.
   a List the sets A, B and C.
   b List $A \cap B$, $B \cap C$ and $C \cap A$.
   c List $A \cap B \cap C$.

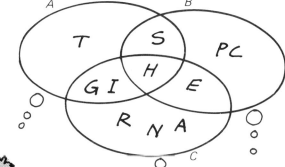

11B a Plot the points O(0, 0) and A(6, 6). Join OA.
  b On the same diagram plot the points B(6, 0) and C(0, 6). Join BC.
  c P = {coordinates of all points on OA}, Q = {coordinates of all points on BC}.
  Copy and complete: $P \cap Q$ = {(..., ...)}.

12B a On your diagram for question **11B** draw the straight line joining
  the points D(0, 2) and E(6, 8).
  b R = {coordinates of all points on DE}.
  Write down: (i) $Q \cap R$ (ii) $P \cap R$.

13C $K = \{-1, -2, -3, -4, -5, -6\}$. Replacing x by suitable numbers
  from K, find these subsets of K:
  a R, the set for which $x > -4$
  b S, the set for which $x < -2$
  c $R \cap S$.

A cube of side 3 cm is painted red. It is then
cut into a set of cubes of side 1 cm.
a How many cubes of side 1 cm will there
be?
b How many members will there be in the
subsets with:
    (i) 3 red sides   (ii) 2 red sides
    (iii) 1 red side   (iv) no red sides.

List all the subsets of $\{a\}$, $\{a, b\}$, $\{a, b, c\}$ and $\{a, b, c, d\}$. Remember that $A \subset A$
and $\emptyset \subset A$.
Copy and complete:

Set	Number of members	Number of subsets
$\{a\}$	1	2
$\{a, b\}$		4
$\{a, b, c\}$		
$\{a, b, c, d\}$		

How many subsets will there be for a set with 5 members, 10 members and
n members?

CHECK-UP ON **THE LANGUAGE OF SETS**

1A Using curly brackets, list the set of the first ten whole
  numbers (starting with zero).

2A $A = \{2, 4, 6, 8, \ldots\}$
  Which of the following are true and which are false?
  a $2 \in A$ **b** $15 \in A$ **c** $29 \notin A$ **d** $44 \in A$ **e** $98 \notin A$

3A Pick out equal sets from:
  a $\{x, z, y\}, \{x, y, w\}, \{w, x, y\}, \{x, y, z\}$
  b $\{0, 1\}, \{1\}, \{0\}, \{1, 0\}$
  c $\{M, E, A, T\}, \{T, A, M, E\}, \{M, E, E, T\}, \{T, E, E, M\}, \{M, A, T, E\}$

4A, B Which of the following sets are empty?

    a The set of even prime numbers.

    b The set of factors of 6 which are odd numbers.

    c The set of multiples of 6 which are odd numbers.

5B List all the subsets of $\{1, 2, 3\}$.

6B $F = \{$factors of 36$\}$. Which of the following are true and which are false?

    a $\{1, 2, 3, 4, 6, 9, 12, 18, 36\} \subset F$ **b** $\{2, 4, 6, 8\} \subset F$

    c $F \subset \{$first 36 natural numbers$\}$ **d** $\{0, 1\} \subset F$

7A

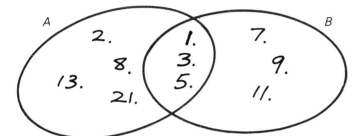

    a List: (i) A

             (ii) B

             (iii) $A \cap B$

    b How many members has each of these three sets?

8A Draw a diagram to illustrate the following sets:

    $A = \{$M, A, C, K, I, N, T, O, S, H$\}$ and $B = \{$F, U, R, N, I, T, E$\}$

9B $P = \{1, 3, 5\}$, $Q = \{1, 2, 3, 4\}$ and $R = \{3, 5\}$. Draw diagrams to illustrate:

    a $P \cap Q$ **b** $Q \cap R$ **c** $P \cap R$ **d** $P \cap Q \cap R$

10C Investigate the number of members in a set which has 64 subsets.

Class discussion

Each of these pictures has something to do with percentages. Explain what the connection is in each case.

THE MEANING OF PER CENT

Per cent means per hundred

> 51% means 51 per hundred, or $\frac{51}{100}$.
>
> 100% means 100 per hundred, or $\frac{100}{100}$, or 1.
>
> 125% means 125 per hundred, or $\frac{125}{100}$.

─────────────── *Exercise 1* ───────────────

1A Write as percentages; for example, $\frac{65}{100} = 65\%$.

  a $\frac{38}{100}$ **b** $\frac{95}{100}$ **c** $\frac{121}{100}$ **d** $\frac{273}{100}$ **e** $\frac{7}{100}$ **f** $\frac{1}{100}$

2A Write as fractions; for example, $5\% = \frac{5}{100}$.

  a 21%   **b** 17%   **c** 9%   **d** 89%   **e** 251%   **f** 100%

3A Write as decimals; for example, $44\% = \frac{44}{100} = 0.44$.

  a 33%   **b** 15%   **c** 10%   **d** 8%   **e** 1%   **f** 150%

4A Each figure has 100 small squares. Copy and complete the calculations:

Fraction shaded $= \frac{20}{100}$ Fraction shaded $= \frac{}{100}$ Fraction shaded $= \frac{}{100}$

$= \_\_\%$ $= \_\_\%$ $= \_\_\%$

Fraction shaded $= \frac{}{100}$ Fraction shaded $= \frac{}{100}$ Fraction shaded $= \frac{}{100}$

$= \_\_\%$ $= \_\_\%$ $= \_\_\%$

5A Copy and complete this table:

Percentage	40%	78%	10%	9%	6%	1%	125%	144%	200%
Fraction	$\frac{40}{100}$			$\frac{9}{100}$			$\frac{125}{100}$		
Decimal	0·40			0·09			1·25		

PERCENTAGES IN ACTION

6A Look at this diagram of all the different costs you have if you own a car.
  a Add up the percentages. Did you expect this answer? Explain why.
  b Arrange the costs in order, from largest to smallest.

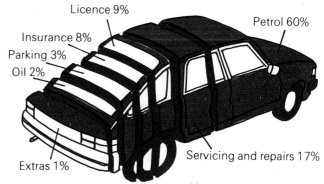

Licence 9%
Insurance 8%
Parking 3%
Oil 2%
Petrol 60%
Servicing and repairs 17%
Extras 1%

7A Write these as fractions in their simplest form; for example, $48\% = \dfrac{\cancel{48}^{12}}{\underset{25}{\cancel{100}}} = \dfrac{12}{25}$.

a 50%	**b** 25%	**c** 75%	**d** 20%	**e** 40%	**f** 10%
g 60%	**h** 90%	**i** 200%	**j** 150%	**k** 5%	**l** 500%

8A List these newspaper cuttings in order, from the smallest to the largest percentage.

only 5pc 167% higher 9.05% 9.25% 0.8% 14.64% 9.50% 8.375% 0.008% 49% 9.52% 9.5% 12% 10.25%

9B Copy and complete this table, giving the fractions in their simplest form.

Percentage	20%	50%	100%	175%	12·3%	11·1%	7·7%	1·5%	6·5%	10½%	12½%
Fraction	$\frac{20}{100}$ $=\frac{1}{5}$				$\frac{12·3}{100}$						
Decimal	0·2				0·123						

USING PERCENTAGES FOR A DISCOUNT

Getting a bargain at the Sales

Discount means 'money off' goods or services. Sometimes you are offered discounts during sales. Can you think of other reasons for discounts?
Cathie and Simon both see this advertisement, and calculate the discount and the cost of the stereo.

Cathie uses her calculator

Discount = 5% of £45

$$\quad (= 0.05 \times £45)$$

$$\quad = £2.25$$

Simon slogs it out

5% of $£45 = \frac{5}{100} \times £45$

$$= £\frac{225}{100}$$

$$= £2.25$$

OR

100% of cost $= £45$

1% of cost $= £45 \times \frac{1}{100}$

5% of cost $= £45^9 \times \frac{5^1}{100_{20_4}}$

$$= £\frac{9}{4}$$

$$= £2.25$$

So the stereo now costs £45 − £2.25 = £42.75.

═══════════════════════════ *Exercise 2* ═══════════════════════════

1A Calculate:
  a 25% of £80   **b** 50% of £26   **c** 75% of £100   **d** 20% of £5
  e 13% of £70   **f** 28% of £80   **g** 36% of £120   **h** 4% of £5
  i 5% of £30   **j** 10% of 50p   **k** 20% of £1   **l** 1% of £1

2A At the sale Margo buys:
  a A notebook usually costing £1·80.
  b A pencil usually costing 60p.
  c A book marked at £2·60.
  What discount does she get on each?

3A

CLOSING DOWN SALE

30% DISCOUNT ON ALL THESE PRICES
ACE COMPUTERS   £150
BLASTEM VIDEO GAMES £8
KWIK CALCULATORS   £3·20
BRILL BADGES   50p

─── * ───

Calculate the discount on each of these items.

PERCENTAGES IN ACTION

4A A shop gives its employees a 10% discount on everything it sells. Calculate the discounts and the employee's prices in this table.

Employee	Item	Usual price	Discount	Employee's price
Mrs Graham	Shoes	£35		
Mr Holmes	Coat	£120		
Miss Johnson	Gloves	£18·50		
Ms Young	Dress	£77		

5A Calculate **a** the discount, **b** What you would have to pay, for each of these:

(i)   (ii)   (iii)

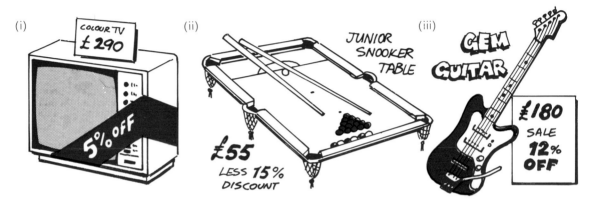

COLOUR TV £290 5% OFF

JUNIOR SNOOKER TABLE £55 LESS 15% DISCOUNT

GEM GUITAR £180 SALE 12% OFF

6B There are 2 adults and 3 children in the Weston family. Gary and Elaine are aged 10 and 12. Mike is 15. How much would their 14 day holiday cost?

2 TAPES FOR THE PRICE OF ONE!

7B What percentage discount is this?

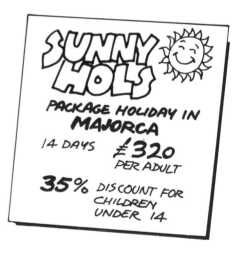

SUNNY HOLS
PACKAGE HOLIDAY IN MAJORCA
14 DAYS £320 PER ADULT
35% DISCOUNT FOR CHILDREN UNDER 14

8B a If a discount of 20% is offered, what percentage of the price has to be paid?

   b Calculate the amount to be paid for each of these.
     (i) Tennis racquet, usually £35; discount 15%.
     (ii) Tracksuit, usually £85; discount $12\frac{1}{2}$%.
     (iii) Sports shoes, usually £28·50; discount 5%.

9C To prepare for a sale, a shop assistant has to reduce
by 10% the price of all items which cost 50p and over.
He uses this flowchart:

To reduce prices of 50p and over by 10%

a Reprice the following items for him.

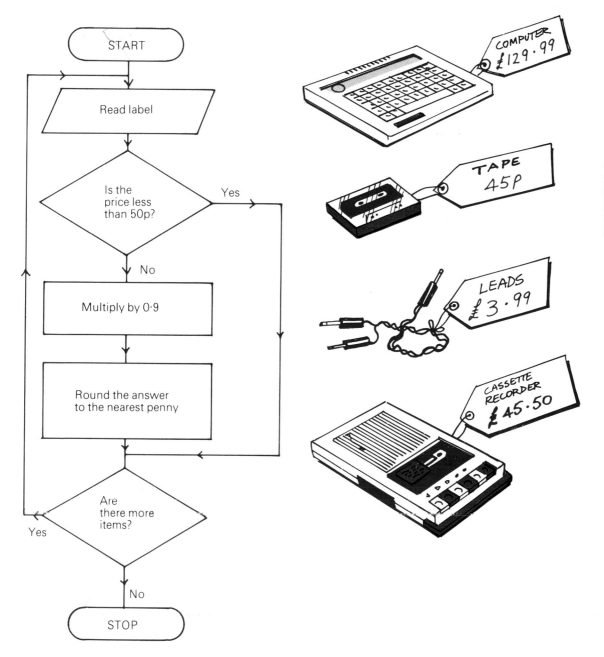

Data: Price list for the store.

b Why did he multiply by 0·9?
What factor would he use if the sales
reduction was:
(i) 20%   (ii) 7%   (iii) 12½%?

USING PERCENTAGES FOR INTEREST

Do you ever save any money?
If you do, put it in an account in a Bank or a
Building Society and get **interest** on it.
The Bank of Brit pays a **rate of interest** of 8% per year.
8% means 8 per hundred, so you get £8 interest on £100 after one year.

IF I PUT £150
IN THE UNION JACK
BUILDING SOCIETY FOR 1 YEAR
HOW MUCH WILL I GET BACK?

Jane's interest = 9% of £150
              = 9% × £150
              = £13·50, after a year.
So she will have £150 + £13·50 = £163·50.

=== *Exercise 3* ===

1A Write down the interest on £100 for 1 year at these rates of interest:
    a 5%   **b** 7%   **c** 9%   **d** 12%

2A Write down the interest you would receive on £200 after leaving it for 1 year in the banks
and building society in the pictures above.

3A Calculate the interest on £75 in the same banks and building society for 1 year.

4A The Safety First Bank offers 6% interest.
    a How much interest would you get in 1 year on £250?
    b How much money would you have altogether?

5A The Shaky Do Building Society offers
14% interest.
    a Calculate your interest on £50 after
      1 year.
    b How much money would you have
      then?

6A Jamie's father put £3600 into the Union
Jack Building Society, hoping that a
year's interest would pay for the family
holiday, costing £350. Did it?

7A Calculate the interest on £1000 after 1 year in:
    a a Building Society at 8·5%   **b** the National Savings Bank at 12·5%

8A Calculate the interest on £25 for 1 year at rates of interest of: **a** 6% **b** 9%.

THE THRIFT BUILDING SOCIETY

The more you put in, the HIGHER the rate of INTEREST!!!

7.0%
UP TO £499
INVEST MORE
– GET MORE !

9.0%
£500 – £4999
INVEST MORE
– GET MORE !

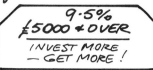

9.5%
£5000 & OVER
INVEST MORE
– GET MORE !

9B Copy and complete this table for the Thrift Building Society above:

Investment	£2500	£350	£1200	£5800
Rate of interest	9%	7%		
Interest in 1 year				

10B £20 is left in a bank for a year. It is then worth £22. Calculate:
    a the interest on the £20 for the year   **b** the interest on £100, that is, the rate per cent.

11B £500 increases to £530 after 1 year in a Building Society. Calculate:
    a the interest for the year   **b** the rate of interest in per cent.

12C a Calculate the interest on £500 for 1 year at 7%.
    b How much would you have altogether at the end of the year?
    c Calculate the interest at 7% on that total amount for the following year.

13C a Calculate the interest on £1200 for 1 year at 9%.
    b What is the total amount you would have at the end of one year?
    c Calculate the interest on this amount for a second year.
    d Repeat this calculation for a third year.

14C Calculate the interest on the following. The annual interest rate holds for any part of a year.
    a £250 at 8% for: (i) 1 year   (ii) 1 month   (iii) 4 months
    b £360 at 5% for: (i) 1 year   (ii) 1 month   (iii) 9 months
    c £1200 at $2\frac{1}{2}$% for: (i) 1 year   (ii) 1 month   (iii) 7 months
    d £800 at 15% for: (i) 6 months   (ii) 11 months.

£1000 is invested at 10% per year. At the end of each year the interest is added on, and the following year's interest is calculated on this total. In which year would the £1000 invested double itself?

USING PERCENTAGES AND FRACTIONS

Penny has to choose her subjects for next
year but she can't tell from her report card
which subjects she is best at. Can you?
She thinks it would be easier if all the marks
were out of 100, that is **percentages**.

Subject	Mark
ENGLISH	15/20
MATHS	42/60
FRENCH	18/30
HISTORY	32/40
SCIENCE	52/75

$100\% = \frac{100}{100} = 1$, so $\frac{15}{20} = \frac{15}{20} \times 100\% = 75\%$ for English.

To change a fraction to a percentage, multiply it by 100%.

Penny uses her calculator

$\frac{42}{60} = \frac{42}{60} \times 100\% = 70\%$ for maths

Penny checks it the hard way

$\frac{42}{60} = \frac{\cancel{42}^{14}}{\cancel{60}_{1}} \times \cancel{100}^{5} = 70\%$

===== *Exercise 4* =====

1A Change the following to percentages, like this: $\frac{2}{5} = \frac{2}{5} \times 100\% = 40\%$.

a $\frac{1}{2}$ **b** $\frac{1}{4}$ **c** $\frac{1}{5}$ **d** $\frac{1}{10}$ **e** $\frac{3}{4}$ **f** $\frac{3}{5}$

g $\frac{7}{10}$ **h** $\frac{9}{10}$ **i** $\frac{4}{25}$ **j** $\frac{11}{20}$ **k** $\frac{19}{50}$ **l** $\frac{6}{5}$

m $\frac{1}{8}$ **n** $\frac{3}{8}$ **o** $\frac{5}{8}$ **p** $\frac{7}{8}$ **q** $1\frac{1}{2}$ **r** $2\frac{1}{4}$

2A Look at Penny's report card again.
   a Calculate all her marks as percentages.
   b List her subjects in order, from best to worst.

3A Calculate as percentages, correct to 1 decimal place:

a $\frac{1}{3}$ **b** $\frac{2}{3}$ **c** $\frac{1}{7}$ **d** $\frac{5}{9}$ **e** $\frac{7}{11}$

4A a Copy this scale, and fill in the missing percentages:

0 —————|———————|———————|———————| 1
        $\frac{1}{4}$ $\frac{1}{2}$ $\frac{3}{4}$
       25%   ____   ____   100%

   b Mark $\frac{1}{3}$ and $\frac{2}{3}$ on the scale, along with their percentages.

Try to remember the fractions and percentages on this scale.

5A These are 'fraction dominoes'. Match the fractions and percentages so that you can put the
dominoes in a straight line.

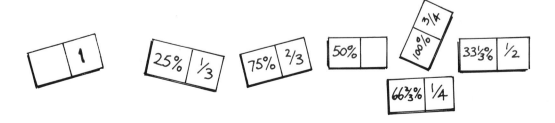

6A In a tray of 20 eggs, 2 were broken.
  a What fraction was broken?
  b What percentage was broken?

7A Petra leaves home at 8 am and returns at 5 pm.
  a How many hours is she away from home?
  b What fraction of 24 hours is this?
  c What percentage is it?

8A This car gains 2 metres in height for every 20 metres it travels up the hill.

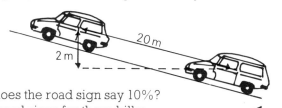

  a Why does the road sign say 10%?
  b Draw road signs for these hills:

  c Which of these is the steeper hill, and why?

9B Out of 150 television sets sold by a store, 140 were colour sets.
  a What percentage of the sets was colour sets?
  b What percentage was black and white?

10B The diagram shows the number of people treated in one day in a hospital accident unit.
  a What was the total number of people treated?
  b Calculate the percentage treated for:
    (i) broken bones
    (ii) sprains
    (iii) eye injuries
    (iv) cuts
    (v) head injuries
  c Add up all the percentages. Why should the total be 100%?

Hospital Accident Unit

Broken bones   Sprains   Eye injuries   Cuts   Head injuries

11B 60 000 tickets are sold for the football cup final. Each of the two clubs playing in the final receives 15 000 tickets. What percentage of the tickets does each club get?

represents one patient

12B Balvinder has to choose five subjects from the eight he is studying this year. His report card looks like this:

English	Maths	History	Geography	French	Science	Art	Technical
$\frac{56}{80}$	$\frac{54}{70}$	$\frac{33}{60}$	$\frac{35}{50}$	$\frac{48}{75}$	$\frac{51}{75}$	$\frac{22}{40}$	$\frac{30}{40}$

  a Can you tell at a glance which subjects he is best at?
  b Calculate all his marks as percentages.
  c Which five subjects might he choose?

USING PERCENTAGES IN PIE CHARTS

1A

2A Last year Caremore High School pupils saved £2500 for charity. The money was divided between several charities, like this.
  a How much did each charity receive?
  b Do you know the full names of any of these charities?

3A The students at a university studied different subjects. 200 students were taking science.
  a How many students were there at the university altogether?
  b How many were studying:
  (i) Computing   (ii) Medicine?

4B In 1985 Strathclyde Regional Council employed 106 553 people. The pie chart shows how they were employed.
  a Check that all the slices add up to 100%.
  b List the job-types in order, from the one employing most to the one employing fewest people.
  c How many were employed as:
  (i) teachers   (ii) police?

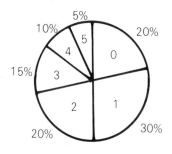

80 pupils in Carbo High School took part in the Duke of Edinburgh's Award Scheme. Their results are shown in this pie chart.
  a 10% of the pupils were awarded the Gold Award. How many pupils was this?
  b How many received Silver and Bronze awards?

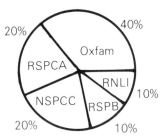

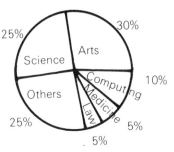

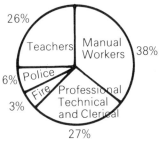

5C The number of goals scored by 80 teams in the English leagues one Saturday were shown in Monday's paper in a pie chart like this.
  a What was the most common number of goals scored?
  b How many teams scored 5 goals?
  c Calculate the total number of goals scored.
  d What was the average number of goals scored?

PROFIT AND LOSS

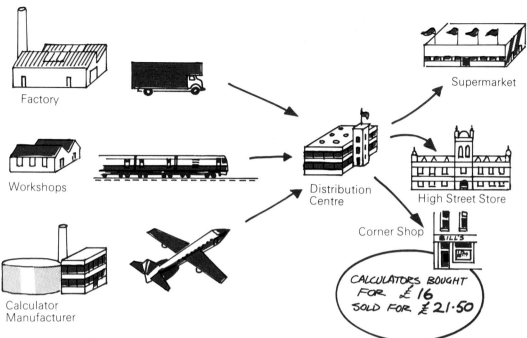

Factory

Workshops

Calculator Manufacturer

Distribution Centre

Supermarket

High Street Store

Corner Shop

CALCULATORS BOUGHT FOR £16 SOLD FOR £21·50

The corner shopkeeper makes a profit of £21·50 − £16 = £5·50 on each calculator.

Exercise 6

1A Find the shopkeeper's profit or loss on a kilogram of each of the items below:

Cost price per kilogram

68p   78p   95p   £2·12

APPLES   GRAPES   ORANGES   TOMATOES

85p   £1·02   £1·32   £1·80

Selling price per kilogram

2A Mr Walker owns a second-hand bicycle shop. Calculate his profit or loss on the following sales:

	Cost price	Selling price
Child's tricycle	£5	£8
Boy's racer	£30	£52
Exercise bike	£34	£51
Girl's racer	£37	£46
Folding bike	£36	£29

163

PERCENTAGES IN ACTION

This car cost the dealer £6675.

a He sold it to Mr Watson for £7900. Calculate his profit.

b Three years later, Mr Watson sold the car for £4250. Calculate his loss.

4A Natasha made toffee for the school fund-raising sale. The ingredients she used cost £6. She divided the toffee into 28 packets, and sold each one for 30p. What profit did she make for the school?

5A Mr Striker bought 50 plastic footballs for £40. He sold them at £1·44 each. Calculate his profit.

6B a A store buys coats at £75 each and sells them at £120.
Calculate the profit on each coat.
b During a sale a discount of 15% is given.
(i) What is the new selling price?   (ii) What profit does the store now make on each coat?

7B Mr Wallace, a mathematics teacher, buys calculators in bulk to save pupils money.
He pays £6 each for them and sells them to pupils for £6·50. He uses the profit to buy spare machines for lending out.
a If he sells 24 calculators, how many extra can he buy?
b If he needs 5 spare calculators, how many will he have to sell?

8C The owner of Bloom'n'Scent flower shop bought 2000 daffodils for £40 and 1500 tulips for £90. He sorted them into bundles of 10. He sold 135 bunches of daffodils at 60p a bunch and 45 bunches of tulips at 90p a bunch. The rest of the flowers were sold off at 35p a bunch. Calculate Mr Bloom's profit.

USING PERCENTAGES FOR PROFIT

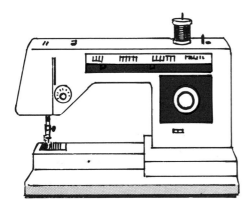

A store bought sewing machines for £175 each, and sold them at £205 each.
Profit on each = £30.
Profit % = $\frac{30}{175} \times 100\%$, based on the cost price
= 17·1%, correct to 1 decimal place.

We will usually calculate profit or loss as a percentage of the cost price, although shops often use the selling price.

1A Calculate the profit or loss, and the percentage profit or loss, based on the cost price of:
  a Pencils costing 15p each, selling at 18p.
  b Books costing £5, selling at £7.
  c Ice cream costing 20p, selling at 35p.
  d Anoraks costing £32, selling at £40.
  e Records costing £3·50, selling at £4.
  f Sweets costing 88p, selling at £1·04.

2A Bottles of lemonade are bought by a supermarket for 50p each, and sold at 65p. Calculate the percentage profit.

3A a This pen was bought for £1, and sold for £2. Calculate the profit, and the percentage profit.

  b This camera was bought for £100, and sold for £101. Calculate the profit, and the percentage profit.

  c Why do shops need to calculate percentage profits, and not just profits in £s?

4A A store buys boxes of crisps for £18, and sells them at £24. Calculate their percentage profit, based on:
  a the cost price   **b** the selling price.

5A Mr Patel owns a furniture store.
  a Calculate his profit or loss on each item.
  b Calculate also his percentage profit or loss on each, based on its cost price.

Item	Bookcase	Bedroom suite	Nest of tables	Coffee table	Dining table
Cost price	£75	£800	£60	£36	£70
Selling price	£90	£1000	£68	£48	£60

6A The school Art Club made Christmas cards for charity. The materials used cost £16. The Club sold 55 cards at 20p each, 40 at 25p each and 30 at 30p each.
  a How much money did they send to charity?
  b What percentage is this of the cost of materials?

7B The owner of a video shop bought some tapes for £3·50 each. How much would he have to sell them at to make a profit of 20%?

8B A stationer bought calendars for £2·25 each. In January he sold them at a loss of 12%. What was his selling price?

9B In the market, Dodger was selling imitation pearl necklaces. He had bought them for £20 each. Often he had to 'think on his feet', so he was good at mental calculations.

FOR A PROFIT OF 5%, HOW MUCH DO I SELL THEM FOR?

HOW MUCH FOR A PROFIT OF 10%? 20%? 25%? 50%? 100%? 200%?

Can you answer all of these mentally?

10B Mr Sharp still runs the school shop. He ordered:

Item	Cost price	Selling price
10 boxes of crisps (50 packets per box)	£60	18p a packet
300 packets of Chewy	£36	15p a packet
280 chocbars	£42	20p a bar
12 dozen apples	£12	12p each
425 tubs of Fruito	£85	22p a tub

All the items were sold. Calculate the percentage profit made for the school shop.

11C A shop bought 80 copies of the TOP 10 Annual for £3·75 each. It sold ten of them at £5 each. To sell the rest quickly the shop reduced the price to a level which gave them an overall profit of 10%. Calculate the reduced price of the remaining copies.

USING PERCENTAGES IN DIFFERENT WAYS

=== *Exercise 8* ===

1A a Do all the slices of this 'pie' add up to 100%?

b What three things is most money spent on?

c Where do you think:
(i) more should be spent
(ii) less should be spent?

National Spending

Industry, energy, trade and employment
Transport
Housing
Defence
Others
Law and order
Education and science
Social security
Scotland
Northern Ireland
Wales
Health and personal social services

3% 4% 4% 10% 14% 6% 6% 3% 2% 13% 31%

2A Alan and his mother each had a set lunch costing £3·40. They gave the waitress 10% of the total as a tip. How much did the waitress get?

3A  This clock radio sells for £22·50, plus 15% VAT (Value Added Tax). Calculate:
a the VAT   **b** the total cost of the radio

4A a £2 pocket money is increased by 50p. What percentage increase is this?
 b What percentage increase is 25p on £1·50?

5A One year there were 10 injuries in Sparks Fireworks Factory. The following year there were 13.
Calculate the percentage increase in injuries.

6A Mr Thomson's business took him to York for four nights. He paid £25 per night in a hotel, plus 5% service charge. Calculate:
a the service charge
b Mr Thomson's bill.

7A Calculate the percentage price reduction for this washing machine.

8A Copy and complete this table which links numbers in fraction, decimal and percentage form. Add three of your own.

Fraction	$\frac{1}{2}$			$\frac{2}{5}$			$1\frac{1}{8}$					
Decimal		0·75			0·3			1·6				
Percentage			25%			120%			$33\frac{1}{3}$%				

9B a Mr Big got a 3% increase in his salary of £25 500. Calculate his increase.
 b Mr Small was given 9% on his salary of £8500. Calculate his increase.
 c Even without doing the calculations you should be able to see that the increases must be the same. Why?

10B The salaries in a company range from £9500 to £19 000. Would it be fair to give them all an increase of 4%? What would the range of salaries be after an increase of 4%?

11B a Would you agree that the new bottle of shampoo has 50% extra in it?
 b If not, sketch the new size as it should be.

12B This microwave oven costs £249·99, plus 15% VAT.

  a Calculate the VAT, and then the total cost.
  b Calculate the cost by multiplying £249·99 by 1·15.
  c Are your two answers the same? Why?

13C Tim's father bought a car for £5000, and sold it three years later for £2400. Owing to inflation the price of new cars rose by 10%, 8% and 5% during these three years. How much money would his father have to find to exchange his old car for a new one?

The old and new sizes of FAB PHOTO prints are drawn to scale.
Is FAB's claim for a 50% increase in area correct?

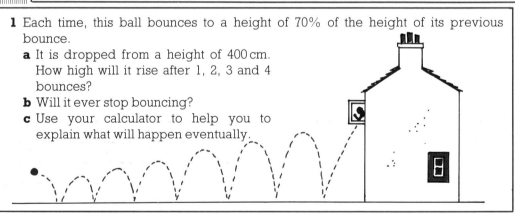

1 Each time, this ball bounces to a height of 70% of the height of its previous bounce.
  a It is dropped from a height of 400 cm. How high will it rise after 1, 2, 3 and 4 bounces?
  b Will it ever stop bouncing?
  c Use your calculator to help you to explain what will happen eventually.

2 The games master at Firth Academy has a problem. He has to award a trophy to the team which has had the most successful season. The teams' results were:

	Games played	Games won	Games lost	Games drawn
Rugby	25	17	7	1
Hockey	20	11	6	3
Golf	12	8	3	1
Basketball	10	7	3	0
Netball	15	11	4	0
Football	18	11	3	4

Investigate ways in which he could choose the winner.
Which team would you choose? Explain why.

1A From fraction to percentage

Write as percentages:

a $\frac{63}{100}$ **b** $\frac{5}{100}$ **c** $\frac{123}{100}$ **d** $\frac{7}{10}$

e $\frac{1}{2}$ **f** $\frac{1}{4}$ **g** $\frac{3}{4}$ **h** $\frac{1}{3}$

2A From percentage to decimal

Change to decimal form:

a 15%   **b** 70%   **c** 6%   **d** 130%

3A A percentage of a quantity

Calculate:

a 40% of 650 g   **b** 25% of £14
c 12% of £2   **d** 65% of 420 m
e 120% of £1000   **f** $2\frac{1}{2}$% of 80p

4A, B Discount

A shop gives a 12% discount on personal stereos priced at £40. Calculate:
a the discount   **b** the new price.

5A, B, C Interest

a Calculate the interest on £25 for 1 year at 7%.
b Which earns more in a year—
£150 at 11%, or £180 at 9%?
c Calculate the interest on £1750 for 4 months at $12\frac{1}{2}$%.

6A, B, C Profit and loss

a John organised a disco. The cost of hiring a hall, lighting and printing tickets was £69·50. He sold 84 tickets at £1.50 each. Calculate his profit or loss.
b Cartons of ice-cream are bought for 28p and sold at 35p. Calculate:
(i) the profit   (ii) the percentage profit.
c A firm's income and expenditure during one month were £18 540 and £21 680 respectively. Calculate the firm's percentage loss, to the nearest 1%.

7A, B, C Using percentages

a A car's price of £5850 is increased by 6%. Calculate:
(i) the increase in price   (ii) the new price.
b A factory increases its workforce from 80 to 96. Calculate the percentage increase.
c Calculate these marks as percentages: 25 out of 40, 44 out of 60, 18 out of 25, 26 out of 35.

8A, B, C

Which of these make sense?

a A discount of 1p in the £ is a discount of 1%.
b Kim scored 105% in her exam.
c The ring was made of 200% pure gold.
d Prices were doubled by increasing them by 100%.
e He gave 110% effort in his work.

CUBOIDS IN ACTION

Mrs Adams has been out shopping. She has put all the things she bought on the table. There are packets of various shapes and sizes.

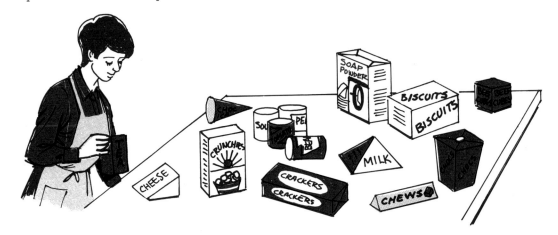

Some of these shapes have special names.

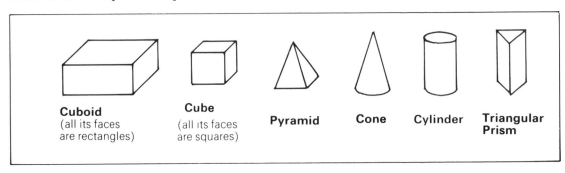

Cuboid
(all its faces
are rectangles)

Cube
(all its faces
are squares)

Pyramid   **Cone**   **Cylinder**   **Triangular Prism**

===== *Exercise 1* =====

1 Copy this table. Fill in all the items Mrs Adams bought.

Cuboid	Cube	Pyramid	Cylinder	Cone	Triangular prism	Other shape
Crackers			Tomatoes		Cheese	

2 Which of these helped you to pick out the cuboids?
   a Their colour   **b** their size   **c** the writing on them   **d** their rectangular faces.

3 a How many faces has a cuboid?
   b How many corners has it?
   c How many edges?
   d What shape is each face?

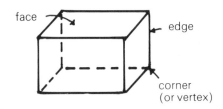

face

edge

corner
(or vertex)

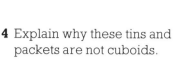
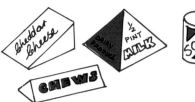

4 Explain why these tins and packets are not cuboids.

5 Many objects in the world around you are in the shape of cuboids.
   a Make a list of the ones you see below.

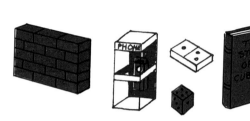

   b Can you think of more examples?

Drawing cubes and cuboids

================= *Exercise 2A* =================

1 Neil found an easy way to draw cuboids. Copy his method and draw your own cuboid.

Stage 1

On squared paper he drew a rectangle for one face of the cuboid.

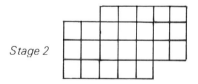

Stage 2

He then drew a congruent rectangle which overlapped the first, like this.

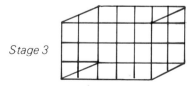

Stage 3

He then joined corresponding corners.

2 Neil noticed an optical illusion in his diagram. He could see the cuboid from above or below. Can you see it in your drawing—first one way, then the other?

3 Follow his instructions for drawing both views.

   a Draw the hidden edges as broken lines.

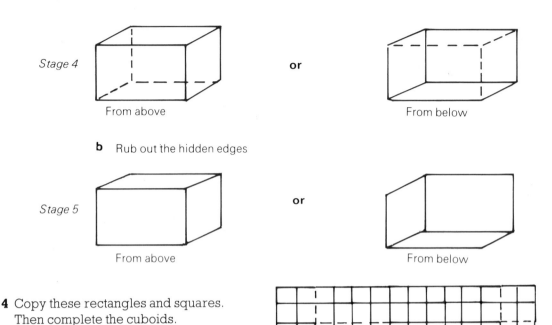

Stage 4

or

From above

From below

   b Rub out the hidden edges

Stage 5

or

From above

From below

4 Copy these rectangles and squares.
Then complete the cuboids.
Colour the different faces.

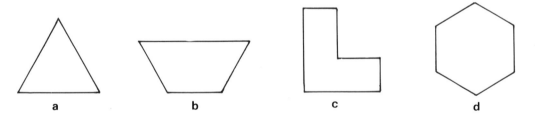

5 Draw two more cuboids of your own, starting with different rectangles. Show the hidden lines in one, and leave them out in the other.

6 Starting with different shapes try to draw some prisms on squared paper. Follow through stages 1, 2, 3 and 4 for each of these shapes.

a   b   c   d

Another optical illusion—or is it?

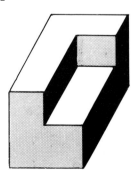

This block of wood has had a piece cut from one corner. But the piece is still there! If you don't believe it, turn your page upside down.

EXPLORING THE CUBOID

1 These solids are made up of wooden cubes of the same size. How many cubes are in each one?

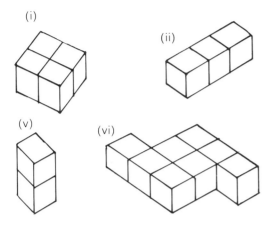

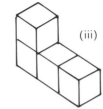

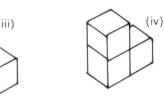

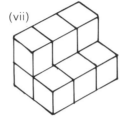

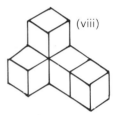

2 For each of the solids above, write down:
  a the number of faces that you can see
  b the number of faces that are hidden.

3 Repeat question **2** for the number of corners in the solids.

4 Take a page of squared paper, and try to cut out a shape which can be folded to make a cube.

Making cubes and cuboids

1 Jack has popped out of his box. The sides of his box have fallen flat on the table.
  Can they be folded up again to form a box? How many squares are there?
  The diagram of squares on the table is called the **net** of the cube they will make.

2 Kate thinks that the net she has drawn could be used to make a dice.
Draw it on squared paper. Make each square 4 cm long, and mark in the dots.
If you are going to glue the edges, draw the flaps.
If you are going to tape the edges, leave out the flaps.
Cut out the shape, and see if Kate is right.

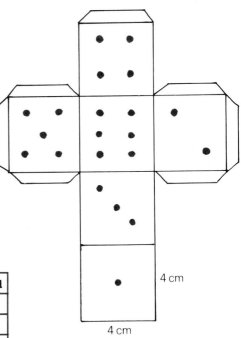

4 cm

4 cm

3 a How many dots are there on the face opposite the one with 2 dots?
  b How many dots are there on the face opposite the one with 4 dots?

4 a Copy and complete this table.

Number of dots on face	Number on opposite face	Total
1	6	7
2		
3		
4		
5		
6		

  b Write a sentence about the results in the table.

5 Here are the nets for five dice. Copy them, and fill in the missing dots.

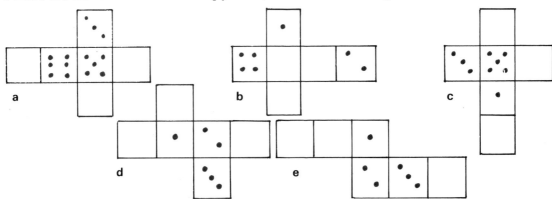

a

b

c

d

e

6 Kate's friend Ruth thought that these four nets could be used to make cubes. Draw them on squared paper, making each square 2 cm long.
Cut them out, and decide which ones will make cubes.

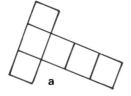

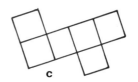

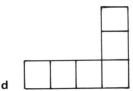

a

b

c

d

Exercise 3B

1 Look at the box of soap powder in Mrs Adams' shopping on page 170.
Kate drew this net for a scale model of the box.
Draw the net on squared paper, with the measurements shown.
Cut it out, and make the box.

2 Calculate: **a** the area of each rectangle in the net in question **1** (ignore the flaps)

b the total area of the net

c the volume of the box.

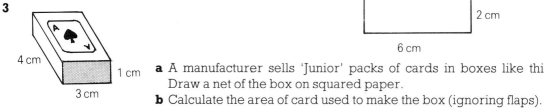

3

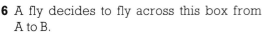

a A manufacturer sells 'Junior' packs of cards in boxes like this. Draw a net of the box on squared paper.

b Calculate the area of card used to make the box (ignoring flaps).

4 Is it possible to make cuboids from the following card rectangles?

a Two rectangles 10 cm by 8 cm, two 8 cm by 4 cm and two 10 cm by 4 cm.

b Four rectangles 5 cm by 3 cm, and two squares 3 cm by 3 cm.

5 Can you find the length, breadth and height of four *different* cuboids which have a volume of 60 cm³? Their edges must be an exact number of centimetres long. Make one of them.

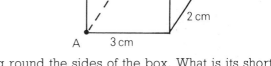

6 A fly decides to fly across this box from A to B.

a Copy the diagram, and draw the line which shows its shortest possible flight.

b The fly returns from B to A by crawling round the sides of the box. What is its shortest route now? *HINT* Draw the net, and mark the points A and B on it.

Exercise 3C

1 Mr Ferguson wants to make a toy-box with a lid that has a hinge at one side. The front of the box will be 100 cm by 50 cm, and the side of the box will be 50 cm by 60 cm. A DIY shop will cut the wood for him.

a List the details of the wood he will need.

b Draw a net for the box, measuring 1 cm on your drawing for 10 cm on the box.

2 Mr Barr is a designer. He has been asked to design small boxes for holding sweets. He decides to make them cube-shaped so that the empty boxes can be used as Alphabet Bricks. Each edge is 3 cm long. Draw this net, cut it out and make one of the boxes. The lid of the box must have a flap to keep it shut.

Calculate the area of material needed (excluding the flap), and the volume of the box.

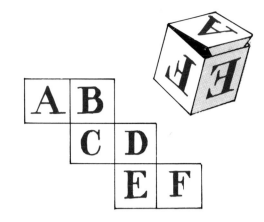

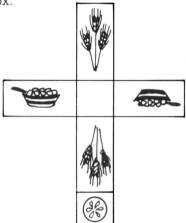

3 Mr Barr has also been given an order for small cereal cartons. The base has to be 4 cm by 5 cm, and the volume of the box has to be 240 cm³.

a Calculate the height of the carton.

b Draw a full-sized net, and use it to make one of the cartons.

4 A cuboid is 30 cm long, 20 cm broad and 10 cm high. Find the size of the smallest rectangular piece of wrapping paper needed to cover it.

---

1 Draw nets for the following items from Mrs Adams' shopping bag.
  a The carton of milk.   **b** The packet of Chews.   **c** The tin of beans.

2 Plan the best way for the sweets manufacturer to stamp out nets of his Alphabet Brick boxes. He uses rectangular sheets of card 36 cm by 18 cm, and wants to waste as little card as possible.

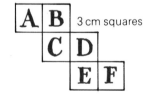

3 Design and make in card a case for holding six stereo cassettes.

Skeleton models

Alan and Mark noticed a wire model of a molecule of salt in the science lab. Alan decided to make his own model, using 12 pieces of straw and 8 pieces of wire pipe cleaner bent in the shape shown. Mark made a model too, using thin canes and plasticine joints.

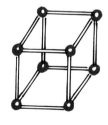

1 Use Alan or Mark's method to make these skeleton models.
Make a list of the lengths and numbers of straws or canes needed for each one.

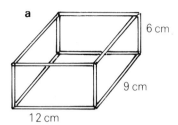

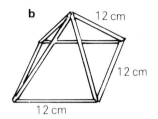

2 These skeleton models are made out of wire. Calculate the total length of wire needed for each one.

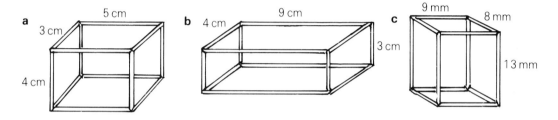

3 a Add together the length, breadth and height of the cuboid in question **2a**. Multiply your answer by 4, and compare this to the length of wire you found you would need in **2a**. Explain why the answers are the same.
  b Check your answers to questions **2b** and **2c** in the same way.

4 Calculate the total length of the rods used for these skeleton models:

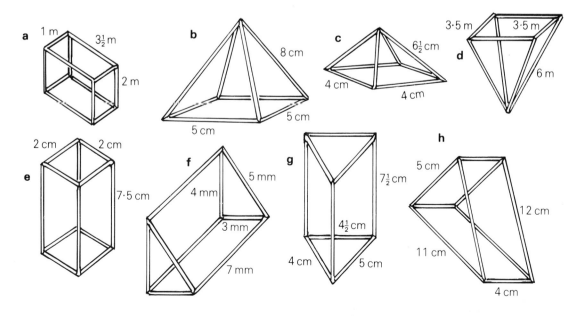

EXPLORING THE CUBOID

1 Meena was given a kit for making a box-kite for her birthday.

When put together, the kite had a frame of thin wooden canes, rigidly fixed at the joints. Cloth was wrapped round the sides, leaving the square top and bottom ends open.

a Make a list of the canes that were part of the kit.

b What is the total length of cane needed to make the kite?

c Calculate the length, breadth and area of cloth in the kit.

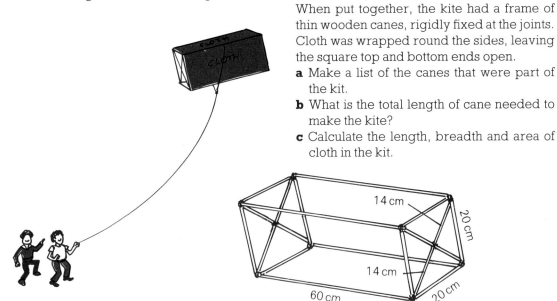

2 A children's playhouse is made of a wire frame covered with painted plastic roof and walls.

a What is the total length of wire needed to build the cuboid part of the house?

b How much more is needed for the roof?

c How many 3-way joints are needed to build the house?

d What other kind of joint is needed?

e The triangular parts of the ends are left open to let light in. What area of plastic cover is needed for the roof and four walls of the house?

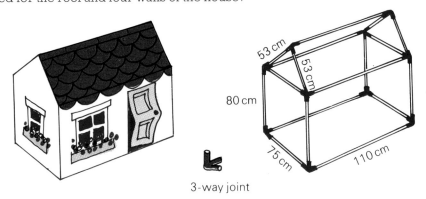

3-way joint

f The manufacturer of the playhouse has to put a list of contents on the box. Make out this list.

Sketch, and then construct, a skeleton model made from six straws, each 8 cm long.

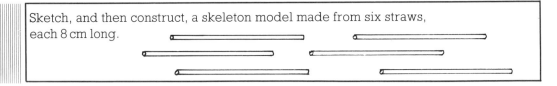

Shoe boxes and match boxes

=== *Exercise 5* ===

1 Miss Walker works in a shoe shop. She is bringing a pair of shoes from the store for a customer to try on. The shoes are in a box.

  a What shape is the box?

  b What shape is the top of the lid?

  c What can you say about the top of the box and the top of the lid?

2 She takes off the lid and puts it on the bottom of the box so that she won't lose it.

  a Will the lid fit as well on the bottom of the box as it did on the top?

  b What can you say about the top and bottom of the box?

  (Remember that two shapes that are exactly the same are congruent.)

3 The customer doesn't like the shoes, so Miss Walker puts the lid back on, and takes the box back to the store.

  a In how many ways could she fit it back in place, with the lid on top?

  b What can you say about the front and back faces of the box?

  c What can you say about the left and right-hand faces of the box?

4 Copy and complete these statements about a cuboid:

  a Number of faces = _____   **b** Number of edges = _____

  c Number of corners = _____   **d** Every face is a_____

  e Opposite faces are_____   **f** All the angles are _____ _____

Explain how these objects work. What properties of cuboids are used?

BURN BRIGHT MATCHES

LIFT

NAMES FOR POINTS, LINES AND ANGLES

You will often find it useful to label points, lines and angles in a diagram.
When this cassette _____ becomes _____ this cuboid ABCDEFGH,

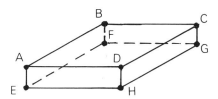

no mathematical information is lost, but faces, edges, corners and angles now have their own letter labels. This makes them easier to discuss.

=========================== *Exercise 6* ===========================

1 In the cuboid above, name:
  a the four top corners   **b** the base
  c the four shortest edges   **d** the angle on top at corner D
  e a line equal in length to AB   **f** the rectangle congruent to CDHG.

2 In this cuboid, name:
  a three lines parallel to AB
  b three lines parallel to AD
  c three lines parallel to AE.

3

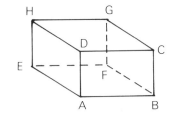

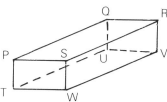

Name:
  a the face which is congruent to PQRS   **b** three edges equal in length to PS
  c three edges parallel to VR   **d** three right angles at corner S.

4

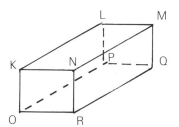

In this drawing, KNRO is a rectangle.
  a Is KLMNOPQR a cube?   **b** Name three edges parallel to KL.
  c Name three faces congruent to KLMN.   **d** Name seven lines equal to OR.

5 A box of tissues sits on a horizontal table.

a Name four vertical edges of the box in diagram (i).

b Are vertical lines always parallel?

c What can you say about the four edges in question **5a**?

d Repeat the above three questions for diagrams (ii) and (iii).

e How many sets of four parallel edges are there on a cuboid?

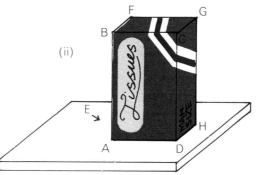

(i)

(ii)

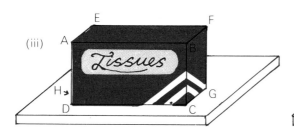

(iii)

A pop-up model

===================== *Exercise 7A* =====================

1 On squared paper cut out a rectangular strip 30 squares long and 8 squares broad. Glue or tape its ends together to make a band like this.

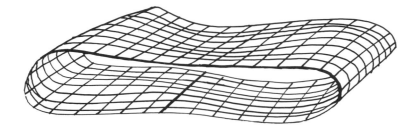

2 Flatten the band carefully, and label the shape you have made as shown below.

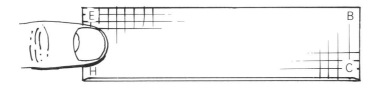

3 What can you say about:

a the lines EB and HC   **b** the lines EH and BC

c the lines EB and EH   **d** the shape EBCH?

EXPLORING THE CUBOID

4 Open out the band, and flatten it again about 4 squares along from the first folds. Label it as shown.

5 a What shape is AFGD?
   b Name three lines equal in length to:
      (i) AD (ii) AE (iii) AB

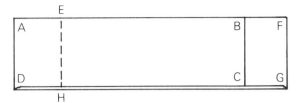

6 Open out the band, and place it on your desk like this.

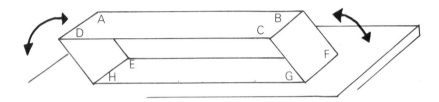

In raising the band to get an open box, some of the faces change shape and others stay the same. As it turns about the 'hinges' HE and GF,

a Which face does not move?
b Which faces change shape?
c Which faces are always rectangles?
d Which faces remain horizontal?

7 How does the idea shown in your open box model help the rocking horse and fairground swing to work?

═══════════ *Exercise 7B* ═══════════

1 Glue or tape your band onto a page of your notebook so that it folds flat as the book closes.
As the band changes shape, so do the 'open faces', and so does the height of the point D above the page. Try this with your model.

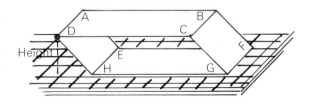

182

2 What path is traced out by D as the model opens out?

3 What can you say about the height of D when the cuboid is formed?

4 What is the shape of the 'open face' DCGH when the cuboid is formed?

5 Which of the following lines change length
as the band changes shape?
  a AB   **b** AC   **c** AD   **d** AE
  e AF   **f** AG   **g** AH

6 As the band changes shape, what other
line always has the same length as:
  a AF   **b** AG?

7 Name two lines that are equal in length to AF only when the model is a cuboid.

8 Repeat question **7** for the line AG.

9 AG, BH, CE and DF are called **space diagonals**.
What can you say about the lengths of the space diagonals of:
  a the cuboid   **b** the band as it changes shape?

Cutting corners

=========================== *Exercise 8* ===========================

1 Lee has joined a woodwork class. She is
practising cutting corners off blocks of
wood. She cuts straight down like this.
  a What will the shape of the cut face, or
    section, of the block be?
  b Draw a sketch to show this.
  c Calculate the number of faces, edges
    and corners on the block, and on the
    piece cut off.

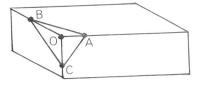

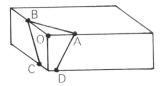

2 Next time she cut the corner at a different
angle. Draw the shape of the block and
the cut-off piece of wood when they are
separated.

3 a How could Lee make sure that she would cut a rectangular section?
  b How could she cut a square section? A sketch might help.

4 Lee then found that she could cut a
triangular section.
  a How could she get a triangle with three
    equal sides?
  b How could she cut the largest possible
    triangle?

5 Is it possible for her to cut a five-sided section?

1 How many cubes are there in this structure?

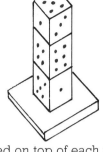

2 Dice are placed on top of each number as shown. What is the total number of dots on the hidden horizontal faces when the column is made up of:

a 1 dice   **b** 2 dice   **c** 3 dice

d 4 dice   **e** n dice?

Looking into every corner

It will help you if you copy this net, and make the cuboid.

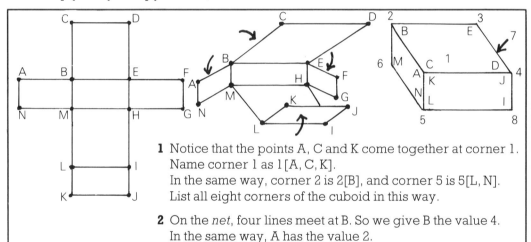

1 Notice that the points A, C and K come together at corner 1. Name corner 1 as 1[A, C, K].
In the same way, corner 2 is 2[B], and corner 5 is 5[L, N].
List all eight corners of the cuboid in this way.

2 On the *net*, four lines meet at B. So we give B the value 4.
In the same way, A has the value 2.
List all the points on the net in this way.

3 The value of a corner is the sum of the values of the points which make it up.
Corner 1[A, C, K] has the value $2 + 2 + 2 = 6$.
Corner 2[B] has the value 4.

4 Copy and complete this table for all eight corners:

Corner	Number of points at corner	Value of corner	Value minus number of points
1[A, C, K]	3	6	$6 - 3 = 3$
2[B]	1	4	
3[E]			

5 What do you notice about the last column of the table?

6 What is the meaning of 3 for the corners of a cuboid?

CHECK-UP ON **EXPLORING THE CUBOID**

1 Copy the diagrams below, including the boxes and the dotted lines.

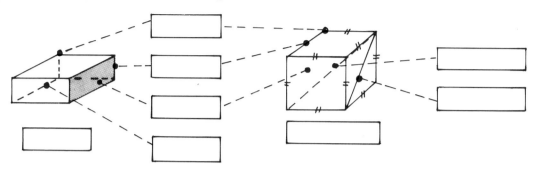

Fill in the boxes in your diagram using these labels:
cube, cuboid, face, edge, corner, hidden line, face diagonal, space diagonal.

2 Copy and complete the following sentences:
 a Both the cube and the cuboid have _____ faces, _____ edges and _____ corners.
 b Each face of a cuboid is a _____.
 c Each face of a cube is a _____.

3 On a cuboid, what is the greatest number
of each of the following that you can see at
any one time?
 a Faces **b** Edges **c** Corners.

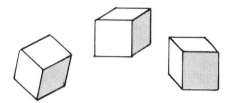

4 Copy the three diagrams below. Use them to show the three sets of four parallel edges to be
found on the cuboid.
The first one is arrowed for you.

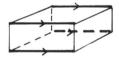 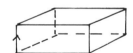 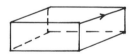

5 How many right angles are there at each corner of a cuboid?

6 Calculate the total length of wire needed to make these skeleton models.

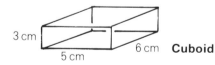
Cuboid

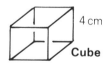
Cube

7 Draw nets of the cuboid and cube in question **6**.

8 Copy the net below, and complete it for the dice shown.

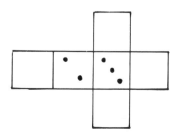

RATIO

Class discussion—comparisons

'I'm 2 feet taller than you, Dormouse', said Alice.
'In fact, I'm *three times* your height!'
'Never mind', said the March Hare. 'I'm only 1 foot taller than you, Dormouse.
I'm just *twice* your height.'
Alice and the March Hare were comparing heights in two different ways— by *subtraction*, and
by *division*.

Alice's height is
three times Dormouse's.
The **ratio** of their heights
is 3 ft : 1 ft, or 3 : 1, or $\frac{3}{1}$.

March Hare's height is
twice Dormouse's.
The **ratio** of their heights
is 2 ft : 1 ft, or 2 : 1, or $\frac{2}{1}$.

A ratio gives the number of times one quantity 'is of another'. The two quantities must be of the same kind.

=== *Exercise 1A* ===

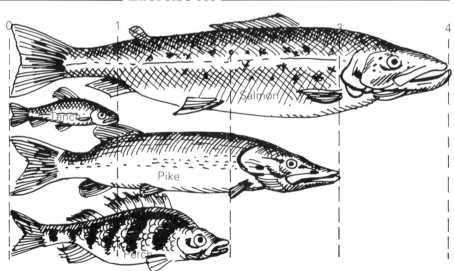

1 Write down the values of these ratios:
  a Length of pike : length of tench
  b Length of perch : length of tench
  c Length of salmon : length of tench
  d Length of salmon : length of pike
  e Length of tench : length of pike
  f Length of perch : length of pike

2 The order of the numbers in a ratio is important. Which of these could be correct?

a Age of father : age of son
= 1 : 3

b Height of car : height of bus
= 1 : 4

c Population of Scotland : population of England
= 10 : 1

d Weight of an elephant : weight of a mouse
= 2 : 1

3

   a   **b**   **c**   **d**   **e**   **f**   **g**

Copy and complete:

Pair of coins	(b, d)	(b, e)	(f, d)	(e, c)	(c, f)	(g, f)	(f, b)	(c, g)	(g, a)	(b, g)
Ratio of values	2p : 10p					100p : 50p				
Simplest form	1 : 5									

4 Alice's height : Dormouse's height = 3 : 1 means that Alice's height is three times that of Dormouse.

Write out in the same way:

a price of pen : price of pencil = 10 : 1

b length of car : length of model = 50 : 1

c weight of baby : weight of sister = 1 : 8

d English mark : French mark = 3 : 4

=========================== *Exercise 1B* ===========================

1 Shirts and blouses are often made from a mixture of cotton and a man-made fibre called polyester. Write these ratios in their simplest form:

a cotton 70% : polyester 30%   **b** cotton 60% : polyester 40%

c cotton 65% : polyester 35%   **d** cotton 50% : polyester 50%

What is your own shirt or blouse made from?

2

Pocket Radio
£7.50

Radio Cassette
£30

Stereo Radio Cassette
£75

Write these price ratios in their simplest form:

a pocket radio : radio cassette

b pocket radio : stereo

c stereo : radio cassette

RATIO AND PROPORTION

3 a 1 cm : 1 m is the same as 1 : 100. Why?

In the same way, write these ratios in their simplest form:

b 1 mm : 1 cm   **c** 1 m : 1 km   **d** 1 kg : 500 g

e 15 seconds : 1 minute   **f** 60p : £2   **g** 0·5 litre : 2 litres

Can you write a ratio in the form 1 : __, or __ : 1?

Example 1   4 : 9 = 1 : 2·25 (dividing each number by 4).
Example 2   5 : 2 = 2·5 : 1   (dividing each number by 2).

════════════════════════ *Exercise 1C* ════════════════════════

1 Copy and complete:

   a 3 : 2 = __ : 1   **b** 2 : 5 = 1 : __   **c** 20 : 40 = 1 : ____
   d 5 : 4 = __ : 1   **e** 5 : 4 = 1 : __   **f** 300 : 200 = ____ : 1

2 Chess is played with these pieces:

     Pawn   Knight   Bishop   Rook   Queen   King

Approximately: 1 Bishop = 3 Pawns   1 Rook = 5 Pawns
                1 Knight = 3 Pawns   1 Queen = 9 Pawns

Choose either 1 : ____ or ____ : 1 to compare the values of:

   a 1 Knight : 1 Queen   **b** 1 Queen : 1 Rook
   c 1 Bishop : 1 Rook   **d** 2 Rooks : 3 Bishops + 1 Pawn

3 Some approximate populations and areas:

   United Kingdom   — 56 million — 240 000 km²
   United States of America — 228 million — 9 300 000 km²
   China   — 975 million — 9 500 000 km²

Use the form 1 : __ : __ to compare:

   a the populations, and **b** the areas of the three countries.

Which is the most densely populated country (most people per km²)?

Gearwheels

════════════════════════ *Exercise 2A* ════════════════════════

1 a Turn A clockwise. Which way will B turn?

   b How many teeth has: (i) A (ii) B?

   c Write in simplest form:
Number of teeth on A : number of teeth on B.

   d Give A 1 full turn. What happens to B?

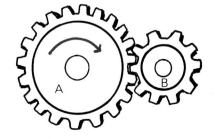

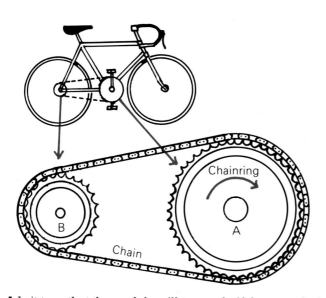

2 A has 48 teeth and B has 24 teeth.
   a Calculate in its simplest form: Number of teeth on A : number of teeth on B.
   b How many times more teeth has A than B?
   c Give chainring A 1 full turn clockwise.
      (i) Which way will B turn?
      (ii) Which direction will the bike go in?
      (iii) How many times will the rear wheel go round?

d Is it true that the pedals will turn at half the speed of the bicycle's wheels?

Exercise 2B/C

1B Two more gears, C and D, are fixed to the bicycle in Exercise 2A, giving:

Gear	B	C	D
Number of teeth	24	20	16

The chainring A still has 48 teeth.

Copy and complete:

Gears in use	Ratio of teeth	Simplest form
A and B	48 : 24	
A and C		
A and D		

2B One full turn of the rear wheel moves the bicycle 2 metres.
   a With gear B, how far will the bike go for 1 turn of the pedals?
   b How many pedal turns would be needed in 120 m?
   c Repeat **a** and **b** for gear D.

3C Travelling at a fixed speed, in which gear (B, C or D) would the pedals be turning: **a** fastest **b** slowest?
Explain your answer.

4C

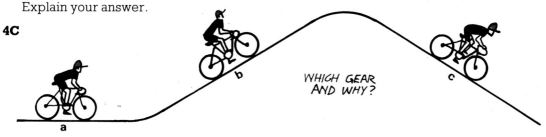

WHICH GEAR AND WHY?

Fair shares for all—proportional division

Colin and Graham buy a box of 24 chocolates. Colin pays £1, and Graham pays £2. How should they share the chocolates?

Colin gets 1 share
Graham gets 2 shares
_____
Altogether 3 shares
_____

Colin gets $\frac{1}{3} \times 24 = 8$ chocolates
Graham gets $\frac{2}{3} \times 24 = 16$ chocolates

=================== *Exercise 3A* ===================

1 '2 parts sand and 1 part cement for this brick wall', thought Denis.
  a What is the total number of parts?
  b What fraction of the mixture is (i) sand (ii) cement?
  c How much of each is needed for 6 cubic metres of the mixture?

2 A coin weighs 12 g. It is made from 3 parts copper and 1 part nickel.
  a What is the total number of parts?
  b What fraction of the coin is (i) copper (ii) nickel?
  c What weight of each metal is used?

3 Susan was making up 10 litres of an orange drink for a party. She decided to use 4 parts of water to 1 part of orange juice.
  a What is the total number of parts?
  b What fraction of the drink is (i) water (ii) orange juice?
  c What volume of each is needed?

4 John and Jim were delivering leaflets in bundles of the same size. John took 3 bundles, and Jim took 2.
  a What fraction of the work did each do?
  b They were paid £20 altogether. How should they share it out?

5 How would you share out this chocolate in the ratios shown?

a 2:1   **b** 3:1   **c** 1:5

6 '2 parts sand and 1 part cement for the brick wall', said Denis. How much of each would he need to make 4 cubic metres?

=================== *Exercise 3B* ===================

1 Sandra wants to buy a home computer costing £210. Her mother promises to pay £5 for every £2 that Sandra can save. How much will each pay?

2 Any goldsmith will tell you that:
  (i) 24 carat gold is pure gold.
  (ii) 18 carat gold contains 18 parts gold and 6 parts alloy.
     What weight of gold is needed to make an 18 carat chain weighing 96 g?

3 What weight of gold would be needed if 22 carat gold was used?

4 Gavin is making apple crumble. He'll need margarine, sugar and flour in the proportions 1:1:2. What weight of each is needed for 360 g of crumble?

5 Denis is now mixing cement, sand and stones in the proportions 1:2:3 to make concrete. What volume of each is needed for 15 cubic metres of concrete?

====== *Exercise 3C* ======

1 Mrs Jones, Mr White, Miss Davis and Mr Baker have formed a pools syndicate. Each week they pay these amounts:
Mrs Jones £1·50, Mr White £2, Miss Davis £1, Mr Baker 50p.
On Saturday they hit the jack-pot, £1 million! How much will they each get?

2 On day trips a school sends 1 teacher for every 15 pupils. What is the largest number of pupils who could travel in a 79 seater bus? Explain why the seats could not all be filled.

3 The sides of a certain right-angled triangle are in the proportions 3:4:5. The perimeter of the triangle is 168 mm. Calculate the length of each side.

Enlarging and reducing

Spider Sam has been increased in the ratio 2:1. The lengths of all the lines have been **doubled**. The scale of the diagram is 2:1, or ×2.

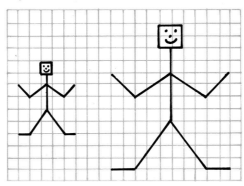

====== *Exercise 4A* ======

1 On squared paper draw diagrams which:
  a increase square A in the ratio 2:1 (scale ×2)
  b enlarge rectangle B in the ratio 3:1 (scale ×3)
  c reduce triangle C in the ratio 1:2 (scale ×½).

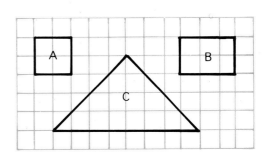

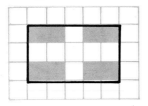

2 Draw and colour this flag on squared paper, with all the lines twice as long as they are in the diagram (scale ×2).

191

3 Anna has two photographs she wants to have enlarged. One is 6 cm by 6 cm, and the other is 8 cm by 5 cm.
  a She has them enlarged in the ratio 2 : 1. What sizes would they be?
  b What would the scale of the enlargement be if the 6 cm by 6 cm photograph becomes 18 cm by 18 cm?

4 This guitar is drawn on $\frac{1}{2}$-cm squared paper.
  Copy it on 1-cm squared paper (scale × 2).

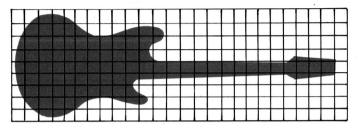

 <!-- sidebar text -->

RATIO AND PROPORTION

=========== *Exercise 4B/C* ===========

Look back at Exercise **4A**.

1B a Calculate the area (in squares) of Spider Sam's head, and also of his enlarged head.
  b Write down the ratio of these areas.

2B a (i) Calculate the area of the square in question **1** on page 191, and the area of its enlargement.
    (ii) Write down the ratio of these areas.
  b Do the same for (i) rectangle B (ii) triangle C.

3B What do you notice about the scales, and the ratios of areas above?

4B The ratio of the side lengths of two squares is 1 : 5. What is the ratio of their areas?

5B The ratio of the side lengths of two squares is 3 : 2. What is the ratio of their areas?

6C The areas of two squares are in the ratio 100 : 1. What is the ratio of the lengths of their sides?

7C The projector enlarges a 35 mm by 25 mm slide to a picture on the screen which is 1·4 m wide.
  Calculate: **a** the scale of the enlargement
       b the height of the picture
       c area of picture : area of slide.

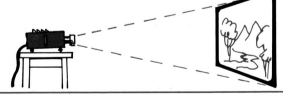

> When planning large storage cubes a designer made models to the scale of 1 : 5. Calculate the ratio of the volume of the model cube to the volume of the real one. Alan said that if the scale was 1 : n, he could write down the ratio of the volumes. Can you?

> Find out how a slide projector works. Describe it with the help of diagrams and calculations.

Maps, plans and models

=== *Exercise 5A* ===

1 This plan of the Simpson's sitting room has a scale of 1 cm : 1 m.
  a Measure the length and breadth of the room in centimetres.
    Then write down its actual size, in metres.
  b Repeat this for (i) the table (ii) the couch.

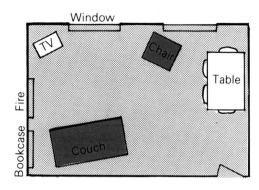

2 Tony is building a model car. The scale is 1 : 20. His model is 8 cm wide.
  a How wide is the actual car?
  b The car is 300 cm long. How long will the model be?

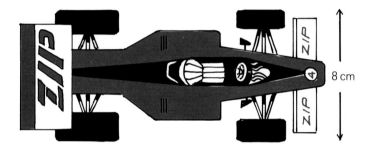

3 The scale of this road sketch is 1 cm : 1 km.
  a How far is it roughly, by road from:
    (i) New Mills to Hayfield
    (ii) Hayfield to Chapel
    (iii) New Mills to Chapel along the A6?
  b It is 14 km from New Mills to Stockport. What distance would this be on the sketch?

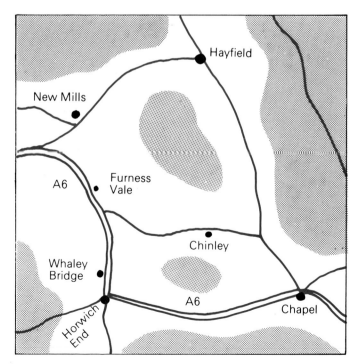

RATIO AND PROPORTION

4

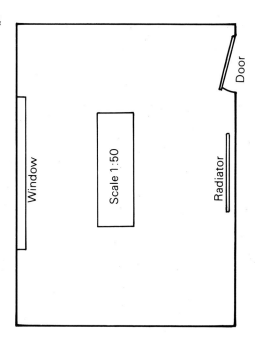

Window

Scale 1:50

Radiator

Door

Mrs Simpson drew a plan of the bedroom to a scale of 1 : 50.

a Measure the length and breadth to the nearest centimetre, and copy the drawing on squared paper.

b Copy and complete this table:

Furniture	Actual size (cm)	Reduced size (cm) (See scale)
Bed	200 by 100	4 by 2
Dressing-table	100 by 50	
Wardrobe	75 by 50	
Desk	50 by 40	

c Draw the furniture to scale on squared paper.

d Cut out the furniture, and arrange it on your plan. Add more items if you wish, and stick them on to the plan.

Exercise 5B/C

1B The scale of this Concorde model is 1 : 200. Its length is 30 cm.

   a What is the actual length of Concorde (in metres)?

   b The wing span of Concorde is 26 m. Calculate the wing span of the model (in centimetres).

2B Michelle's Dad is going to make her a doll's house the same shape as their own house, which is 15 m long, 12 m broad and 9 m high.

   a What scale would be used to make the doll's house 50 cm long?

   b What would the breadth and height of the doll's house be?

3C The scale of this map is 1 : 10 million.

a Copy and complete:

1 : 10 million

= 1 cm : 10 000 000 cm

= 1 cm : _____ m

= 1 cm : ____ km

b How far are the actual distances in a straight line between:

(i) Bristol and London

(ii) London and Glasgow

(iii) Land's End and John O'Groats?

c Manchester is on a straight line between Birmingham and Edinburgh, and is about 100 km from Birmingham. How far would it be from Edinburgh on the map?

DIRECT PROPORTION

Number of apples	Cost
1 ⟷	10p (⟷ 'corresponds to')
2 ⟷	20p
3 ⟷	30p
4 ⟷	40p
5 ⟷	50p
6 ⟷	60p

Doubling the number of apples **doubles** the cost.

Trebling the number of apples **trebles** the cost.

Halving the number of apples **halves** the cost.

The number of apples and their cost increase, or decrease, in the same ratio.

The cost is directly proportional to the number of apples.

1

Copy and complete these tables. The cost is always directly proportional to the number of items of fruit.

a Number of apples	Cost	**b** Number of bananas	Cost	**c** Number of oranges	Cost
1	13p	1	16p	1	18p
2	26p	2	32p	2	......
3	39p	3	......	3	......
4	......	4	......	4	......
5	......	5	......	5	......

2 Prices are not always directly proportional to the number of items bought. Which of these *are* in direct proportion?
   a 2 chocolate biscuits for 24p, or 5 for 60p. (Calculate the cost of 1 in each case.)
   b 2 comics for £1, or 4 for £2.
   c 2 records for £3, or 4 for £5.
   d 1 video tape for £5, or 10 for £45.
   Why are prices not always in direct proportion?

3 Dave walks 12 km in 3 hours.
   At the same speed, how far would he walk in:
   a 1 hour   **b** 2 hours   **c** 5 hours?

4 Anne cycles 80 km in 4 hours.
   At the same speed, how far would she cycle in:
   a 1 hour   **b** 2 hours   **c** 3 hours?

5 Phyllis knits 300 stitches in 10 minutes.
   How many would she knit in:
   a 1 minute   **b** 5 minutes   **c** 15 minutes?

6 A 200 g portion of chips contains 600 calories.
   How many calories would 300 g contain?

7 10 records need 4 cm of shelf space.
   How much space would be needed for 25 records?

8 Here is Mrs Watson's bill at the fruit shop.   Copy and complete Mrs Black's bill.

3 oranges	60p	4 oranges
4 grapefruit	100p	3 grapefruit
6 peaches	72p	5 peaches
TOTAL £2·32		

9 A rate of 6% in a bank gives £90 interest in a year on a sum of money. How much would 7% give on the same sum of money?

A short cut

Peggy was pleased. She had found a short cut. To convince Susan she worked out this problem in two ways:

'In 15 minutes I travelled 18 km. How far could I go in 20 minutes at the same speed?

   (i) In 15 minutes, I travelled 18 km
       In 1 minute, I would travel $\frac{18}{15}$ km = 1·2 km
       In 20 minutes, I would travel $20 \times 1·2$ km
                       = 24 km

  (ii) 15 minutes $\longleftrightarrow$ 18 km
       20 minutes $\longleftrightarrow$ $18 \times \frac{20}{15}$ km (*More* km, so
                            multiply by $\frac{20}{15}$.)
                    = 24 km

RATIO AND PROPORTION

=========== *Exercise 6B* ===========

Use Peggy's short cut for these questions.

1 5 newspapers cost 100p. Find the cost of 9 of them.

2 500 pencils cost £22. How much would 750 cost?

3 15 cassette tapes cost £18. How much would 10 cost?

4 Jenny knitted 300 stitches in 12 minutes. How many would she knit in 20 minutes at the same rate?

5 7·25 dollars can be bought for £5. How many dollars can be bought for £12 at the same rate?

6 John took 150 minutes to travel 186 km. How far would he go in 200 minutes, at the same speed?

7 Mr Jones earns £56·34 in $7\frac{1}{2}$ hours. What would he earn in $37\frac{1}{2}$ hours at the same rate?

8 30 m of carpet cost £250. How much would 24 m cost?

9 Which is the better buy:
  a a 300 g jar of coffee for £4·44, or
  b a 200 g jar at £2·94?

10 Archie's calorie sheet tells him that:
    200 g baked potatoes .... 170 calories
       1 sausage .... 120 calories
    440 g tin of baked beans.... 212 calories
    Calculate the calorie count for his meal of 300 g baked potatoes, 2 sausages and 110 g of beans.

RATIO AND PROPORTION

1 Write down the missing words.

a

The distance travelled is directly proportional to the _____ and the _____.

b The cost of running the fire is directly proportional to the _____ and the _____.

c

The distance on the map is directly proportional to the _____.

2 5 miles = 8 kilometres approximately.
  a How many kilometres (to the nearest km) are there in 11 miles?
  b How many miles (to the nearest mile) are there in 18 km?

3 Renting a TV set for a year costs £105·50. What would it cost for 5 months, at the same rate, to the nearest penny?

4 Which contains more calories per gram?
  a 150 g chips containing 350 calories, or
  b 27 g of crisps containing 140 calories.

5 A train travelled 360 km in 2 hours 30 minutes. How long would it take to travel 300 km at the same speed?

6 A 252·6 m long video tape lasts 3 hours
  a What length of tape would last 4 hours?
  b For how many minutes would 10 m of tape play?

7 2500 Italian lira = £1. How many £s would you need to become a lira millionaire?

GRAPHS OF QUANTITIES IN DIRECT PROPORTION

This table shows the cost of apples given on page 195.

Number of apples	1	2	3	4	5	6
Cost (p)	10	20	30	40	50	60

The points lie on a straight line which passes through the origin.

This is always true for two quantities which are in direct proportion.

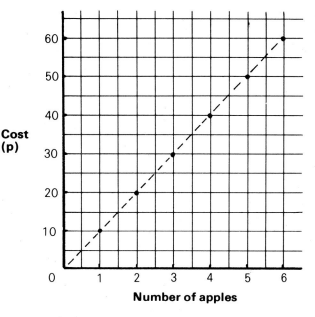

Cost (p)

Number of apples

═══ *Exercise 7* ═══

1 a Copy and complete this table.
b Using the same scales as in the example above, plot the points.
c Draw a line through the points. Does the line pass through the origin?

Number of oranges	1	2	3	4	5
Cost (p)	15	30	45	60	

2 a Copy and complete this table for a car travelling at 40 km/h.

Time (hours)	1	2	3	4
Distance (km)	40	80	120	

b Using scales of 2 squares to represent 1 hour on the horizontal axis, and 40 km/h on the vertical axis, plot these points and draw a line through them.
c Use your graph to find the distance travelled in 6 hours.

3 a Copy and complete this table for interest on money in a bank.

Money in bank (£)	0	100	200	300	400
Interest (£)	0	10	20		

b Using scales of 2 squares to represent £10 interest on the horizontal axis, and £100 in the bank on the vertical axis, plot these points and draw a line through them.
c Use your graph to find the interest on: (i) £500 (ii) £150.

4 a Using scales of 1 square to represent 14 cents on the horizontal axis, and 10p on the vertical axes, plot these two points.

Number of cents	0	140
Number of pence	0	100

b Join the points, to make a conversion graph between cents and pence.
c How many cents equal: (i) £1 (ii) 50p?
d How many pence equal 35 cents?

5 a Copy and complete this table for the number of words read at a constant rate.

Time (mins)	5	10	15	20	25
Number of words	600				

b Draw a graph, and estimate (i) the time for 1000 words (ii) the number of words read in 32 minutes.

INVERSE PROPORTION

Anne can go to school in four different ways.
She can walk, run, cycle, or go by car.

	Walk	**Run**	**Cycle**	**Car**
Speed	walking	2 × walking	3 × walking	8 × walking
Time (mins)	24	12	8	3

TWICE THE SPEED ½ THE TIME
INVERSE OF 2 IS ½

THREE TIMES THE SPEED ⅓ OF THE TIME
INVERSE OF 3 IS ⅓

EIGHT TIMES THE SPEED ⅛ OF THE TIME
INVERSE OF 8 IS ⅛

Increasing the speed in the ratio $\frac{3}{1}$ decreases the time in the ratio $\frac{1}{3}$.
The speed is inversely proportional to the time.

Example. Anne takes 15 minutes to walk to school at 4 mph.
How long would she take at 3 mph?
At 4 mph Anne takes 15 minutes.
At 1 mph she takes 15 × 4 minutes (less speed, so more time).
At 3 mph she takes $\dfrac{15 \times 4}{3}$ minutes (more speed, so less time) = 20 minutes.

━━━━━━━━━━━━━━━━━━ *Exercise 8A* ━━━━━━━━━━━━━━━━━━

1 Iain takes 10 minutes to walk to school at 6 km/h. How long would he take at:
  a 1 km/h   **b** 5 km/h   **c** 20 km/h?

2 Isobel takes 24 minutes to cycle to the youth club at 15 km/h. How long would she take at 18 km/h?

3 Four pupils take 20 minutes to set out chairs for the assembly. How long should:
  a 1 pupil take   **b** 5 pupils take?

4 On Monday Hassan took 60 minutes for his paper round. On Tuesday Robin helped him. How long should they take?

5 A double glazing firm estimated that 2 men could fit new windows in a house in 3 days.
  a One of the men took ill before starting. How long would the job take now?
  b How many men would be needed to fit the windows in 1 day?

Another short cut

Peggy did it again! She calculated that if 25 pupils in the class took 24 minutes to put letters about the school play into envelopes, then all 30 pupils could do it in 20 minutes. Here's how she did it:

25 pupils ⟷ 24 minutes.

30 pupils ⟷ $24 \times \frac{25}{30}$ minutes (less time, so multiply by $\frac{25}{30}$)

       = 20 minutes.

1 Carbo High school has a 6 period day with 60-minute periods. For the same length of day, how long would each period in a 5-period day last?

2 At 300 words a minute, John took 6 hours to read a detective story.
How long should Melanie take to read the same book at 400 words a minute?

3 A contractor estimates that 3 men could rewire the Samson's house in 4 days. To please Mr Samson he puts 4 men onto the job. How long should they take?

4 A car takes 3 hours for a journey at an average speed of 80 km/h. What average speed would it need to do the journey in $2\frac{1}{2}$ hours?

5 A maths department had £600 to spend on textbooks.
  a How many could be bought at £4 each?
  b A few years later the price of the books had gone up to £8 each, but the department still had just £600 to spend.
    How many could be bought then?
    Describe the relation between the cost of a book and the number that can be ordered.

6 Which of these are in inverse proportion?
  a The number of workers on a job and the time it takes them.
  b The time taken for a journey and the speed of travel.
  c The time taken and the distance travelled at a fixed speed.
  d The age and height of a person.
  e The population of a country and the area of land per person.
  f The length of a side of a square and the perimeter of the square.

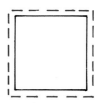

RATIO AND PROPORTION

RATIO AND PROPORTION

1 The population of the United Kingdom is about 56 million, giving a density of about 240 people to 1 km².
Calculate the density if the population fell by 7 million.

2 A space probe travelling at $\frac{1}{2}$ the speed of light would take 8·6 light years to reach the nearest star, Proxima Centauri.
  a How long would it take at $\frac{5}{8}$ the speed of light?
  b How many light years away is Proxima Centauri?

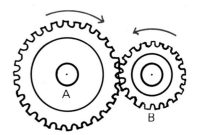

3 Gear wheel A has 30 teeth and is turning 120 times per minute. It engages wheel B which has 20 teeth. Calculate the number of revolutions per minute (rpm) made by B.

4 The wavelength of a radio signal is inversely proportional to its frequency. Radio 1 has a wavelength of 275 m, and a frequency of 1089 kHz. Radio 2 has a wavelength of 433 m. Calculate its frequency.

Take an A4 sheet of paper, and fold it like this:

A4

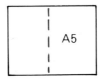
A5

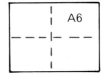
A6

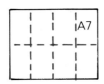
A7

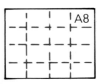
A8

Copy and complete this table, giving the ratios in the form ___: 1, correct to 1 decimal place:

Paper size	A4	A5	A6	A7	A8
Length (cm)					
Breadth (cm)					
Length : Breadth					

What do you find? Compare your answer with the ratio of the diagonal to the side of a square. Investigate the ratio length: breadth for envelopes, newspapers, books, telephone directories, magazines, etc.

INVESTIGATION

CHECK-UP ON **RATIO AND PROPORTION**

1A Ben has 5p, Tony has 15p and Kerry has 25p. Write these ratios in their simplest form:
   a Ben's money : Tony's money   **b** Tony's money : Kerry's money
   c Kerry's money : Ben's money.

2A Share 60p in the ratio: **a** 2 : 1 **b** 3 : 2 **c** 1 : 5

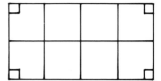

3A On squared paper, draw a rectangle
   with sides one and a half times the size
   of the rectangle shown (scale × $1\frac{1}{2}$).

4A A model of a coach is made with a scale of 1 : 40.
   a If the model is 6 cm wide, how wide is the coach?
   b If the coach is 800 cm long, how long should the model be?

5A If £1 sterling is worth 3·5 German marks:
   what is the value, in marks, of: **a** £4   **b** 10p?

6B At the same rate as in question **5A**, what is the value of:
   a 1 mark, in pence   **b** 200 marks, in £s?

7B 25 g of cheese spread contain 80 calories. How many calories would 15 g contain?

8B A car journey takes 30 minutes at an average speed of 50 km/h. If the speed was increased
   to 60 km/h how long would the journey take?

9C A model aircraft is 12 cm long. The actual length of the aircraft is 8·64 m. The wing span of
   the model is 8·5 cm. What is the actual wing span?

10C An electric fire costs 12p per hour to run.
   a Make a table of costs for 1, 2, . . . , 6 hours.
   b Why would you expect the graph drawn by joining the points to be a straight line?
   c Draw a graph of cost against time. Why does it pass through the origin?

RATIO AND PROPORTION

Reminder

Weighing machine		Equation	
	A balanced weighing machine.	$3x = x + 4$	An equation.
	Remove x weights from each side; the machine is still balanced.	$3x - x = x - x + 4$	Subtract x from each side; we still have an equation.
	Keep half of each side.	$2x = 4$	Divide each side by 2 (or 'cover-up' x).
	There must be 2 weights in the bag.	$x = 2$	The equation has been solved.

The problem:

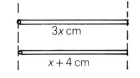

3x cm

$x + 4$ cm

What are the lengths of these straws?

Make an equation $\left\{ \begin{array}{l} 3x\text{ cm and }x + 4\text{ cm are the same length.} \\ \text{The number } 3x \text{ equals the number } x + 4. \\ 3x = x + 4. \end{array} \right.$

Solve the equation $\left\{ \begin{array}{l} 3x - x = x - x + 4. \text{ (Subtract } x \text{ from each side.)} \\ 2x = 4. \\ x = 2. \end{array} \right.$

Explain the solution $\left\{ \begin{array}{l} \text{When } x = 2, 3x = 3 \times 2 = 6, \text{ so } 3x \text{ cm is } 6 \text{ cm.} \\ \text{The straws are } 6 \text{ cm long.} \end{array} \right.$

Check the solution $\quad \left\{ \text{When } x = 2, x + 4 = 2 + 4 = 6, \text{ so } x + 4 \text{ cm is also } 6 \text{ cm.} \right.$

Another problem:

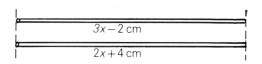

Find the lengths of these straws.

Equation $\{\ 3x-2 = 2x+4$

Solving $\begin{cases} 3x-2+2 = 2x+4+2 & \text{(Add 2 to each side.)} \\ 3x = 2x+6 \\ 3x-2x = 2x-2x+6 & \text{(Subtract $2x$ from each side.)} \\ x = 6 \end{cases}$

Solution $\begin{cases} \text{When } x = 6,\ 3x-2 = 3\times6-2 = 16,\ \text{so } 3x-2 \text{ cm is } 16 \text{ cm.} \\ \text{The straws have a length of } 16 \text{ cm.} \end{cases}$

Checking $\{$ When $x = 6$, $2x+4 = 2\times6+4 = 16$, so $2x+4$ cm is also 16 cm.

═══════════ **Exercise 1   Two short straws** ═══════════

Make an equation for each of the following pairs of equal straws.
Solve it, and then find the lengths of the straws.

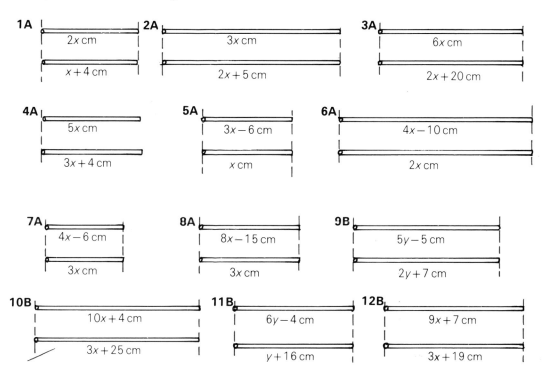

13C Six centimetres more than five times the length of a straw is the same length as 12 centimetres more than twice the length of the straw. Find the length of the straw.

EQUATIONS AND PROBLEM SOLVING

A straw model kit

The problem: Make Model No. 1 using one 60 cm straw length.

Understand the problem ⎰ How should the 60 cm straw length be cut?
⎱ The model needs 6 short straws and 3 larger straws.

Use a letter {

x cm
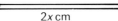
$2x$ cm

Rewrite as an equation {
The 6 straws of length x cm and the 3 straws of length $2x$ cm have to be cut from the 60 cm straw length,
$6x + 3 \times 2x = 60$

Solve the equation {
$6x + 6x = 60$
$12x = 60$
$x = 5.$

Understand the solution {
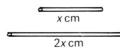
x cm
$2x$ cm

The short straws are 5 cm long.
The longer straws are 2×5 cm $= 10$ cm long.

Check the the solution { $6x + 3 \times 2x = 30 + 3 \times 10 = 60.$

═══════ *Exercise 2 Straw skeleton models* ═══════

Follow the instructions to make these models, always using 60 cm of straw. In each question make an equation, solve it and decide how to cut the straw. All faces with the same shape in each question are congruent.

1A

Model No 2
(Tetrahedron)

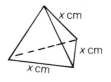
x cm
x cm
x cm

Model No 3
(Cube)

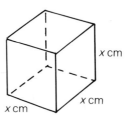
x cm
x cm
x cm

Model No 4
(Cuboid)

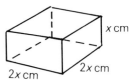
x cm
$2x$ cm
$2x$ cm

Model No 5
(Octahedron)

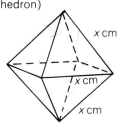

x cm
x cm
x cm

Model No 6
(Triangular Prism)

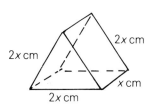

$2x$ cm
$2x$ cm
$2x$ cm
x cm

Model No 7
(Pentagonal Pyramid)

x cm
x cm

Model No 8
(Pentagonal Pyramid)

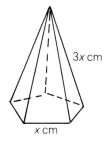

$3x$ cm
x cm

Model No 9
(Octahedron)

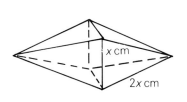

x cm
$2x$ cm

Model No 10
(Cube and Square Pyramid)

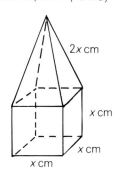

$2x$ cm
x cm
x cm
x cm

Model No 11
(Dodecahedron)

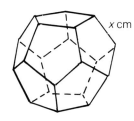

x cm

Model No 12
(Square Pyramid)

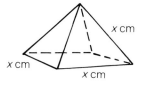

x cm
x cm
x cm

Model No 13
(Octagonal Prism)

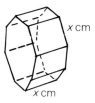

x cm
x cm

3C The straw must be cut in whole numbers of millimetres.

If your calculator gives 3·78 cm, would you cut a length of 3·8 cm or 3·7 cm? Remember that you cannot have *more* than 60 cm of straw for each model. Now use these ideas for models 14–19.

Model No 14
(Triangular Dipyramid)

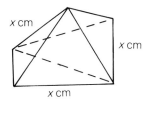

x cm
x cm
x cm

Model No 15
(Hexagonal Pyramid)

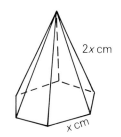

$2x$ cm
x cm

Model No 16
(Cuboid)

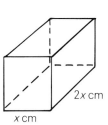

$2x$ cm
x cm

EQUATIONS AND PROBLEM SOLVING

Model No 17
(Triangular Prism)

Model No 18
(Rectangular Pyramid)

Model No 19
(Church)

$5x$ cm

x cm

$2x$ cm

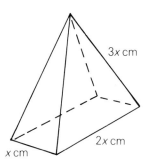

$3x$ cm

$2x$ cm

x cm

$2x$ cm

$3x$ cm

x cm

x cm

x cm

$3x$ cm

$3x$ cm

x cm

4C a If the church (Model No. 19) is made from two straw lengths of 60 cm each, explain how best to cut these into the required number of pieces so that as little straw as possible is wasted.

b Make a similar investigation for three straw lengths.

This is the net of a solid called a truncated tetrahedron.

The net could be cut out and folded to form the solid.

Can you work out, without cutting out and folding, how many edges the solid will have? If you were building a model from straw with one 60 cm straw length what lengths would you need to cut?
Draw an accurate copy of this net, and fold it to check your results.

Triblocks

Here are some building bricks. The numbers on the ends show the number of sections in them.

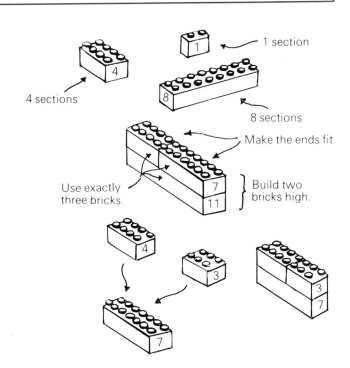

1 section

4 sections

8 sections

Make the ends fit.

Use exactly three bricks.

Build two bricks high.

A *triblock* is made from three bricks, like this:

These three bricks

4   3   7

can make a triblock because
$4+3=7$.

1A Which of these are triblocks, and which are not? Give reasons.

a   b   c   d   e

   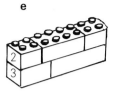

2A Some bricks in question **1A** have their numbers covered. Write down the lengths, in sections, of these bricks.

3A Which of the following sets of bricks can be made into triblocks? Give reasons.

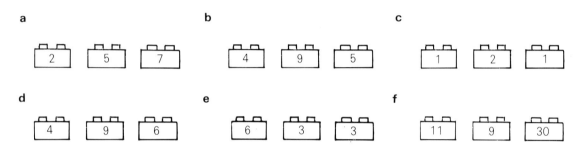

4A 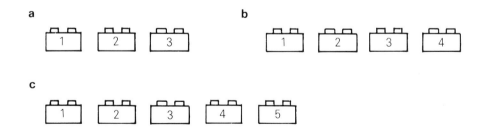 These bricks could build two different triblocks. What are the possible lengths of the third brick?

5B How many different triblocks can be made from each of these sets of bricks?

a

b

c

6C Continue the pattern of questions in question **5B**. Investigate the sequence of answers that you get. Your investigation might help you answer this question:
How many different triblocks can be made from these 100 bricks?

     ...

What does your answer mean?

The problem { These bricks can be made into a triblock. Find the length of the unknown brick.

Understand the problem {

First arrangement (6 as the base)	**Second arrangement** (x as the base)	**Third arrangement** (4 as the base)
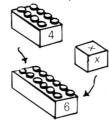	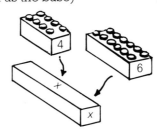	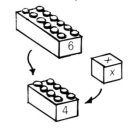

Rewrite as an equation {

$x + 4 = 6$

$x = 4 + 6$

$x + 6 = 4$

Solve

$\begin{cases} x + 4 - 4 = 6 - 4 \\ x = 2 \end{cases}$

$x = 10$

$\begin{aligned} x + 6 - 6 &= 4 - 6 \\ x &= -2 \end{aligned}$

Understand the solution { The unknown brick has a length of 2 sections.

The unknown brick has a length of 10 sections.

A brick cannot have a length of -2 sections. This arrangement is impossible.

Check {

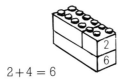

$2 + 4 = 6$

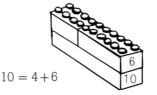

$10 = 4 + 6$

The 6 section brick is longer than the 4 section base of the wall!

========= *Exercise 4   Unblocking* =========

For each of these triblocks write an equation, solve it, then check your answer.

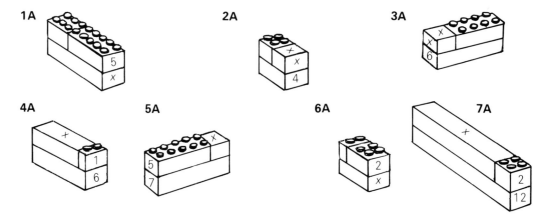

1A

2A

3A

4A

5A

6A

7A

In questions **8A–13B**, triblocks can be made from the three bricks shown. Write down an equation for each possible way that you could put the bricks together. Solve the equation, and say what the solution tells you about the length of the unknown brick.

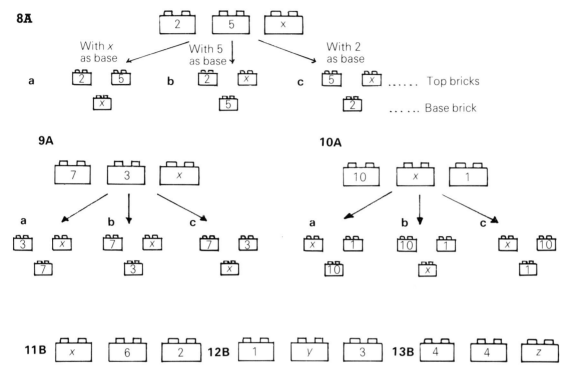

11B x | 6 | 2 **12B** 1 | y | 3 **13B** 4 | 4 | z

14B Find the number of different triblocks that can be made from each of these sets of bricks, using all the possible values of x. Explain your answers, using equations.

a 1 | 2 | x

b 1 | 2 | 3 | x

15C Extend question **14B** by considering the number of different triblocks that can be made from:

a 1 | 2 | 3 | 4 | x

b 1 | 2 | 3 | 4 | 5 | x

Investigate the sequence of numbers that you get from these answers.

16C Investigate the possibilities of making triblocks from these rows of bricks, finding all the possible values of *x*.

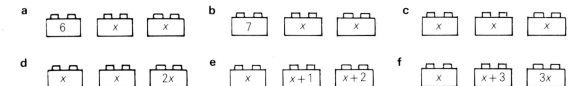

a 6 | *x* | *x*
b 7 | *x* | *x*
c *x* | *x* | *x*

d *x* | *x* | 2*x*
e *x* | *x*+1 | *x*+2
f *x* | *x*+3 | 3*x*

More equations

The problem
{ A triblock can be made from these bricks:

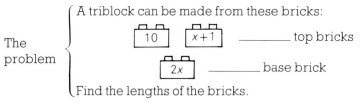

10 | *x*+1 ——————— top bricks

2*x* ——————— base brick

Find the lengths of the bricks.

Equation { $2x = x + 1 + 10$

Solving { $2x = x + 11$
$2x - x = x - x + 11$

Solution { $x = 11$

Meaning of the solution
{ *x*+1 $11 + 1 = 12$

2*x* $2 \times 11 = 22$

The three bricks have lengths of 10, 12 and 22 sections.

Check   { $10 + 12 = 22$

═══════════════ **Exercise 5   Round the triblock** ═══════════════

Each set of bricks can make a triblock, *arranged as shown*. Find the lengths of the bricks by making equations, and solving them.

1A

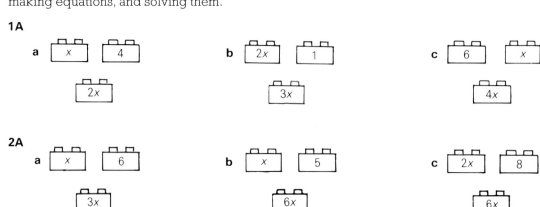

a   *x* | 4   **b**   2*x* | 1   **c**   6 | *x*

2*x*   3*x*   4*x*

2A

a   *x* | 6   **b**   *x* | 5   **c**   2*x* | 8

3*x*   6*x*   6*x*

EQUATIONS AND PROBLEM SOLVING

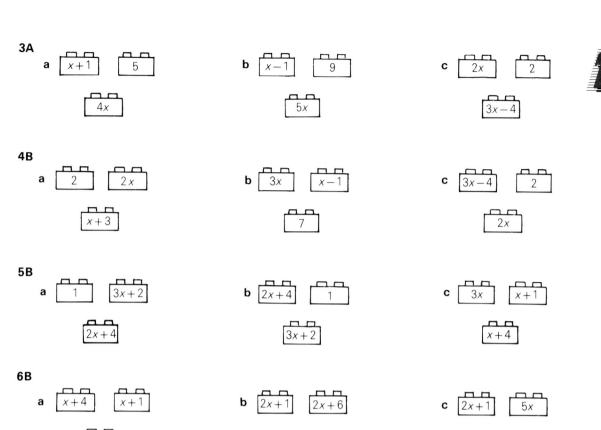

3A

a $x+1$ 5
  $4x$

b $x-1$ 9
  $5x$

c $2x$ 2
  $3x-4$

4B

a 2 $2x$
  $x+3$

b $3x$ $x-1$
  7

c $3x-4$ 2
  $2x$

5B

a 1 $3x+2$
  $2x+4$

b $2x+4$ 1
  $3x+2$

c $3x$ $x+1$
  $x+4$

6B

a $x+4$ $x+1$
  $3x$

b $2x+1$ $2x+6$
  $5x$

c $2x+1$ $5x$
  $2x+6$

7C Investigate the possibilities for making triblocks from:

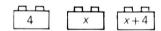

4 x $x+4$

8C

These six bricks all have different lengths.

They are all less than 11 sections long. It is impossible to make a triblock from them. Can you find their lengths?

9C Find the largest set of bricks of different lengths of 20 sections or less, from which it is impossible to make a triblock.

A triblock wall

Investigate how to build triblock walls. Part of one is shown here. The number of sections in each brick is marked on its *side*. Write the length of each wall you investigate, in sections, beside it, and also its height, in bricks.

Colour the walls if you wish.

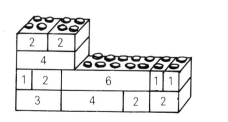

EQUATIONS AND PROBLEM SOLVING

213

CHECK-UP ON **EQUATIONS AND PROBLEM SOLVING**

These cards are in the wrong order. Sort them.

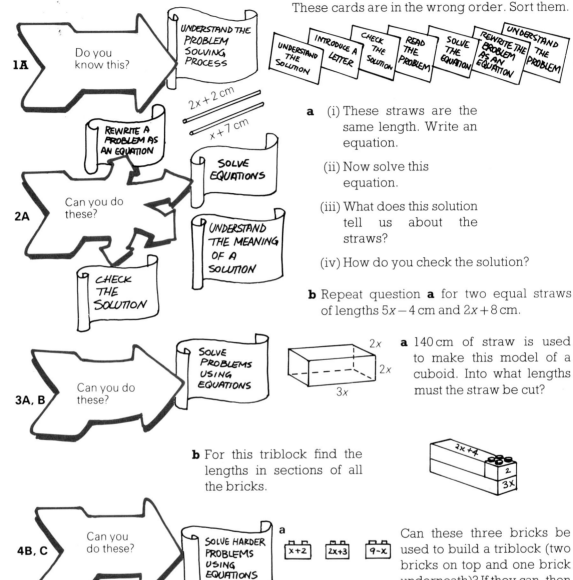

1A Do you know this?

UNDERSTAND THE PROBLEM SOLVING PROCESS

UNDERSTAND THE SOLUTION

INTRODUCE A LETTER

CHECK THE SOLUTION

READ THE PROBLEM

SOLVE THE EQUATION

REWRITE THE PROBLEM AS AN EQUATION

UNDERSTAND THE PROBLEM

REWRITE A PROBLEM AS AN EQUATION

2x + 2 cm

x + 7 cm

SOLVE EQUATIONS

2A Can you do these?

UNDERSTAND THE MEANING OF A SOLUTION

CHECK THE SOLUTION

a (i) These straws are the same length. Write an equation.

(ii) Now solve this equation.

(iii) What does this solution tell us about the straws?

(iv) How do you check the solution?

b Repeat question **a** for two equal straws of lengths $5x - 4$ cm and $2x + 8$ cm.

3A, B Can you do these?

SOLVE PROBLEMS USING EQUATIONS

$2x$

$2x$

$3x$

a 140 cm of straw is used to make this model of a cuboid. Into what lengths must the straw be cut?

b For this triblock find the lengths in sections of all the bricks.

$2x + 4$

2

$3x$

4B, C Can you do these?

SOLVE HARDER PROBLEMS USING EQUATIONS

a $x+2$ $2x+3$ $9-x$

Can these three bricks be used to build a triblock (two bricks on top and one brick underneath)? If they can, then find all the possible lengths for the bricks.

b Bricks of length 4, 6, 6 and 8 are arranged in a square:

The outside perimeter is 32 sections.

In a similar way a rectangle is made from four bricks of lengths x, $x-2$, $2x-2$, $x+2$ sections with an outside perimeter of 36 sections.

Find the lengths of the four bricks, and draw the rectangle.

1A How many triangles can you count in each picture?

2A In real life, which of these triangles is smallest, and which largest?

3A Copy and complete this table for the types of triangle in each picture.

Picture	Only 2 equal sides	3 equal sides	3 acute angles	1 right angle	1 obtuse angle
(i) (ii) (iii) (iv) ⋮	✓	✓	✓		

4A a Look at picture (vii) above. The bar across the gate makes it stronger. Why is this?

  b Where else have you seen triangles used to make things stronger?

5A

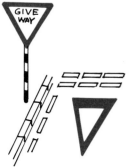

Why is the triangle on the road longer than the one on the road sign? Keep a lookout for these and other road signs with triangles round them.

RIGHT-ANGLED TRIANGLES

1A 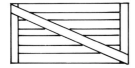 This rectangular gate has been drawn with single lines instead of bars.

    a How many triangles can you count in the line drawing?
    b How many of them have a right angle?
    Each of these triangles is called a **right-angled triangle**.

2A  Repeat question **1** for the line drawing of the St Andrew's cross.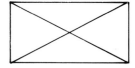

3A The drawings of the gate and the flag both contain a rectangle with a diagonal, like this:
    a Name the two right-angled triangles.
    b Name the right angles in these triangles.

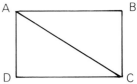

4A a Take a rectangular sheet of paper, or cut out a rectangle from squared paper.
    b Cut it along a diagonal so that you have two right-angled triangles.

    c Tear off the corners of one of the triangles, and fit them together like this. How many degrees do the three angles make when you add them together?

    d Make three folds in the other triangle as shown below. How many degrees do the three angles of this triangle make?

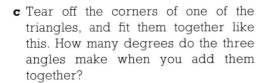

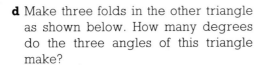

5A a On squared paper draw a right-angled triangle with sides at least 5 cm long. Measure the sizes of its angles. Add all three together.

   b Repeat **a** for a different right-angled triangle. What do you find?

6B Study the diagrams. Then copy and complete what follows.

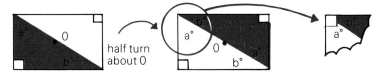

half turn about 0

Each angle of a rectangle = _____°

So $a° + b° =$ _____°

The three angles of each right-angled triangle add up to $a° + b° +$ _____°

$=$ _____° $+$ _____°

$=$ _____°

> **The angles of a right-angled triangle add up to 180°**

=========================== *Exercise 3* ===========================

1A Which of these triangles could be right-angled?

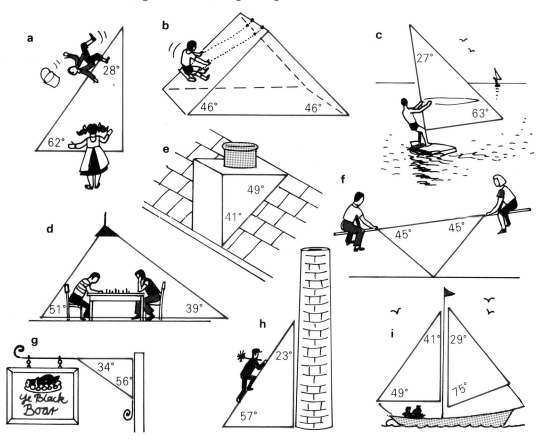

2A Calculate the sizes of the angles marked with letters; for example $a° = 30°$.

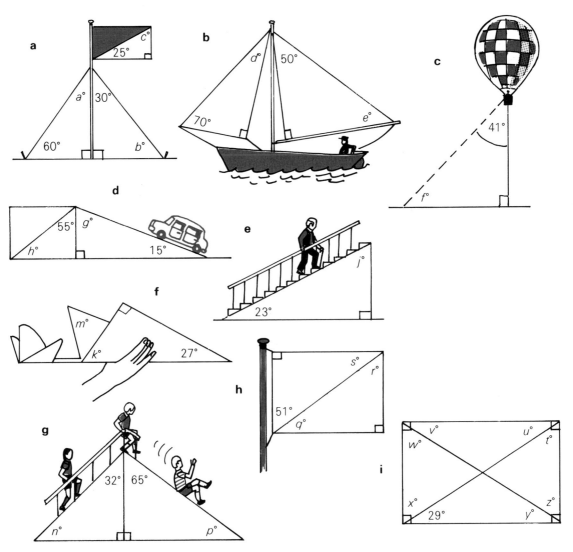

3B For the diagrams below make equations, and find the numbers x and y stand for. Then write down the sizes of the angles.

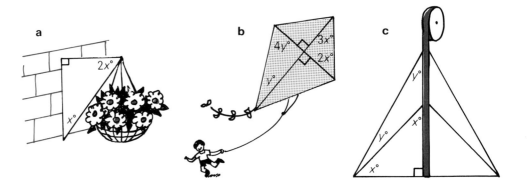

TRIANGLES EVERYWHERE

AREA—FROM RECTANGLE TO TRIANGLE

Rachel and Marc were talking about how to calculate area. Rachel said that rectangles were easy—'just length × breadth'. Marc then said that right-angled triangles were easy too—'half the area of the rectangle'.

Area of rectangle $= 20 \times 10 \, \text{cm}^2$
$= 200 \, \text{cm}^2$
So area of triangle $= \frac{1}{2} \times 200 \, \text{cm}^2$
$= 100 \, \text{cm}^2$

A formula

Area of rectangle $=$ length × breadth
Area of triangle $= \frac{1}{2}$ base × height $= \frac{1}{2}b \times h = \frac{1}{2}bh$.

The area of a right-angled triangle $= \frac{1}{2}$ base × height

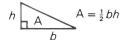

Exercise 4

1A Copy these right-angled triangles on squared paper, and complete a rectangle for each one. Then calculate the areas of the triangles.

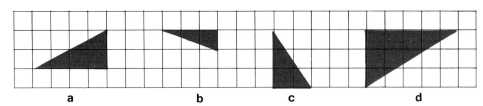

a   b   c   d

2A Calculate the area of each shaded right-angled triangle.

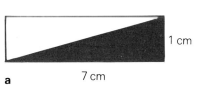

a   7 cm   1 cm

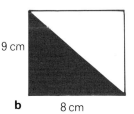

9 cm   b   8 cm

13 cm
c   15 cm

3A Calculate the areas of these right-angled triangles.

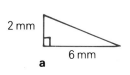

2 mm   6 mm   a

15 cm   8 cm   b   12 mm

12 mm   c

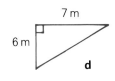

7 m   6 m   d

4A Calculate the area of each sail.

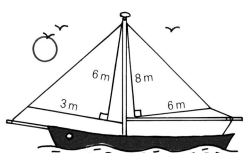

6 m 8 m
3 m 6 m

5A What area has to be painted below the stairs?

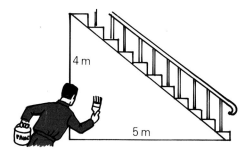

4 m
5 m

6A The area below the slide is made of two right-angled triangles.
Calculate **a** the area of each triangle
b the total area below the slide.

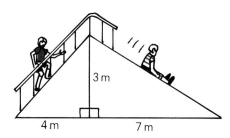

3 m
4 m 7 m

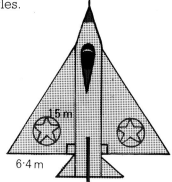

5 m
6·4 m

7A Find the *total* wing area of the plane.

8A Why might people need to know the different areas you have calculated in questions **4A–7A**?

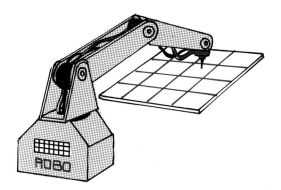

9A A cutting machine has been programmed to cut out a triangular piece of metal.
The coordinates of the triangle's corners are (1, 1), (7, 1) and (7, 10).
Calculate the area of metal cut out.

10B The same machine is programmed to cut out a square.
The coordinates of its corners are (6, 1), (10, 5), (6, 9) and (2, 5).
a Plot the points, and join them to make the square.
b Join the diagonals, and calculate the area of each small triangle.
c Calculate the area of the square.
d Calculate the length of a side of the square as accurately as you can.

11C The height of a right-angled triangle is twice its base. Calculate the height and base if its area is: **a** $100 \, cm^2$ **b** $64 \, mm^2$ **c** $1 \, m^2$ **d** $20 \, cm^2$

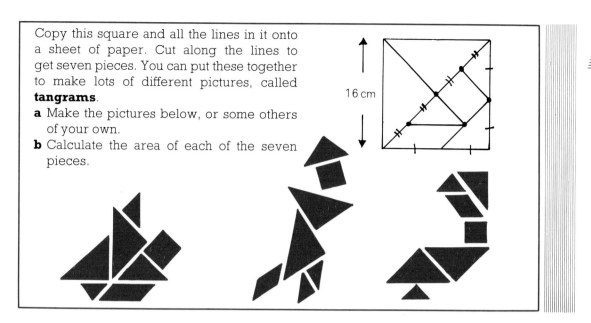

Copy this square and all the lines in it onto a sheet of paper. Cut along the lines to get seven pieces. You can put these together to make lots of different pictures, called **tangrams**.

a Make the pictures below, or some others of your own.

b Calculate the area of each of the seven pieces.

16 cm

ISOSCELES TRIANGLES

The steps used by ABC Airways have sides which are congruent right-angled triangles. When they are not in use, two sets of steps are parked back-to-back.

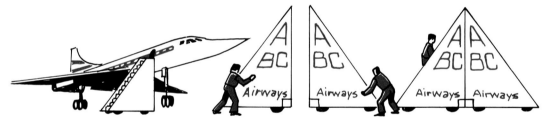

Put together, the two right-angled triangles make an **isosceles triangle**.
The line joining the two right-angled triangles
is an **axis of symmetry**.

═══════════════════ *Exercise 5* ═══════════════════

1A a Copy this figure, and fill in as many lengths and angles as you can. Remember that BD is an axis of symmetry.

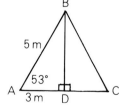

b Draw the triangle again, this time without its axis of symmetry BD. Mark in the lengths of the sides and the sizes of the angles.

An isosceles triangle has one axis of symmetry.
It has two equal sides, and two equal angles.

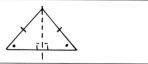

2A a Draw a large isosceles triangle on squared paper.
   b Cut it out, and fold it along its axis of symmetry.
   c Check that it has two equal sides and two equal angles.
   d In how many ways will it fit its outline?

3A Sketch each of the isosceles triangles below. Fill in all the angles, and add them up like this:

Angle at A = 40°
Angle at B = 70°
Angle at C = 70°
_____
Sum of angles of triangle = 180°

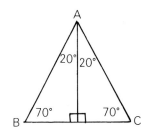

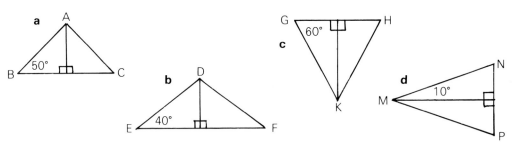

4A Sketch these isosceles triangles, and fill in as many lengths and angles as you can.

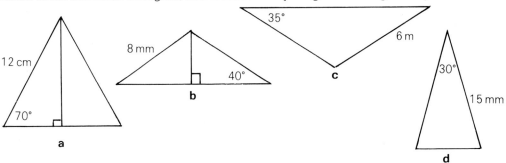

5B

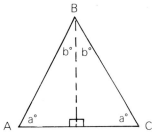

Copy and complete:
The 3 angles of a right-angled triangle add up to _____°.
So $a° + b° =$ _____°
and $a° + b° + b° + a° =$ _____°

$\angle A + \angle B + \angle C =$ _____°.
The angles of triangle ABC add up to _____°.

> **The angles of an isosceles triangle add up to 180°.**

6B Draw a right-angled isosceles triangle. Fill in the sizes of all of its angles.

7B B is the point $(-2, 0)$ and C is $(2, 0)$. A is a point (x, y) so that AB = AC.
   a Name: (i) the axis of symmetry of triangle ABC
             (ii) two equal angles in the triangle.
   b What can you say about the numbers x and y stand for?

1A Sketch the isosceles triangles below, and fill in the sizes of all the angles.

a 70°

b 28°

c 50°

d 110° 110°

2A Sketch the isosceles triangles below, and fill in as many lengths and angles as you can.

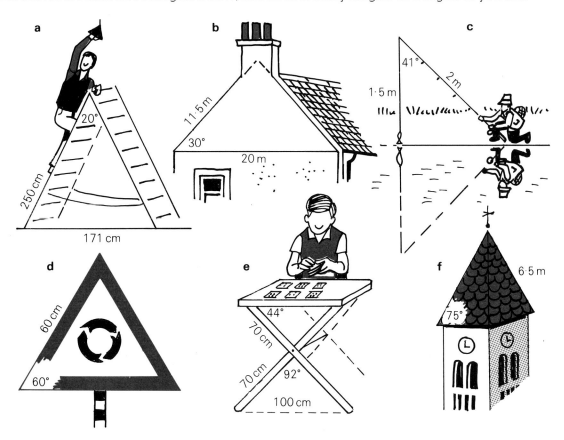

a 20° 250 cm 171 cm

b 11·5 m 30° 20 m

c 41° 2 m 1·5 m

d 60 cm 60°

e 44° 70 cm 70 cm 92° 100 cm

f 6·5 m 75°

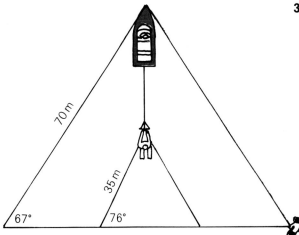

70 m

35 m

67°   76°

3B A speed-boat goes out to sea at right angles to the shore, pulling a water skier. The two wakes behind the boat and the skier both make isosceles triangles with the shore.

a What line do the boat and skier follow?

b Make a sketch, and mark in as many lengths and angles as you can.

c How far from the man on the shore is the front of the boat?

4C The canopy above the door of the Hair-dresser's opens out as shown in the picture. There are congruent isosceles triangles on the side. Fully open, ∠ABC is a right angle.

a Calculate the size of each angle in the triangles, when fully opened.

b Calculate the size of each angle when the canopy is half open, assuming that the shapes stay as triangles, and the canopy opens uniformly.

c Repeat **a** and **b** for a canopy with four triangles in its side.

d Can you do it for five triangles?

e Brainstormer! Try it for *n* triangles.

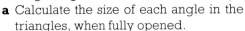

A
B
C

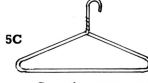

5C   A company makes wire coat hangers, using 1 metre of wire per hanger.
Fifteen centimetres of wire are needed for the hook.

a Some hangers are 40 cm wide. How much wire is needed for each shoulder?

b Others are 42 cm wide. How much wire is needed for each shoulder in this case.

c The manager asks for a width of 43 cm. The foreman says 'Impossible'. Why does he say this?
The manager insists. How can the foreman solve the problem?

THE AREA OF AN ISOSCELES TRIANGLE

===== *Exercise 7* =====

1A Fold a rectangular piece of paper along one of its axes of symmetry. This makes a smaller rectangle.

Cut this smaller rectangle along one diagonal.

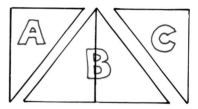

Open it out. You have made three triangles.

a What kind of triangles are triangles A and C?
b What kind of triangle is triangle B?
c You should be able to place A and C so that they cover B exactly. Do this.
d Thinking about *area*, what can you say about A, C and B?
e What fraction of the original rectangle is the isosceles triangle B?

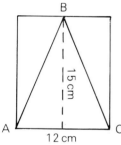

2A The dotted line is an axis of symmetry.
   a Write down the length and breadth of the rectangle.
   b Calculate the area of the rectangle.
   c Now calculate the area of triangle ABC.

3A Repeat parts **a**, **b**, and **c** of question **2A** for the following:

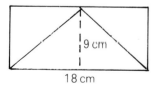

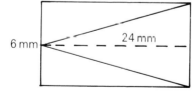

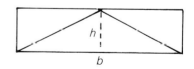

The area of an isosceles triangle $= \frac{1}{2}$ base × height $= \frac{1}{2}bh$

4A In each of the following, calculate the area of the rectangle, and then the area of the isosceles triangle.

a
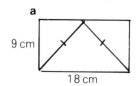

b
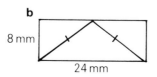

c

d
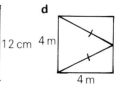

5A Calculate the area of each isosceles triangle.

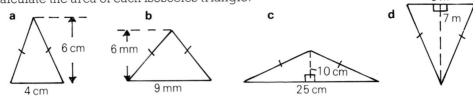

a — 6 cm / 4 cm
b — 6 mm / 9 mm
c — 10 cm / 25 cm
d — 5 m / 7 m

6A Calculate the areas of these isosceles triangles.

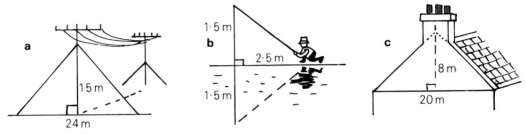

a — 15 m / 24 m
b — 1·5 m / 2·5 m / 1·5 m
c — 8 m / 20 m

7A a A is the point (2, 1), B is (6, 1) and C is (4, 7).
  (i) What kind of triangle is ABC?
  (ii) Calculate the area of the triangle.
  b D is the point (4, 0). Calculate the areas of:
  (i) triangle ABD   (ii) the shape ADBC.

8B Calculate the areas of these shapes:

a — 5 cm / 5 cm / 4 cm / 3 cm / 3 cm
b — 25 m / 25 m / 24 m / 14 m / 25 m / 25 m
c — 8 cm / 6 cm / 3 cm
d — 15 mm / 4 mn / 12 mm

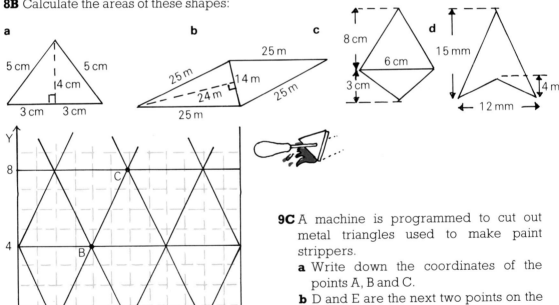

9C A machine is programmed to cut out metal triangles used to make paint strippers.
  a Write down the coordinates of the points A, B and C.
  b D and E are the next two points on the line ABC. What are their coordinates?
  c Calculate the area of each metal triangle.
  d Notice that there is wastage along the sides. What is the total area of metal wasted in each strip.
  e The triangles have to be isosceles to make sure that the pressure is even when the paint stripper is used. Is there an isosceles triangle which would avoid wastage? By moving the positions of A, F and G in the bottom strip, you can get 6 isosceles triangles instead of five! Each triangle will have the same area as the original triangles, but there will be no wastage. Draw this strip and give the new coordinates of A, F and G.

EQUILATERAL TRIANGLES

Jill can change the angle of her drawing board any way she likes. But the easel's legs will always make an isosceles triangle with the ground.

In one position the distance between the feet (B, C) is the same as the lengths of the legs (AB, AC).

This is called an **equilateral triangle**. An equilateral triangle is a special kind of isosceles triangle.

Exercise 8

Equilateral

Isosceles

Isosceles

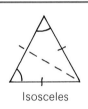

Isosceles

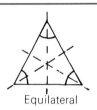

Equilateral

1A a How many axes of symmetry has an equilateral triangle?
  b What do the angles of an isosceles triangle add up to?
  c What size is each angle in an equilateral triangle?

2A a Draw an equilaterial triangle of side 8 cm.
  You may use compasses . . .   or a protractor . . .

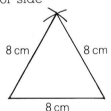

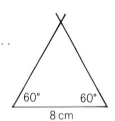

  b Cut it out, and fold it to check the 3 axes of symmetry.
  c Find how many ways it will fit into its space.

An equilateral triangle has three equal sides and three equal angles. Each angle is 60°. It has three axes of symmetry.

3A Where can you see equilateral triangles:
  a in an orchestra   **b** on road signs   **c** in other places?

4A a Draw a circle with radius 3 cm.

b Use your compasses to mark points on the circle 3 cm apart, as shown. Join the points to make a hexagon.

c Write down the length of each of its sides.

d Calculate the sizes of all the angles of the hexagon.

HINT Join each corner to the centre of the circle first.

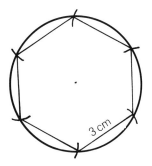

5B A record is playing on a turntable. The record label has an equilateral triangle printed on it.

a If the record spins once, how many times will the triangle be in a position like the one in the picture?

b This tells you that an equilateral triangle has another kind of symmetry. What kind?

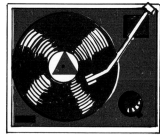

c

Here is a diagram of the label.
Calculate the size of each angle at O.

6B Matthew is setting up the balls for a game of snooker.

a Without measuring, he knows that the triangular frame is equilateral. How does he know this?

b What is the size of each angle?

c How many different ways can the frame fit over the arrangement of snooker balls?

7C Which of the following are possible? A triangle which:

a has 2 right angles

b has one obtuse angle

c is isosceles and right-angled

d is equilateral and right-angled

c is equilateral and has exactly 2 axes of symmetry

f is isosceles and obtuse-angled.

---

1 Draw a net of equilateral triangles, like this. Use it to make a tetrahedron (triangular pyramid).

2 An icosahedron is a 'solid' with 20 faces, all of which are equilateral triangles. Can you design and make one?

OTHER TRIANGLES

An acute-angled triangle has all its angles acute.
How many obtuse angles has an obtuse-angled triangle?
Which kinds of triangles can you see in these pictures?

Factory roofs

Crane   Deckchairs

═══════════════ *Exercise 9* ═══════════════

1A Copy and complete:

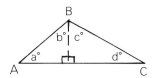

The 3 angles of a right-angled triangle add up to _____°.
So $a° + b° = $ _____°
$c° + d° = $ _____°
$a° + b° + c° + d° = $ _____°
↓ ⌣ ↓
$\angle A + \angle B + \angle C = $ _____°.
The angles of triangle ABC add up to _____°.

> **The sum of the angles of every triangle is 180°**

2A Calculate the missing angles in each of these triangles. Then say whether the triangle is right-angled, isosceles, equilateral, acute-angled or obtuse-angled (or more than one of these).

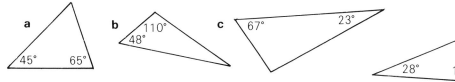
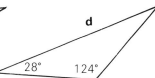

3A Copy the following diagrams and fill in all the angles. Then show what kind of triangle each one is.

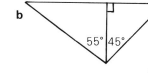
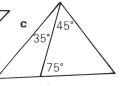
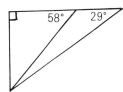

4A Find an equation with *x* and the other letters in the following triangles:

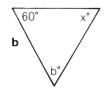
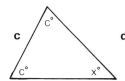
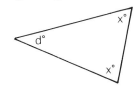

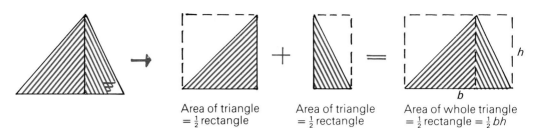

Area of triangle = ½ rectangle

Area of triangle = ½ rectangle

Area of whole triangle = ½ rectangle = ½ bh

| **The area of every triangle = ½ base × height = ½bh** |

TRIANGLES EVERYWHERE

=========================== *Exercise 10* ===========================

1A Calculate the areas of these triangles:

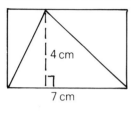

a

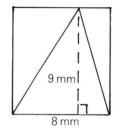

b

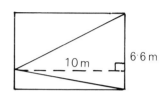

c

2A Calculate the areas of these triangles:

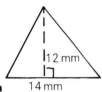

a

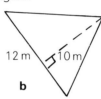

b

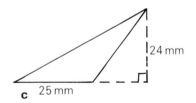

c

3A Arrange the following triangles in order, smallest area first:

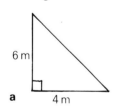

a

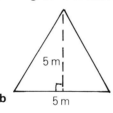

b

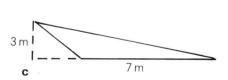

c

4B a On squared paper draw the triangle ABC, where A is the point (1, 1), B is (3, 4) and C is (4, 2).
  b Draw the rectangle around it with its sides parallel to the x and y-axes.
  c (i) What is the area of the rectangle?
    (ii) What are the areas of the triangles 1, 2 and 3?
    (iii) What is the area of triangle ABC?

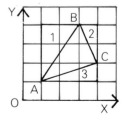

5B Use the same method to find the area of the triangle PQR, where P is (−2, −1), Q is (3, 0) and R is (2, 2).

6B Find the area of the 'boomerang' shape with corners D(−3, −1), E(−1, 0), F(1, −1) and G(−1, 1).

Drawing triangles, using ruler, compasses and protractor

Jacqueline was asked to draw a triangle ABC with sides

$$AB = 3\,cm, \quad BC = 4\,cm \quad and \quad CA = 6\,cm.$$

First she made a rough sketch, to get an idea of what was needed.

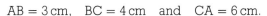

This allowed her to draw her triangle bit by bit, like this:

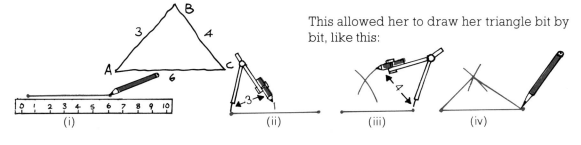

=== *Exercise 11* ===

1A Follow Jacqueline's method, and draw triangle ABC accurately. Measure its angles.

2A Try to use the same method to draw the following triangles. One of them is impossible; which one is it? Measure the angles in each triangle.
  a △STU, where ST = 4 cm, TU = 5 cm, US = 7 cm.
  b △XYZ, where XY = 6 cm, XZ = 6 cm, YZ = 1 cm.
  c △MAP, where MA = 3 cm, AP = 7 cm, MP = 2 cm.
  d △PQR, where PQ = 10 cm, QR = 5 cm, PR = 6·5 cm.
  e △DEF, where DE = 7·5 cm, EF = 7·5 cm, DF = 7·5 cm.

3A Archie, the joiner, drew a triangle with sides 3 cm, 4 cm and 5 cm long. He said that it was a 'trick of the trade' to draw a right angle. Draw the triangle, and use a protractor to check that he is right.

> **Three sides fix a triangle.**

Adam was asked to draw the triangle JKL where angle J = 30°, JK = 6 cm and JL = 5 cm. First he drew a rough sketch!

He drew a triangle and called it JKL. He put in the given data . . . and the steps became clear.

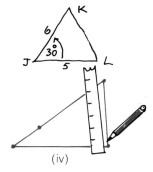

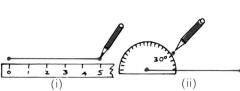

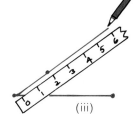

4A Follow Adam's steps to draw triangle JKL accurately.
  Measure the length of the third side to one decimal place.

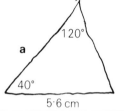

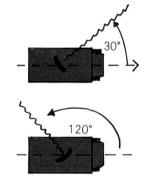

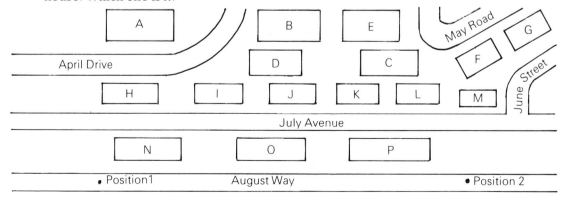

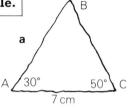

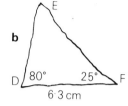

TRIANGLES EVERYWHERE

5A Draw these triangles accurately, and measure the third side of each one to one decimal place.

   a △DEF, where ∠D = 42°, DE = 7 cm, DF = 8 cm.

   b △GHI, where ∠H = 85°, HI = 5·5 cm, HG = 7·3 cm.

   c △PQR, where ∠R = 120°, QR = 6·5 cm, PR = 8 cm.

Two sides and the included angle fix a triangle.

6A a Make accurate drawings from these sketches.

   b Measure the third angles. Check your answers by calculation.

a — A 30° ... 50° C, 7 cm, B

b — D 80° ... 25° F, 6·3 cm, E

7B

a — 120°, 40°, 5·6 cm

b — 40°, 8·2 cm

Think out how to make accurate drawings from these sketches.

Two angles and a side fix a triangle.

8B A ship sails 8 km north from A to B, then 6 km east from B to C.

   a Using a scale of 1 cm to represent 1 km, draw AB and BC.

   b How far is the ship from A?

   c Remembering that bearings are measured clockwise from North, what is the bearing of C from A?

9B Repeat question **8B** for a journey of 7 km south, then 7 km east.

10B A TV detector van is driving along a straight road, August Way, when it picks up a signal. At that point, Position 1, its aerial is pointing at an angle of 30° to the road.
100 metres further on, at Position 2, this angle has increased to 120°.

   a Take 1 mm for 1 m. Make a careful drawing of the triangle you'll need to find the house the signal is coming from.

   b Make a tracing of your triangle. Place it on the map to fix the house. Which one is it?

Alice was puzzled. She was trying to draw a triangle ABC with AB = 4 cm, AC = 6 cm and angle ACB = 20°. She had stumbled on an example of the 'ambiguous case'. Look up 'ambiguous' in the dictionary, then investigate Alice's problem.

Computer graphics

When Jeff types TRIANGLE(7, 6) the flashing dot moves to the point (7, 6) and colours in the triangle formed by this point and the last two points visited by the dot. For example,

MOVE(1, 6)
MOVE(1, 1) ⎫ produces
TRIANGLE(7, 6) ⎭

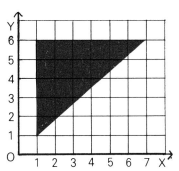

TRIANGLES EVERYWHERE

═══════════════ *Exercise 12* ═══════════════

1A a Copy Jeff's diagram. Label the corners A, B, and C to show the order in which they were visited by the flashing dot.
   b What command could Jeff add to his list to make his drawing a coloured-in rectangle?

2A

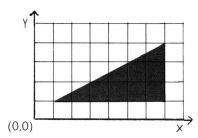

For his next attempt, Jeff typed
MOVE(7, 1)
MOVE(7, 4)
TRIANGLE(1, 1).
Repeat question **1** for the triangle he got this time.

3A a List the commands needed to draw this triangle. Visit the points in the order 1 → 2 → 3.
   b What shape will it become if you add the command TRIANGLE(3, 2)?

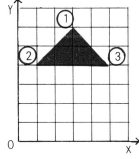

4B Anita thought she was colouring in a square when she gave the commands:

MOVE(2, 1)   MOVE(2, 4)   TRIANGLE(5, 4)   TRIANGLE(5, 1).

   a Follow the steps carefully to see what shape she *did* get. (Remember 'TRIANGLE' uses the last two points visited.)
   b Can you rearrange Anita's list to make it do what she wants?

CHECK-UP ON **TRIANGLES EVERYWHERE**

1A Describe each of these triangles: right-angled, isosceles, equilateral, right-angled and isosceles, or none of these:

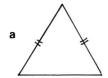

2A Copy the triangles above that have axes of symmetry, and draw in these axes.

3A What numbers do these letters stand for?

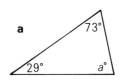 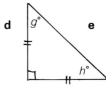

4A, B Calculate the shaded areas.

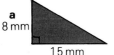 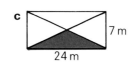 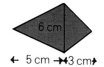

5A, B a Calculate the area of the triangle ABC where A is the point $(1, 3)$, B is $(6, 1)$ and C is $(6, 5)$.
   b D is the point $(4, 3)$. Calculate the area of ABDC.

6A, B a Copy this diagram, and fill in the sizes of as many angles and the lengths of as many lines as you can. SR = 5 cm.
   b What is the sum of the angles of the quadrilateral PQRS?

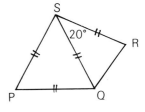

7A Draw the triangle ABC with $\angle A = 40°$, AB = 5 cm and AC = 6 cm. Measure BC.

8C A ship is 10 km from a lighthouse. After it sails 12 km in a straight line it is 13 km from the lighthouse.
How close did it get to the lighthouse?

9C Why is it impossible to actually make this wooden triangle?

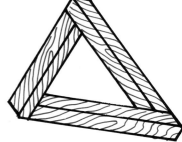

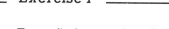

1 Describe the circles in these pictures. Try to find examples of:
a radius, a diameter, a circumference, a centre, an arc and a chord.

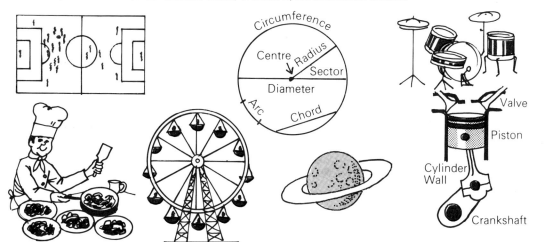

2 a Why are the following objects usually circular?

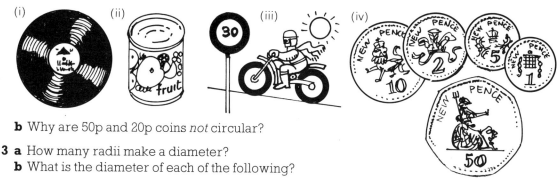

(i)   (ii)   (iii)   (iv)

b Why are 50p and 20p coins *not* circular?

3 a How many radii make a diameter?
b What is the diameter of each of the following?

(i)
Radius 1 cm

(ii)
Radius 6 inches

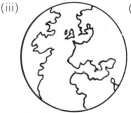
(iii)
Radius 4000 miles

(iv)
Radius 40 cm

4 Calculate the radius of each of the circles shown below.

a
Diameter 28 mm

b
8 cm

c
Diameter 0·6 m   Diameter 1·4 m

CIRCLES AROUND US

CIRCLES AROUND US

1 a Stand a 2p or a 10p coin at the start of the line below. Roll it carefully along the line. **Don't let it slip!**

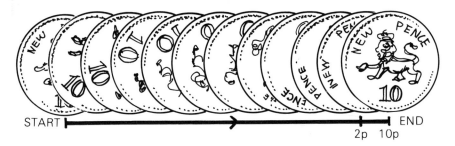

START ▶━━━━━━━━━━━━━━━━━━━━▶━━━━━┥ END
2p 10p

b Can you see that the distance rolled along the line is the same as the circumference of the coin?

Measure the line. Then copy and complete:

Circumference of __p coin = __ cm.

2 Each wheel of a bicycle has a circumference of 2 metres. How far will the bicycle go in:

a 1 turn of a wheel   **b** 10 turns   **c** 100 turns   **d** $\frac{1}{2}$ turn?

3 The diameter of a wheel is 60 cm. The wheel has 30 spokes, each 3 cm shorter than the radius of the wheel. Calculate the total length of all the spokes, in metres.

4 'It is easier to measure the diameter of a circle than the circumference.' Investigate.

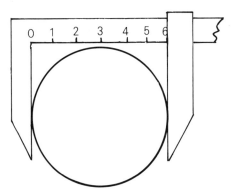

0 1 2 3 4 5 6

THE CIRCUMFERENCE OF A CIRCLE

(i) Astronauts orbiting the earth 150 miles above its surface need to know the circumference of their orbit if they want to calculate their position.

(ii) Antarctic explorers measure the distance they travel by the number of turns made by a wheel pulled along by their sledge.

(iii) The manufacturer needs to know the circumference of the can to calculate the length of the label.

Estimating the circumference

================ *Exercise 3A* ================

1 In the picture below a 5p coin is rolled along a straight line.

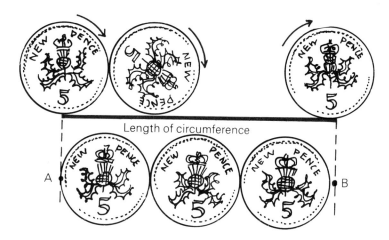

Length of circumference

a How many coins fit between A and B?
b So, roughly, how many times longer than the diameter is the circumference?

2 The line below has the same length as the circumference of the 1p coin.

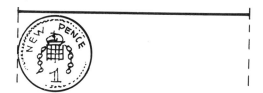

a How many 1p coins fit side by side between the dotted lines?
b How many times does the diameter divide into the circumference?

3 Each line has the same length as the circumference of the coin shown beside it.

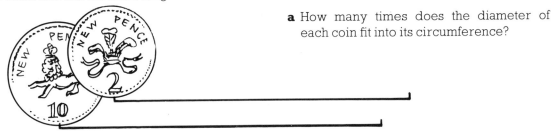

a How many times does the diameter of each coin fit into its circumference?

b Copy and complete the following:

The circumference of a coin is about ____ times its diameter.

4 Make several cardboard circles, and compare their diameters with their circumferences.

> **For all circles, the circumference is about '3 × diameter'**

5

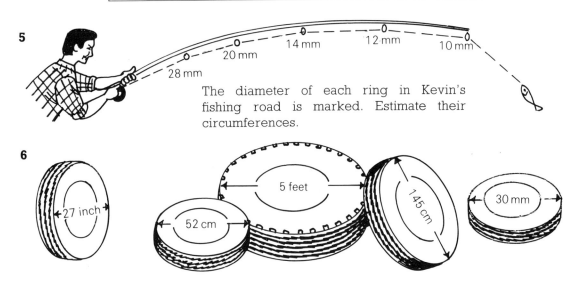

The diameter of each ring in Kevin's fishing road is marked. Estimate their circumferences.

6

Estimate the circumference of each of these tyres.

7 The radius of the ring at the top of a basketball net is 22·5 cm.
  a Calculate the diameter of the ring.
  b Estimate its circumference.

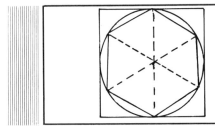

This diagram contains a square, a circle and a regular (equal-sided) hexagon.
The circle has radius R cm, diameter D cm and circumference C cm.
Show that: **a** $C > 3D$ **b** $C < 4D$.

More accurate estimates of the circumference

Use the life-sized pictures and the circumference lengths drawn below to complete the table. Measure to the nearest millimetre.

Coin	Circumference (C mm)	Diameter (D mm)	$C \div D$ (to 1 decimal place)
1p			
2p			
5p			
10p			
£1			

If you measure carefully, you will find that $C \div D$ is between 3·1 and 3·2. If you are *very* careful you might even find that it is 3·14 or 3·141 . . .. In fact the ratio $\dfrac{C}{D}$ is the same for all circles and is a never ending decimal, 3·141 592 653 589 793 . . .. It is impossible to write it out in full. Because of this we use a special symbol, π (pronounced **pi**), to represent it.

$\pi = 3\cdot14$ to 3 *significant figures*, so answers cannot be given with greater accuracy than this.
In the same way, 3 has 1 *significant figure*,
> 3·1 has 2 *significant figures*, and
> 3·1416 has 5 *significant figures*.

$$\frac{C}{D} = \pi, \text{ so } C = \pi D$$

The circumference of a circle is $C = \pi D$
---

1 How many significant figures in the decimal forms of the following would give good approximations for π? **a** $\frac{22}{7}$ **b** $\frac{355}{113}$.

CIRCLES AROUND US

2 Try this program in a computer, and watch it slowly calculating π.

```
1Ø LET N = 1: LET P = 2
2Ø LET D = 4 * N * N
3Ø LET T = D/(D − 1)
4Ø LET P = P * T
5Ø PRINT N; "2 spaces"; P
6Ø LET N = N + 1
7Ø GOTO 2Ø
```

Example

The diameter of this tin is
6 cm. Find its circumference.
$D = 6$
$C = \pi D$
   $= 3 \cdot 14 \times 6$, using $3 \cdot 14$ for π
   $= 18 \cdot 84$
The circumference is $18 \cdot 8$ cm, to 3 significant figures.

Note: Measurements are not exact. At this stage, however, they are assumed to be. For example, a radius of 6 cm is taken to be exactly 6 cm, and the approximation in the answer follows from the approximation made for π.

═══════════════ **Exercise 3B** ═══════════════

Complete the following questions *using $3 \cdot 14$ as an approximation for π, or the π key on your calculator. Round off your answers to 3 significant figures* unless there are other instructions.

1 Calculate the circumference of each of these objects.

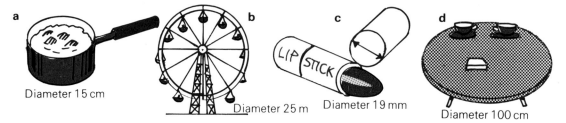

a Diameter 15 cm   **b** Diameter 25 m   **c** Diameter 19 mm   **d** Diameter 100 cm

2 Calculate the diameter, and then the circumference, of each of the following:

a Radius 5 cm   **b** Radius 15 cm   **c** Radius 46 cm   **d** Radius 9 inches

3 Here are some knitting needle sizes:

Size	0	2	4	6	8	10
Diameter (mm)	8	7	6	5	4	3·25

a Calculate the circumference of each needle.
b Which size of needle would be used to knit a chunky sweater?

Circles in the home

4 A rough estimate. Use 3 for π to calculate the circumference of:

a the ribbon round the hat

b the flex-holder

c the tape spool

d the reel.

Diameter 12 cm

Diameter 16 cm

Diameter 9 cm

Diameter 30 mm

5 A better estimate. Use 3·1 for π to calculate the length of:

a the edges of the biscuits being coated with brown sugar

b greaseproof paper strips to go round the inside edges of the tins

c the frill round the edge of the cushion.

Diameter 6·5 cm

15 17½ 30 22½ 25 27½

Diameters of tins in millimetres

Diameter 450 mm

6 Better still. Use 3·14 for π to calculate the length of:

a the rubber seal round the washing machine door

b the fancy trim round the 3 tiers of cake

c the edging on this lace mat.

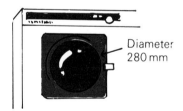

Diameter 280 mm

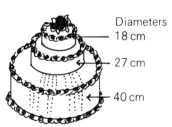

Diameters
18 cm
27 cm
40 cm

Diameter 162 mm

7 Four significant figures! Use 3·142 for π to calculate the length of:

a the inlay round the hole in the guitar

b the expensive gold trim round this china.

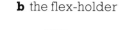

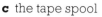

Cup 73

Saucer 130

Dinner plate 220

Diameter 14·3 cm

Diameters (mm)

Side plate 163

Soup plate 220

16

8

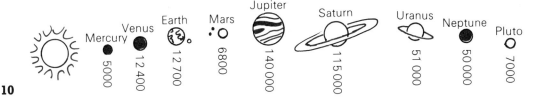

a The radius of the moon is 1740 km. Calculate its circumference.

b The radius of the sun is 696 000 km. Calculate its circumference.

c There is a big difference between the circumferences of the sun and moon. Why do they appear to be the same size during an eclipse?

9 The diameter of the earth across the equator is 12 760 km, and from pole to pole is 12 710 km. Using 3·142 for π, calculate the earth's circumference to 4 significant figures:

a round the equator   **b** round the poles.

What does this suggest about the shape of the earth?

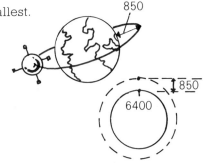

Jupiter   Saturn   Uranus   Neptune

Earth   Mars   Pluto

Venus

Mercury

Sun   5000   12 400   12 700   6800   140 000   115 000   51 000   50 000   7000

10

The picture above shows the planets in our solar system, in order from the sun outwards. The figure beside each planet gives its diameter in kilometres.

a Calculate the circumferences of the planets.

b Rearrange them in order from largest to smallest.

11 NOAA9 is a satellite which orbits the earth 850 km above the surface. Taking the radius of the earth to be 6400 km, and π to be 3·142, calculate:

a the radius of the orbit

b how far the satellite travels in one orbit

c how much further it would travel if the orbit was one kilometre higher.

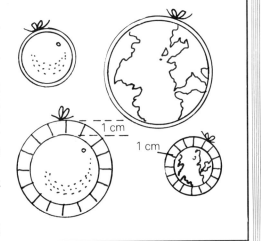

850

850

6400

Imagine a thread tied round an orange (diameter 10 cm), and a similar thread tied round the earth (diameter 12 700 km).

a Forgetting the knot, how long is each piece of thread?

b Imagine that spacers, 1 cm long, are put around the surface of the orange and the earth, and that the pieces of thread are lengthened to fit round these larger objects (as shown in the picture on the right).

How much thread has to be added in each case?

c Investigate a similar situation around:

(i) Saturn   (ii) Jupiter   (iii) the Universe!

1 cm

1 cm

CALCULATING THE DIAMETER

Example: Calculate the diameter of a circle with circumference 25 m.

$$C = \pi D$$

$$25 = 3 \cdot 14\, D$$

$$D = \frac{25}{3 \cdot 14} \text{ (dividing both sides by 3·14)}$$

$$= 7 \cdot 96, \text{ to 3 significant figures.}$$

The diameter is 7·96 m.

═══════════════ *Exercise 3C* ═══════════════

1 If you wanted to draw a circle with circumference 24 cm,
  a what would the diameter of the circle be?
  b What distance apart would you set the points of your compasses?

2 Draw circles with circumferences:
  a 27 cm   **b** 18 cm   **c** 12 cm.

3 A hatter is measuring a customer's head. If he assumes the head to be circular, what diameter of hat should he make for a customer whose head measures:
  a 20 cm   **b** 22 cm   **c** 25 cm?

4 Collar sizes in a catalogue are recorded as $14\frac{1}{2}$ inch, 15 inch, $15\frac{1}{2}$ inch, 16 inch, $16\frac{1}{2}$ inch. If the collars are circular, what diameter of neck is each of the above sizes meant for?

5 After a bank robbery, the police found a track left by the getaway car.

They measured the distance between two marks on the tyre track.
The distance was 5495 mm. What was the diameter of the wheel?

Wind a piece of thread ten times round a circular object such as a tin can or jar. Keep the windings close together.
Measure the length of the thread, and divide it by 10. This gives you the circumference of the object.
Now measure the diameter of your object.
Calculate π $(C \div D)$.
How accurate is the value for π which you find?
Try more windings. Does this improve your results?
Devise a similar experiment using a trundle wheel.

THE AREA OF A CIRCLE

Estimating the area

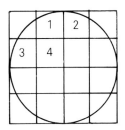

This circle has a radius of 2 cm.
Estimate its area like this:
count half a square or more as one
square, and don't count the others.
Check that the area of the circle is
approximately 12 cm².

═══════════════════ *Exercise 4A* ═══════════════════

1 On 1 cm squared paper draw circles with radii 2, 3, 4 and 5 cm. Estimate their areas by counting squares. Copy and complete the table.

Radius (R cm)	Area (cm²)	R^2	$3R^2$
2	12	$2 \times 2 = 4$	12
3		$3 \times 3 = 9$	27
4			
5			

Check that in each case the area is equal to, or slightly more than, $3R^2$.

> **The area of a circle is about 3 × Radius × Radius, or $3R^2$.**

2

Use this result to estimate the areas of the circular parts of these objects.

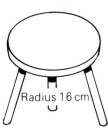
Radius 16 cm

Radius 6 cm

Radius 5·5 cm

Radius 14 mm

3 a The radius of an LP is 15 cm. Estimate the area of one side.
  b What shape is the record sleeve? What area of cardboard is needed to make it?

4 A single has a radius of 8·5 cm. Repeat question **3** for a single.

5 Estimate the areas of the rug, which has a radius of 2 m, the table, with diameter 80 cm and the table mat, with diameter 66 mm.

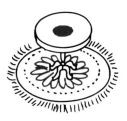

More accurate estimates of the area

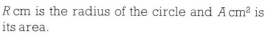

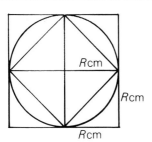

R cm is the radius of the circle and A cm² is its area.

The area of each triangle is $\frac{1}{2}R \times R$ cm² = $\frac{1}{2}R^2$ cm².

The area of the circle is more than 4 triangles and less than 8.

So $2R^2 < A < 4R^2$.

CIRCLES AROUND US

Here is the circular end of a roll of kitchen paper.

 Using a sharp knife we cut along the top of the roll, down to the centre:

 We straighten out the layers of paper:

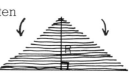

The layers of paper form an isosceles triangle.
The base of the triangle is the circumference of the roll of paper.
Why can we say its length is $2\pi R$?
What is the area of the triangle?
So what is the area of the circle?

The investigation above suggests that the area is πR^2. This is, in fact, true.

> **The area of a circle is $A = \pi R^2$**

Example

Calculate the area of the circular cover for the speaker.
Its diameter is 16 cm.

$D = 16$
So $R = 8$
$A = \pi R^2$
$\quad = 3\cdot14 \times 8 \times 8$, using $3\cdot14$ for π
$\quad = 201$, to 3 significant figures.

The area of the cover is 201 cm².

=========== *Exercise 4B* ===========

Take $3\cdot14$ for π, or use the π key on your calculator, and round off your answers to 3 significant figures.

1 Calculate the circular areas of these three objects and three more (**d**, **e** and **f**) on page 246.

a

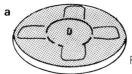

Radius 17 cm

b

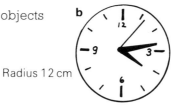

Radius 12 cm

c

Radius 15·5 cm

d

e

Sanding Discs
Radius 8·5 cm

f

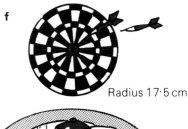

Radius 17·5 cm

Radius 3·5 cm

2 This circular table has a glass centre.
The diameter of the table is 1·5 m, and the
diameter of the glass circle is 1 m.
Calculate the area of:
a the whole table top   **b** the glass
b the wooden surround.

3

The opening at the top of the lampshade
is 60 mm in diameter. The opening at the
bottom is 360 mm across.
a Calculate the area of both openings.
b How much bigger is the bottom opening
than the top?

Air rising inside the shade is heated by the bulb and escapes
through the top opening.
c What do you think would happen if the area of the top opening
was too small?

4

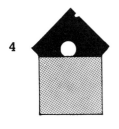

Here is a floppy disc for a home computer.
The two most popular sizes of disc are $5\frac{1}{4}$ inches and $3\frac{1}{2}$ inches
in diameter. The actual disc sits inside a protective black sleeve
like this:

The shaded part of the disc
is coated with a special
magnetic material.

For each size of disc calculate:
a the area of the outer circle
b the area of the hole (diameter 1 inch)
c the area that is coated
d the area inside the sleeve which is 'lost'.

5 Calculate:
a the area of the label
b the area available for recording on each
side of the record.

10 cm

30 cm

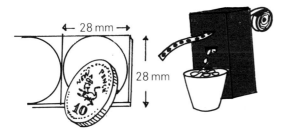

← 28 mm →

28 mm

6 At the Royal Mint 10p coins are stamped
out of strips of metal.
a Calculate the area of waste for each
coin.
b How much waste will there be when £50
worth of coins have been stamped out?

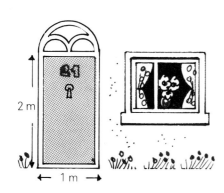

2 m

← 1 m →

Calculate the area of the whole doorway in this picture.

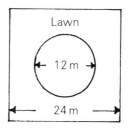

Lawn

← 12 m →

← 24 m →

8 This diagram shows a square lawn with a circular flower bed in a park. Calculate:
 a the area of the flower bed
 b the area of the lawn.

9 In this diagram the arcs are parts of equal circles with centres at the corners of the square.
 a What shape do parts 1, 2, 3 and 4 make if they are cut out and put together?
 b Calculate the area of the asteroid (the shaded part).

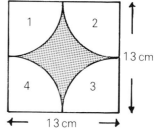

1   2

13 cm

4   3

← 13 cm →

Exercise 4C

1 The back of an Underground train looks like this.
 a What area of the back is *not* door?
 b What fraction of the back is taken up by the door?

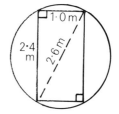

1·0 m

2·4 m

2·6 m

2 The goal area of a hockey pitch is bounded by the goal line and two quarter circles which are joined by a straight line 4 yards long. Calculate:
 a the length of the arc AB
 b the perimeter of the goal area
 c the area of the goal area
 d the percentage of the whole pitch, (a rectangle 100 yards by 60 yards), made up by the goal area.

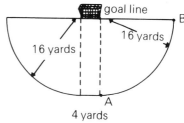

goal line

B

16 yards

16 yards

16 yards

A

4 yards

If you have to compare areas of circles it is best to leave π in each answer like this:
For a circle radius 5 cm, $A = \pi r^2 = 25\pi$.

3 The dial of a telephone has a radius of 4 cm. The label has a radius of 2 cm. Each fingerhole has a radius of 5 mm.
  a What is the ratio of:
    (i) the label's radius to the dial's radius
    (ii) the label's area to the dial's area?
  b How many times larger is the dial than the label?
  c Repeat parts **a** and **b** for one of the fingerholes and the dial.

4 Mohammed is fitting new copper water pipes in his house. He is using the two sizes of piping shown, one for cold water and one for hot. The copper in each pipe is 1 mm thick. Calculate:
  a the inside radius of each pipe
  b the ratio of these radii, in the form 1 : __.
  c the inside cross-sectional area of each pipe (the shaded part)
  d the ratio of these areas, in the form 1 : __.

5 Repeat question **4** for pipes measuring 15 mm and 28 mm in diameter. How could you calculate **d** without calculating **c**?

Sport and design

===== *Exercise 5A* =====

Use 3 as an approximation for π in the following questions.

1

7 ft

  a Estimate the circumference of the shot putt circle.
  b What is the radius of the circle?
  c Estimate the area of the circle.

2 The centre circle of a football pitch has a radius of 10 yards.
  a Estimate its area.
  b What is its diameter?
  c Estimate its circumference.

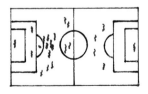

3

O is the centre of this circle which has a radius of 5 cm.
  a Draw the design, which is based on semi-circles.
  b Explain why the shaded and unshaded areas are equal.
  c Calculate the shaded area.

4

The diameter of this circle has been divided into six equal parts, each 2 cm long.

a Draw the design, also based on semi-circles.

b Calculate the area of every semicircle that you can find in the design.

5

Copy the pattern on the left, which consists of circles and arcs of circles.
In it colour the pattern on the right.

Exercise 5B/C

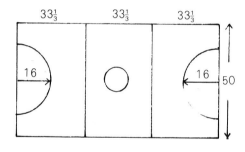

$33\frac{1}{3}$ $33\frac{1}{3}$ $33\frac{1}{3}$

16   16   50

1B In netball you must be in the opponent's semicircle to score. The dimensions in the diagram are in feet.

a Calculate the area of one of the semi-circles.

b What percentage is this area of the whole pitch?

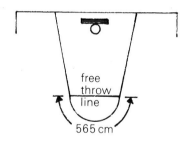

free throw line

565 cm

2B In basketball the semicircle behind the 'free throw line' must be 565 cm long. Calculate, to the nearest centimetre, the radius of this semicircle.

3B An archery target has a gold centre 24·4 cm in diameter, ringed by four concentric bands, each 12·2 cm wide. Calculate:

a the gold area

b the diameter of the target

c the circumference of the target.

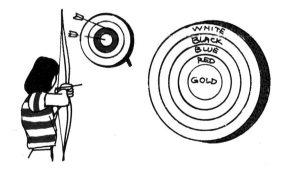

4C Calculate the area of the blue ring in the archery target.

5C A farmer has 100 m of flexible fencing.

a Which would give him the larger enclosed area—a square pen or a circular pen?

b Calculate the difference between the two areas.

CHECK-UP ON **CIRCLES AROUND US**·

1 a The radio dish has a diameter of 3 metres. What is its radius?
 b The radius of the cymbal is 12 inches. What is its diameter?

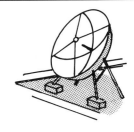

2 a Use this picture to get an approximation for the circumference of a 5p coin.

 b Describe how you got your answer.

3 What formula connects the circumference and the diameter of a circle?

4 a What is the circumference of the fishing net if its diameter is 18 inches?
 b What is the circumference of the tin of shoe polish if its radius is 4·5 cm?

5 a A coin rolled through an ink blot and left a trail as shown below.

 A   B   C

   With the help of a ruler calculate the radius of the coin.
 b Draw a circle with circumference 29 cm.

6 What formula connects the radius and the area of a circle?

7 a Taking π as 3, what is the area of glass covering the front of the barometer? (Its radius is 10 cm.)

 b Use 3·14 for π to find the area of the lid with diameter 35 cm.

 c (i) The 80 mm lens is a precision instrument. If you wanted to be very precise about its area what value would you use for π?
    (ii) If 80 mm is the diameter, what is the area of the lens?

FROM POINTS TO CURVES

As the sailor raises his arm, it makes a larger angle with his body.

A

B

GRAPH

Height of hand

B

A

O Size of angle

The points on this graph represent situations A and B, above.

GRAPH

Height of hand

B

A

O Size of angle

The curve shows the gradual change from A to B.

=========== Exercise 1   Joining points ===========

In each of these questions: **a** Copy the axes and their titles.
b Plot and label two points to show situations A and B.
c Join the points A and B to show the gradual change from A to B.
d Copy and complete the sentence.

1A

A 5 years old   B 50 years old

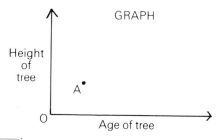

GRAPH

Height of tree

A

O Age of tree

As the tree grows older, its height _____ .

2A

A Six months old   B One year old

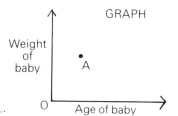

GRAPH

Weight of baby

A

O Age of baby

As the baby grows older, its weight _____ .

3A

 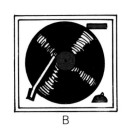 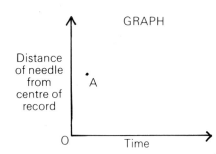

As time passes, the distance of the needle from the centre _____.

4A

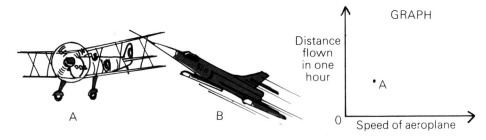

The greater the speed, _____.

5A

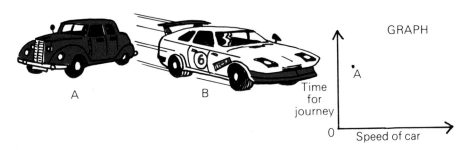

The greater the speed, _____.

6A

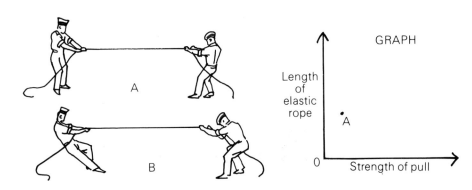

As the pull increases, the length of the elastic rope _____.

7B

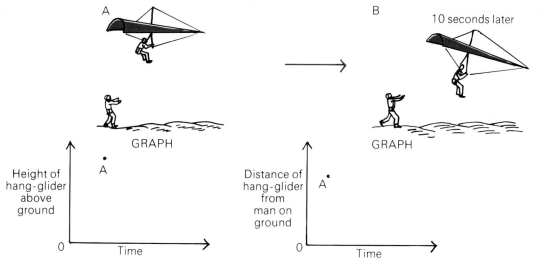

As time passes, the height of the glider
_____ .

As time passes, the distance of the glider from the man on the ground _____ .

8B

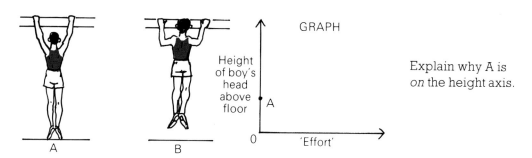

Explain why A is *on* the height axis.

9B When drawing these graphs, think whether any of the points lie *on* the axes.

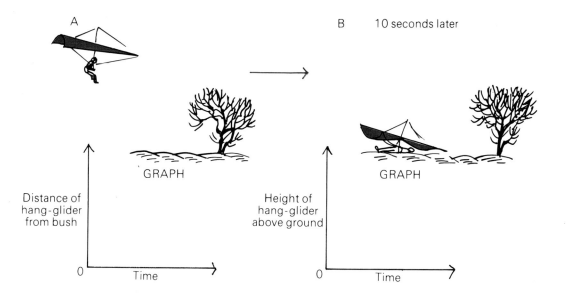

10C Copy and complete the graphs below for the movements of the boy on the parallel bars.

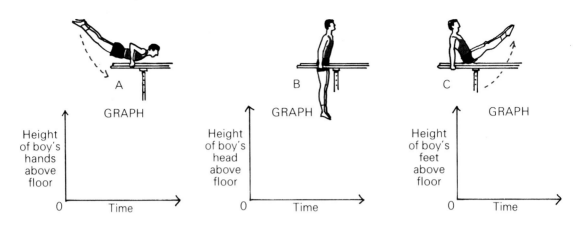

SPEED GRAPHS

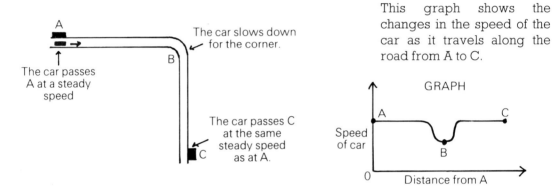

The car slows down for the corner.

The car passes A at a steady speed

The car passes C at the same steady speed as at A.

This graph shows the changes in the speed of the car as it travels along the road from A to C.

GRAPH

Speed of car — Distance from A

Exercise 2   Road work

In questions **1A–5A** copy the axes and titles. Then copy and complete the graphs to show the speed of the car as it travels from A to C or D.

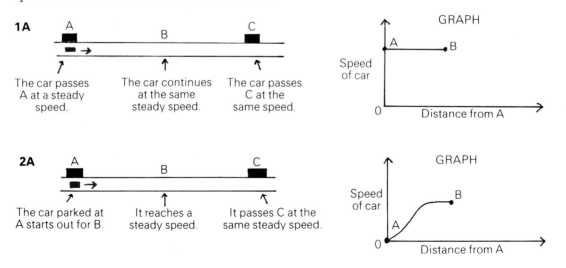

1A

The car passes A at a steady speed.

The car continues at the same steady speed.

The car passes C at the same speed.

GRAPH

Speed of car — Distance from A

2A

The car parked at A starts out for B.

It reaches a steady speed.

It passes C at the same steady speed.

GRAPH

Speed of car — Distance from A

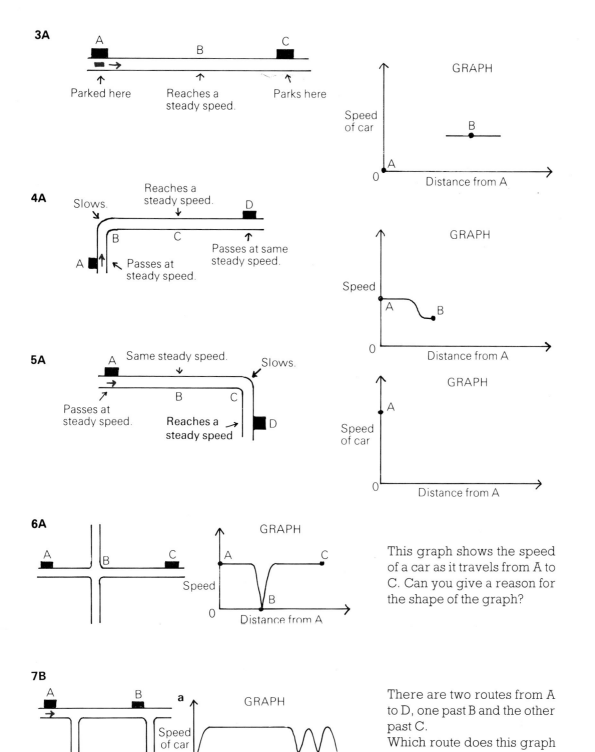

3A

A   B   C

Parked here   Reaches a   Parks here
           steady speed.

GRAPH

Speed of car

B

A

0   Distance from A

4A

Slows.

Reaches a steady speed.

B   C   D

A   Passes at   Passes at same
    steady speed.   steady speed.

GRAPH

Speed

A   B

0   Distance from A

5A

A   Same steady speed.   Slows.

Passes at   B   C
steady speed.   Reaches a   D
        steady speed

GRAPH

A

Speed of car

0   Distance from A

6A

A   B   C

GRAPH

A   C

Speed

    B

0   Distance from A

This graph shows the speed of a car as it travels from A to C. Can you give a reason for the shape of the graph?

7B

A   B

C   D

a GRAPH

Speed of car

A   D

0   Distance from A

There are two routes from A to D, one past B and the other past C.
Which route does this graph show?

b Draw a graph for the other route, showing the speed of the car as it travels from A to D.

FROM COORDINATES TO GRAPHS

GRAPHS AND RELATIONS

Far away in time and space a planet named Graff spins around a pale green sun. Above its jagged surface a deadly battle is raging. Here is a world inhabited by two races: the evil and cruel flying Graffins and the good and wise bouncing Pointlings.

This Pointling is bouncing along, quite unaware that this Graffin

is flying towards it. Their positions were plotted from the coordinates shown. *t* is the time in 'Graff seconds'. Will the Graffin catch the Pointling?

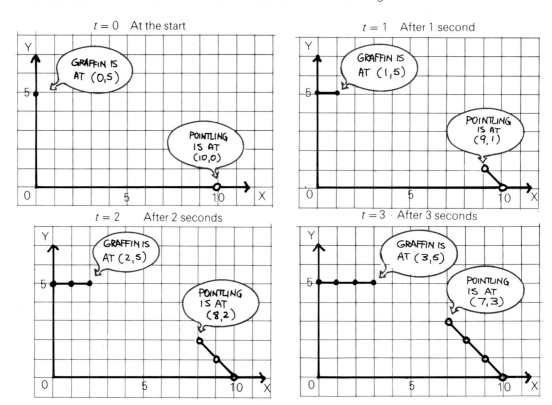

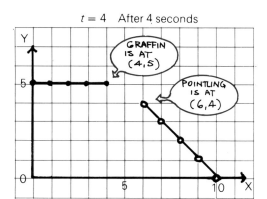

$t = 4$ After 4 seconds

GRAFFIN IS AT (4,5)

POINTLING IS AT (6,4)

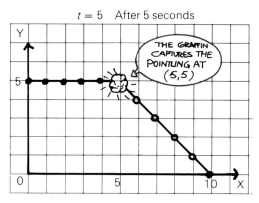

$t = 5$ After 5 seconds

THE GRAFFIN CAPTURES THE POINTLING AT (5,5)

Exercise 3   Graffins and Pointlings

1A Copy the axes and scales on squared paper. Plot the points shown in the table, one row at a time, for the positions of the Graffin and the Pointling.

$(t, 8)$

$(8-t, 2t)$

$t = 0$	$(0, 8)$	$(8, 0)$
$t = 1$	$(1, 8)$	$(7, 2)$
$t = 2$	$(2. 8)$	$(6, 4)$
$t = 3$	$(3, 8)$	$(5, 6)$
$t = 4$	$(4, 8)$	$(4, 8)$

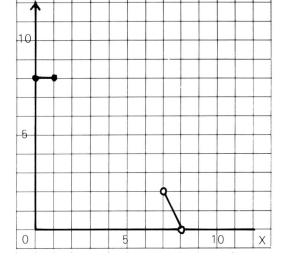

Does the Graffin capture the Pointling?

2A Copy and complete this table and graph, plotting the positions of the Graffin and Pointling after each row.

$(2t, 5)$

$(4+t, t)$

$t = 0$	$(0, 5)$	$(4, 0)$
$t = 1$	$(2, 5)$	$(5, 1)$
$t = 2$	$(4, 5)$	$(6, 2)$
$t = 3$	$(6, 5)$	$(7, 3)$
$t = 4$	$(8, 5)$	$(8, 4)$
$t = 5$	$\ldots$	$\ldots$

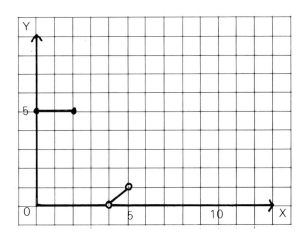

Will the Graffin catch the Pointling this time?

3A Two Pointlings travelling along together
are spied by a Graffin . . . . What happens?

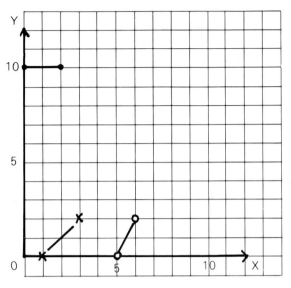

$t = 0$	$(0, 10)$	$(5, 0)$	$(1, 0)$
$t = 1$	$(2, 10)$	$(6, 2)$	$(3, 2)$
$t = 2$	$(4, 10)$	$(7, 4)$	$(5, 4)$
$t = 3$	$(6, 10)$	$(8, 6)$	$(7, 6)$
$t = 4$	. . .	. . .	. . .

Copy and complete the table and graph to find out.

These graphs show how this Pointling bounces through the air:

$t = 0$ The Pointling starts to bounce

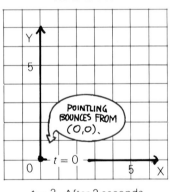

POINTLING BOUNCES FROM (0,0).

$t = 1$ After 1 second

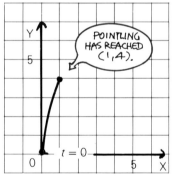

POINTLING HAS REACHED (1,4).

$t = 2$ After 2 seconds

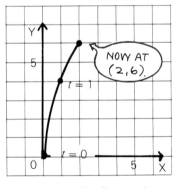

NOW AT (2,6).

$t = 3$ After 3 seconds

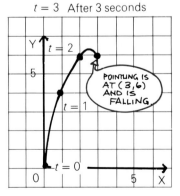

POINTLING IS AT (3,6) AND IS FALLING.

$t = 4$ After 4 seconds

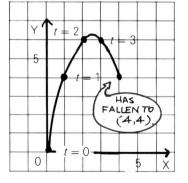

HAS FALLEN TO (4,4).

$t = 5$ After 5 seconds

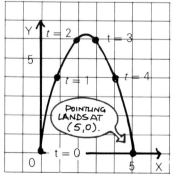

POINTLING LANDS AT (5,0).

4B

Draw the following axes:

x-axis, with scale 0–6, y-axis with scale 0–10.

a Plot the bounce of the Pointling until it lands back on Graff.
b Where does it land?
c After how many 'Graff seconds' does it land?
d What was the highest point in its bounce?

$t = 0$	$(0, 0)$
$t = 1$	$(1, 5)$
$t = 2$	$(2, 8)$
$t = 3$	$(3, 9)$
$t = 4$	$(4, 8)$
$t = 5$	
$t = 6$	

5B Is this bouncing Pointling captured by the evil Graffin?

Draw axes with x-axis scale 0–20 and y-axis scale 0–20.

As you complete each row of the table plot the new positions of the Graffin and the Pointling.

$t = 0$	$(0, 15)$	$(10, 0)$
$t = 1$	$(3, 15)$	$(11, 7)$
$t = 2$	$(6, 15)$	$(12, 12)$
$t = 3$		
$t = 4$		

6C

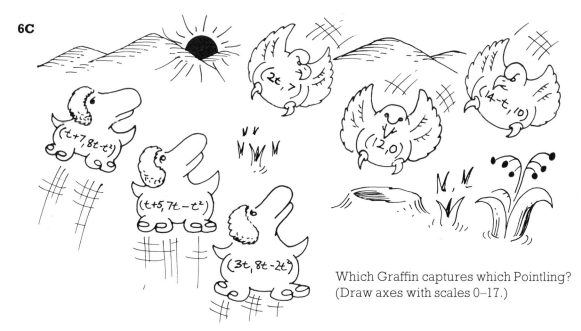

Which Graffin captures which Pointling?
(Draw axes with scales 0–17.)

GRAPHS AND RELATIONS

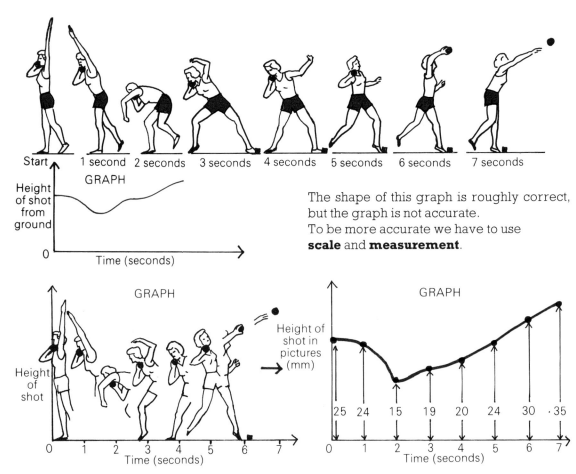

The shape of this graph is roughly correct, but the graph is not accurate.
To be more accurate we have to use **scale** and **measurement**.

You cannot put the pictures on your graph, but you *can* measure them with your ruler. Then, using squared paper, you can plot the points and draw the graph.

═══════════════════ *Exercise 4   Measure for measure* ═══════════════════

1A Copy the axes and their titles on squared paper.
Use the measurements shown on the graph above to plot the points for the positions of the shot every second.
Join the points with a smooth curve.

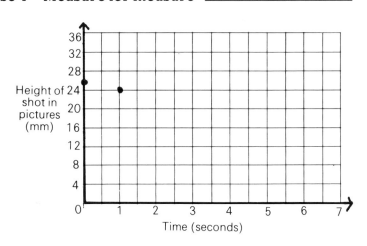

2A The heights of the athlete's left hand at different times are shown in this table.

Time (seconds)	0	1	2	3	4	5	6
Height (mm)	36	32	10	24	24	20	20

a Copy the axes and titles.
b Plot the points for the heights of the left hand.
c Join the points with a smooth curve.

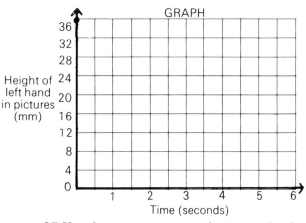

3A Use the measurements shown to plot the distances of the shot putter's right foot from the block every second. Join the points with a smooth curve.

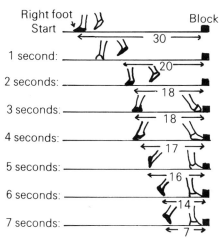

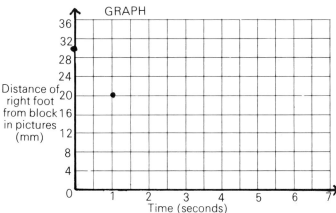

4B Mr Toad is going for a walk. These pictures show the distances in millimetres, every second, between his right legs and his left legs as he walks.

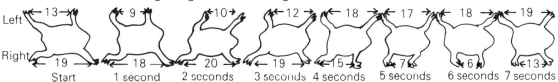

a Copy and complete this table for the distances between the right legs.

Time (seconds)	0	1	2	3	4	5	6	7
Distance (mm)	19	18	20					

b Copy and complete the graph.
c On the same diagram draw a graph of the distance between the left legs.
d What do the graphs tell us about the way Mr Toad walks?

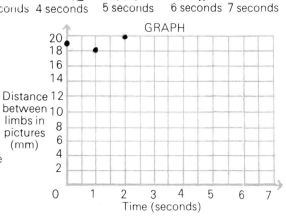

5C Mr Newt also takes a walk. Each drawing shows Mr Newt's position one second after the previous one.

a Measure the distances between the right and left limbs of Mr Newt as he walks, and draw two tables and graphs as in question **4B**.

b Use all four graphs to describe the differences in the ways Mr Toad and Mr Newt walk.

6C a Draw a circle with radius 40 mm and draw in a clock-face.

b Copy and complete this table by measuring the distance from the tip of the hour hand to the base-line each hour.

Time	12	1	2	3	4	5	6
Distance (mm)	80						

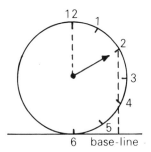

c Draw a graph on squared paper, taking
1 hour every cm on the horizontal axis
and 10 mm every $\frac{1}{2}$-cm on the vertical axis.

d Describe the graph in a sentence.

A Class/Group Graph

Set up a pendulum in an open doorway, or in a higher space, if possible. You can make the pendulum from strong thread and a metal weight, like a key.

Count the number of swings from side to side during one minute for pendulum lengths of 25 cm, 50 cm, 75 cm, ...

Enter the number of swings and lengths in a table.

Plot the points on squared paper, marking the horizontal axis 'Length (cm)', and the vertical axis 'Number of swings per minute'.

Join them up with a curve. Can you give any reason why this might not be a smooth curve?

Would it be sensible to continue the curve in both directions?

═══════════════ *Exercise 5   Every graph tells a tale* ═══════════════

1A a What is the usual depth of the river?

b What was its depth when the floods from the heavy rain were at their worst?

c What was the increase in depth due to the rain?

d For how long was the depth: (i) increasing (ii) decreasing?

e How long after the start of the rain did the river return to normal?

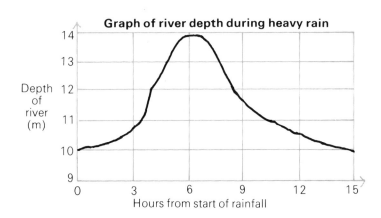

2A a What is the normal body temperature?

b How many days after the bite does the fever start?

c Why is sand-fly fever sometimes called 'three-day fever'?

d What is the patient's highest temperature during the fever?

e There are two spells of fever in an attack. Which is worse?

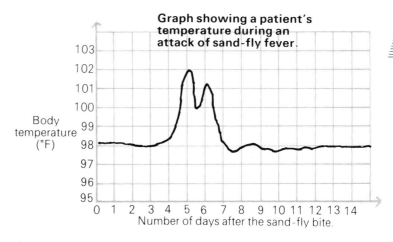

Graph showing a patient's temperature during an attack of sand-fly fever.

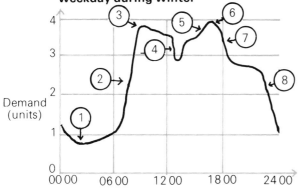

Graph showing demand for electricity from the National Grid on a typical weekday during winter

3A Match the numbers 1–8 on the graph with the letters **a–h** below. For example 1–**e**.

a Afternoon peak demand.

b Morning peak demand.

c Greatest increase in demand.

d Increase due to lighting being switched on.

e Demand is small.

f Decrease due to factories closing down.

g Decrease due to families going to bed.

h Decrease due to factory lunch hour.

4B

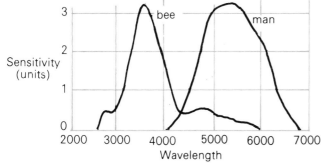

Graph showing the sensitivity of a man's eye and a bee's eye to different wavelengths of light

Table of colours and wavelengths	
Below 3800	ultra-violet
3800–4299	violet
4300–4699	blue
4700–4999	blue-green
5000–5399	green
5400–5599	yellow-green
5600–5949	yellow
5950–6199	orange
6200–7600	red

Use the graph and the table to answer these:

a Can a bee 'see' green?

b Can we see ultra-violet?

c Name a colour that we can see but a bee cannot.

d To which colour are we most sensitive?

e To which colour is a bee most sensitive?

f To which colour are we equally as sensitive as a bee?

5B a Mount Everest is nearly 9 km high. Estimate the temperature at its top.

b In 1961 a man called Malcolm Ross went up in a balloon to a height of $34\frac{1}{2}$ km. Describe the changes in temperature he would have felt during his ascent.

c The ozonosphere stretches from a height of 30 km to 80 km.
Estimate the warmest and coldest temperatures in this layer.

d Between what heights is there a warm layer between two freezing layers?

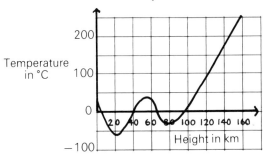

Graph showing the temperature of the atmosphere of the earth

6C These graphs of wind speed, wind direction, temperature and rainfall were recorded on the 24th October at Kenmore on Loch Tay in Scotland.

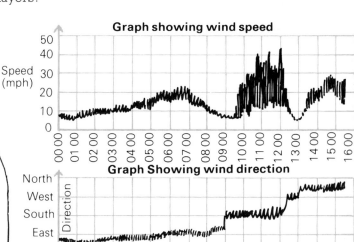

Graph showing wind speed

Graph Showing wind direction

WEATHER REPORT FOR 24TH OCTOBER

JUST AFTER MIDNIGHT IT WAS FAIR WITH A LIGHT EASTERLY WIND (7-8 MPH), AND THE TEMPERATURE SETTLED TO A STEADY 10°C. AT 01 00 HOURS IT STARTED TO RAIN STEADILY UNTIL 02 00 HOURS WHEN IT STOPPED. BUT BY 03 00 HOURS IT WAS RAINING AGAIN HEAVIER THAN BEFORE AND THE WIND WAS INCREASING. BY 05 00 HOURS WITH THE EASTERLY WIND NOW BETWEEN 15 - 20 MPH THE RAIN STOPPED AGAIN AT 06 00 HOURS...

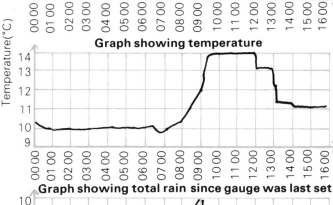

Graph showing temperature

Using the information in the graphs try to continue this weather report, mentioning all the main changes during the day until 16 00 hours.

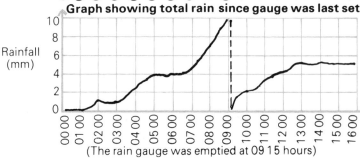

Graph showing total rain since gauge was last set

(The rain gauge was emptied at 09 15 hours)